PADRE PRO

PADRE PRO

BY **Fanchón Royer**

P. J. KENEDY & SONS

NEW YORK

✠ Nihil Obstat: RT. REV. MSGR. JOHN M. A. FEARNS, S.T.D.,
Censor Librorum

✠ Imprimatur: FRANCIS CARDINAL SPELLMAN, *Archbishop of New York*

New York, February 2, 1954

The nihil obstat and imprimatur are official declarations that a book or pamphlet is free of doctrinal and moral error. No implication is contained therein that those who have granted the nihil obstat and imprimatur agree with the contents, opinions or statements expressed.

In conformity with the decree of Pope Urban VIII, we do not wish to anticipate the judgment of the Church in our appraisal of the characters and occurrences spoken of herein. We submit wholeheartedly to the infallible wisdom and judgment of Holy Mother Church.

FOR

THEODORE LE BERTHON

A CHAMPION OF THE
"PEOPLE OF PRO."

CONTENTS

"MADRE MÍA,
GIVE ME BACK MY SON!"

MAMÁ BIBI'S house was a sturdy adobe structure whose two-story façade, thrusting above its humbler neighbors, confronted Guadalupe's plaza with decided dignity. Its upper floor boasted a wrought-iron balcony, a peerless vantage point from which to look out upon a small Mexican town. Year in and out Mamá Bibi's provincial world had been traversing the green square under her sharp but compassionate gaze. She knew it in all its moods and fortunes—and loved it.

She also loved her splendid view of Guadalupe's glorious monument to a more distinguished day, the massive hulk which had once been the famous Franciscan Colegio Apostólico de Propaganda Fide.[1] Indeed, the ancient sanctuary was an intimate part of Mamá Bibi's life because, during the 1880's, her own brother, Fray Crisóstomo Gómez, had served it as chaplain while, an *ex-claustrado*,[2] he shared her house along with the motherless Juárez children, their nieces and nephews. The great heart and willing hands of Mamá Bibi took care of them all.

One of the young nieces who grew up under the protection of Mamá Bibi was Josefa Juárez. It is certain that Josefa was both

[1] Founded in 1707 by the Venerable Fray Antonio Margil de Jesús.

[2] According to Bernardo Portas, S.J.: *Vida del Padre Pro, S.J.*, p. 7. Although Adolfo Pulido, S.J.: *Alborada de un Mártir*, p. 5, says that Fray Crisóstomo was "the last cloistered Guardian" of the Monastery, this situation probably changed before his death, in the late 1880's.

a lovable and estimable girl for it was she to whom Fray Crisóstomo willed his most cherished possessions, his crucifix and instruments of penitence. And when Josefa was eagerly sought in marriage by the stalwart youth Miguel Pro, whom Mamá Bibi knew well as the meritorious son of Don Hilario Pro, the mining engineer and manager of the Hacienda Maguey, the old lady's resistance to the loss of her favorite niece occasioned an unfortunate strain in their previously close and affectionate relations. Nevertheless, following the wedding of Josefa and Miguel in March 1886, Mamá Bibi's love triumphed over her injured feelings. As soon as she understood Josefa to be in a "delicate" state of health, she insisted that the newlyweds move into her commodious home where she might keep a vigilant eye upon the bride. The young Pros accepted her invitation, which is how it came about that their first three babies were born in the big house on the plaza. The little ones were: María de la Concepción, María de la Luz and—he whose appearance was to bring little Guadalupe its later-day claim to glory— Miguel Agustín Pro Juárez.

The Guadalupe of which we speak is about four miles southeast of the city of Zacatecas and, since the earliest days of her colonial epoch, the center of one of México's richest silver-mining districts. Since the young husband, Miguel Pro, like his father, was a mining engineer, he was presumably employed in the Zacatecas mines during the first years of his marriage. Theirs was a happy life in Guadalupe which was crowned by the birth of their first son on January 13, 1891. Enormous was the rejoicing of the Pro Juárez clan headed by good old Mamá Bibi when, three days later, the promising infant received the "waters of the Jordan" in the Franciscan monastery's Nápoles Chapel where his sisters and parents had likewise been baptized. Miguel Agustín's godparents were Hilario Pro and Ricarda Romo, his paternal grandparents.[3] The baptismal water poured over

[3] Register of baptisms for the *Vicaría de la Parroquia del Sagrario* (now *de los Sagrados Corazones de Jesús y de María*), book 5, p. 135. Guadalupe, Zacatecas, México.

the tiny head by Padre Luis de las Piedras had been another gift to Josefa from her deceased uncle, Fray Crisóstomo. Immediately thereafter the rafters of the house on the plaza were ringing with the felicitations, the merriment, and the joyous fiesta that, in México, invariably welcome "the new little Christians" into its large families.

But the first gaiety and ensuing happy tranquillity that ushered small Miguel Agustín into the world and the house of Mamá Bibi were soon affected by a trio of sorrowful incidents. These were the deaths in rapid succession of the baby's maternal grandfather, of his aunt, Josefa's only sister, and, as the greatest loss of all, that of Mamá Bibi herself. The passing of three such close relatives within ten months cut many of the bonds which had held Miguel Pro and his wife to their home village. Now they determined to make a new start with their little family in the national capital.

Thus it was in the proud "City of Palaces" that Miguelito learned to walk; and, with almost his first independent steps, he exhibited the temerity which was to characterize him throughout his action- and danger-filled life. The marvelous discovery that he could ramble where he pleased about the spacious México City house was eagerly seized by the infant. One morning while his mother and Concepción were at Mass, he escaped the eye of his nursemaid to make his way on an unsteady toddle out of the nursery and down a long hall toward an entrancing floor-length window. Having attained this goal, he contrived to pass his diminutive body through the railing guard. A moment more and he was well beyond reach, lurching triumphantly along a cornice which held him precariously suspended three stories above a busy thoroughfare.

Here is where the shocked Josefa found him upon her return from church. Praying desperately, the young mother crawled out upon the insecure ledge. As her trembling knees, impeded by the capacious petticoats of the nineteenth century, inched their way down the length of the old cornice, the thin margin, literally, of their lives, she must have despaired of saving her tiny son. His slightest motion might so easily prove to be the last. Dare she risk a few soft words of direction? Would her lively, impetuous baby see in her creeping pursuit only the humor of some exciting new game and make a dash for escape that must certainly hurl his little frame into space to be shattered upon the cobblestones so fearsomely far below? Afterward could Josefa Juárez ever understand how she did manage to rescue her intrepid infant? We only know that years later she was to say that this was merely the first time she had offered her life for that of her beloved first-born son. . . .

There was no denying that Miguelito's investigative impulses and incessant physical activity constantly drew him into mischief, but his little heart was also a wellspring of the love that tempers willfulness, and from the beginning his obedience to his adored *mamacita* was remarked by everyone.

There were no front lawns, or even back yards, in which to play in México City, because the fortresslike edifices which housed her population rose flush with the streets and were set wall to wall on the other three sides. Games shared with one's sisters were therefore conducted in the patios made colorful by a profusion of flowering plants and the tropical "painted birds" which trilled merrily in the cages that festooned the heavy columns of the *corredores*. These galleries ran about three, and frequently four, sides of the bright and gracious main patio which formed the heart of the Mexican home. Through the massive double doors opening upon them and the balconies the high-ceilinged rooms received their air and most of their light. In only those rooms which ran across the front of the house were to be found any save occasional windows. A little boy must be resigned to whatever he could manage to see and hear of the great humming city rising outside through these few openings upon a restricted segment of the narrow, wall-lined street.

It was through the windows of the Pro residence flung open to the sun-soaked Mexican mornings that Miguelito first learned to listen for the rhythmic cries of the ambulant vendors who made a bedlam of the invigorating early air as they sought the attention of the housewife or the housekeeper for their wares.

"Mangos of Manila . . . and very fine strawberries?"

"Sweet potatoes, tomatoes, string beans, very beautiful?"

"*Bis—co—chos,* sweet bread of quality?"

"Brooms and feather dusters . . . a great bargain truly?"

The cajoling, singing syllables of the Indian-slurred Spanish that rose to every pause on a note of lingering query might be offered tentatively, or insistently thrown forth against the close-built walls. Some were deep, brave shouts from brown, half-naked chests; others no more than thin plaints whose shrillness was lost through the women's inevitable, all-enveloping *rebozos.* But none fell harshly upon the ear as they lifted on the clear, lightly gilded atmosphere across the iron grillwork to penetrate the deep recesses of the weathered residences which had once been the glittering mansions of colonial México's fabled Imperial City.

The hawkers' calls tickled the easy humor of Miguelito's genial nature. One and all, they charmed him into responses expressed in baby chuckles and gleeful handclappings. But he always waited most eagerly for one certain voice in which he found a special magic, took a delight that soon deepened into the stubborn, wholly trustful love known only to very young children. The voice which achieved all this, which inspired the little one's first extra-familial devotion, was that of the humble *Azteca* who supplied the Pro table with its luscious tropical fruits. And the fruit peddler loved the little Pro boy, almost fanatically. *"Mi niño Almiguelito,"* she called him, indulging the Indians' penchant for picturesque contraction. To her, he was "little Miguel, my soul baby."

It was a strange attachment, this bond of love between the carefully nurtured toddler and the lowly *Indita* who was too shy to reveal her name or the slightest circumstance of her existence to his naturally interested parents. But it was a very strong attachment, plainly seen in the ardor that her singsong calls evoked in the infant as they heralded her daily approach to his parents' door. The child could elude anyone's arms, would even abandon those of his wonderful mother, to run excitedly to meet his friend. And although he was strictly forbidden to approach the window rails, he soon discovered a splendid spot from which to glimpse her figure as she entered the *zaguán* or entryway. This was a capacious jardiniere into which he would clamber to wait patiently in the midst of a luxuriant plant. Well he knew that his imperative calls would bring the devoted woman to his side. But this happiness was fated to attract a mishap which very nearly cost Miguelito his life.

One day the little fellow's enthusiastic welcome made him disregard all caution. He fell out of the jardiniere. It is not clear just where the flowerpot was located, but Father Pulido affirms: "A little more and he would have been killed," [4] then and there. The frightened woman hastened to pick up and comfort her *"Almiguelito"* with caresses and words of endearment.

We do not know that an injury from this accident contributed to his later woes, but it surely marked a notable increase in the Indian's attentions to Miguelito which were to result disastrously. In her overpowering desire to please the little boy she now began to shower upon him every indulgence at her command. And this is what led to his undoing. One morning of sorrowful memory the two great friends were seated on the tile floor of the *corredor.* Were they playing little games together, or was she telling him stories of her own infancy in some faraway hill village of her forefathers? No one knows. But it was during this visit that she made him a very injurious gift. This was a big gourd jar filled to the brim with a chalky-tasting small fruit which the Mexicans call *tejocote.* And the child fell upon this windfall with such greedy enthusiasm that by the time the family discovered what was afoot, he had consumed no less than half a hundred of the *tejocotes!*

His pleasure was of short duration. After the chagrined withdrawal of his generous guest before Josefa's scolding, he suffered a violent congestion. The worried Pros passed a sleepless night over the crib of a very sick little boy.

[4] *Alborada de un Mártir,* p. 9.

Upon her arrival at the house the following morning, the Indian was stricken to learn what her affection had wrought and, sobbing with remorse and fear, she ran directly to the nursery without hesitating to ask permission. Nor, shy as she was, would she submit to ejection. She sat in stoic agony at the head of his bed, her ebony eyes glazed with pain as they watched the grim battle being waged within the tiny body. Night and day she clung to her post, punishing herself for her great fault toward *"Almiguelito"* as he wavered between life and death before his grief-shaken parents, who had frantically called in several physicians. The chief diagnostician believed the case to be hopeless. For, even if the Pro baby managed to escape the grave, he would surely be left feeble-minded! Under these doleful dictums which the Indian may or may not have understood, and the suffering of the family, which she certainly did, she sat on, without sleep, refusing nourishment. The only one she addressed in all this time was the Virgin of Guadalupe, to whom she intermittently raised her voice to implore the life of her little friend.

There came a day when the anguish of the Pros was granted a measure of mitigation. The fierce clutch of the disease loosened and they dared hope that their baby might survive. Just how much the Indian read into this slight improvement would never be known. But apparently her primitive blood, that blood which always runs *with* nature, suggested that Miguelito was out of danger. Were his parents somewhat comforted to see her now arise and, lips still sealed, slip out of the room? Perhaps, for they would have been acquainted with the intuitive aboriginal mind. Their son's friend had simply disappeared, never to return. But, young as he was, Miguel Agustín never forgot her.

However, for him, all memories, whether joyous or sorrowful, were to be long postponed. It seemed the doctor had been right in his terrifying prediction. The passing of these earliest pains and fevers left their small victim with the vacuous stare, the hanging head, and the open mouth of an imbecile. Although he sometimes seemed to respond interiorly to the afflicted Josefa's loving voice, he was incapable of enunciating a syllable. For a long, sad year his mind was a dark, only conjecturable mystery.

It seems sure that Miguelito's initial congestion had been compounded by an attack of brain fever because Father Pulido [5] avers that "a new cerebral fever" developed at the end of the year, following intervening bouts with measles and whooping cough which he had somehow managed to resist. This time, however, the threat to his life proved the most drastic of all. He went into a series of convulsions. Again the doctors announced that death was inevitable. Gathered about his bed on the day which would bring the crisis, they and the household watched him stiffen into the rigidity that really must bring a definitive end to the ills he had now sustained for nearly a third of his short sojourn in the world.

Might it not be best for his loved ones to resign themselves, quietly submit their little one to Heaven? Surely he had suffered enough and, if he was destined to a witless existence here below, far too much! But a good father's heart is a strange, deep well of emotion, not the least part of which is his stubbornness in defense of his young. Suddenly snatching his baby son's insensible form from the bed, Don Miguel stumbled toward an aged likeness of Our Lady of Guadalupe. Before the pensive, downcast gaze of his country's Patroness, he presented in his outstretched arms the piteous sight of the child whom all there now believed to be beyond recall. Then he gave vent to his no-longer controllable pain in an anguished outcry which sounded more like a demand than a prayer:

"*Madre mía,* give me back my son!"

In the dead silence which followed, the startled witnesses saw Miguelito's immense shudder as he came out of his death trance and fairly bathed his father in a great vomit of blood. Such a spectacular physical manifestation reanimated the physicians, who declared at once that the child's recovery, both physically and mentally, was now a strong possibility. And this was the second of their many predictions to prove accurate.

Following a few days' convalescence, Miguelito was restored to

[5] *Ibid.,* p. 10.

full health, a felicity presaged by his first words, clearly articulated, soon after the working of the miraculous cure.

"*Mamá,* I want a *cocol,*" he said, naming a variety of roll which had always been his favorite bread.

Josefa ordered that the bread be brought him and then, half delirious with love and gratitude, she caught him up into her embrace, crying, "Come here, my little *cocol!*"

Years later, when he was dodging the Calles police in the midst of México's frightful religious persecution, he frequently signed his perilous letters to his brothers in the Faith: "*Cocol.*"

THE FAMILY THAT STOOD ALONE

BETWEEN his fourth and fifth birthdays Miguel Agustín's constitution so vastly improved that no one would have suspected that this lively lad had twice been snatched from the arms of death—who could deny it?—by Our Lady of Guadalupe. The remainder of the Pros' stay in the capital saw their eldest man-child assuming his place with exceptional verve. This was the greatest of blessings for his parents for, besides their delight in seeing their son in perfect health and spirits once more, they were deeply grateful that, with new babies coming along at regular intervals, Josefa was relieved of the worry of a sick child which would have been disadvantageous to her health and the welfare of her infants. Before 1897 little Josefina and Ana María (and quite possibly baby brother, Edmundo, as well) were joyously welcomed into this again wholly happy home.

The playfulness which had characterized Miguelito's infancy had developed into a disposition not only sunny, but diverting to all. His jokes, pranks, and impersonations combined to form a highlight of the evenings which, in the Mexican family tradition, the Pros passed together in the intimacy of their home. His facile memory and gift for imitation were especially outstanding. To his doting parents that long year in which they had accustomed themselves to the idea that their Miguel would never be a nor-

mally "bright" child seemed nearly incredible. He was the live-
liest child in the house. Enthusiastically and incessantly he staged
skits and charades, recited verses—many of them improvised—
which warmed the chill highland evenings with laughter and
kept the Pro *sala* noisy with fun. He was a born clown. Recognizing that his five-year-old possessed a very real talent, Don
Miguel presented him with a tiny theater, exquisitely made and
complete with curtains, scenery, and effects. But alas, it lacked
actors! His indulgent *mamacita* promised that they should be
supplied without delay.

Setting out upon a shopping expedition to this end, Josefa
and Miguelito, accompanied by Concepción and María de la Luz,
directed themselves to the Alameda, that broad, central city park
whose promenades were lined by colorful *puestos* or booths overflowing with toys, sweets, and other items to delight the younger
generation of the capital. Juvenile shopping was in those days a
fresh-air outing. One strolled or skipped along beneath the
verdant Alameda's thick canopy of ancient trees and found all the
most intriguing offerings of the skills and arts of México's justly
famed toymakers piled high in the open *puestos*. And meanwhile
one might enjoy the elegant fountains and fine statuary that the
Porfiriana Era had scattered throughout the park with a lavish
hand. A boy could absorb unforgettable lessons in his country's flora, art, and history during a simple quest for playthings
in that day before the effects of commercialism and advertis-
ing had touched the masses, or the classes, of México—when
there was still time enough and to spare for everything best in
life.

They had no difficulty in locating a display of the figures
which, under Miguel Agustín's small nimble fingers and gigantic
imagination, would bring the miniature stage alive. The lad was
entranced by the cleverly executed *muñequitos* or small dolls,
representations of México's typical, colorfully garbed natives, and
he excitedly pleaded to be permitted to purchase them all. Since
this ambitious transaction brought the cost to a figure in excess
of his budget, Concepción and María de la Luz generously emp-

tied their small purses to make up the difference. This detail concluded, Miguelito threw himself on the pavement in the midst of his treasure, intent upon nothing but the immediate rehearsal of his cast in the dance he had recently seen performed by Indian pilgrims at the shrine of his special protectress, Our Lady of Guadalupe. However, as Josefa had other errands it was needful to persuade the young director to collect his actors and move along. And the sooner they arrived home the better, inasmuch as he had already announced a full production for that same evening.

This counsel produced the desired effect, but such is the predilection of the true theatrical genius that Miguelito had soon spotted, in a store window, some absolutely indispensable additions to his proposed "spectacle." The group of elegantly clad puppets was just what he needed to lend class to a variety show! Josefa patiently acceded to his importuning. They entered the modest establishment behind the eye-catching window to make the purchase, this time from *her* purse. But apparently this latest indulgence turned the head of the five-year-old because, usually the most amiable of the Pro progeny, Miguelito was, upon this occasion, quite undone. Inside the store the first object he saw made him forget all about the puppets. The new attraction was a desk ornament, a beautiful horse of white marble.

"*Mamá,* I don't want the puppets now. What I *really* want is this magnificent white horse!" clamored Miguel Agustín.

Josefa looked at him in astonishment but replied calmly, "No, *mi hijito,* the horse is not a toy—nor for you."

"*Pues sí,* I want it, I want it!" he cried in an obstinacy he had never previously exhibited. And thereupon the age-old struggle between parental authority and youthful caprice was joined. Before it was concluded, the proprietress of the shop was commiserating with the chagrined young woman whose unreasonable child was "bound to achieve the premature whitening of his mother's hair."

Josefa, who scarcely recognized Miguel in such a mood, managed to answer quietly, "We shall hope in God that it won't be like that." [1] And with this, she called a carriage in which to take her perturbed children home.

The frustrated boy persisted in his self-pity and thus the countenance, usually so merry, which he lifted for his father's homecoming embrace was tearstained and resentful. When Don Miguel understood the circumstances, he said ominously, "Very well, my little *caballero,* we shall have to settle this matter between ourselves." He directed his wife and daughters to leave them alone together that he might not have "to show them the disrespect" of spanking "this stupid *niño*" in their presence. Taking her uneasy little girls by the hands, Josefa forthwith marched them out of the house to the astonishment of a small boy who had never before received any such drastic punishment as a paddling. But merely three not very severe spanks brought the tender-hearted mother and sisters back again, for they had stationed themselves just behind the street door. In the soft solicitude typical of Mexican women and girls toward their sons and brothers, they joined their pleas that *papá* desist and pardon Miguelito's naughtiness.

This had the desired effect, and a chastened Miguel asked pardon of each of them individually, of his father, his dear *mamacita,* Concepción, and María de la Luz. It was a never-to-be-forgotten evening. His ordinarily jolly and affectionate father managed to maintain a sober mein and, for the first time in his son's memory, presided at the supper table with an exceedingly long face.

The following day Josefa returned to the shopping district with the three children. Much to Miguelito's chagrin, they went directly to the store which housed the coveted marble horse. When the proprietress recognized them, she exclaimed, *"Ave María Purísima!* That rude *niño* of yesterday!"

"Sí, Señora," replied Josefa blandly, "the same. And I am here to ask you to show us all the toys that you have in stock. Of course, I expect to recompense you for the work this will cause you."

[1] Pulido, p. 12.

"Humph!" snorted the shopkeeper. "This is how children are brought up nowadays. What sort of policy is this, *Señora?*"

"That which I use with my children," observed Don Miguel's loyal helpmate noncommittally.

"*Bueno,* as you are willing to pay, and if this is how you coddle your children, so be it," grumbled the woman as she commenced taking the toys from her shelves and pointedly addressing her comments upon the attractions of each exclusively to Miguel Agustín. Saving the controversial horse for the very last, she presented it in mockery. "Oh, yes, here it is. Take it!"

"*No, Señora, gracias*"—in a small stifled voice.

"What? It's the same horse!"

"*No, Señora,* I don't wish it, thank you very much."

"All right, I make you a present of it."

"*No, no, Señora, no, muchas gracias!*" Trembling with emotion, the little boy clasped his sisters with both hands to prevent himself from being tempted to extend them toward the fascinating object, and his round dark eyes were full of tears.

Comprehension dawned upon the shopkeeper and, in Latin effusiveness, she ran out from behind her showcase to embrace Josefa and kiss Miguel. Then she applied to the mother for permission to make her little boy a formal gift of the white horse. She was sure that each time he gazed upon it he would be reminded of how greatly it pays to conquer oneself and to be obedient.

In the end, the horse went home with them, but Miguel declined to carry it. And thereafter it stood for many years on Don Miguel's desk in splendid isolation. Actually, the mere sight of it caused the boy pain. One day he was heard to exclaim, "For this *thing* I made my mother weep!" His father had always taught him that only a coward causes the tears of a woman. After that, no one of the family ever again alluded to the "affair of the white horse."

On the whole, however, there were surprisingly few punishments in the home of Don Miguel and Doña Josefa. They were never aloof or formidable parents. Their whole life was the love they bore one another. On the part of the husband, it enriched and deepened his natural chivalry. Although he did, on rare occasions, deem it his duty to castigate his sons, it is known that he never lifted a hand against the little girls. He had devised a much pleasanter method for keeping his children's deportment on a high level. Each Saturday evening over the cups of foaming chocolate and plates heaped with sweet rolls, the little Pros' recurrent excitement would mount, sometimes on grins of confidence, sometimes in nervous doubts and soul searchings—to the point of tension. This was the big event of the week. They knew that just as soon as the cups and plates were finally empty, Don Miguel would make the announcement which never grew commonplace, would never lose its thrill of suspense.

"It just so happens," he would begin, "that certain very good and wise angels of my acquaintance have sent word to me that they have deposited in this house some very special gifts for those of my children who have been exceptionally well-behaved during the past week. I understand, too, that these gifts may be found this evening behind the portrait of your great-uncle, Fray Crisóstomo, in the cupboard near the photograph of Mamá Bibi's house in Guadalupe where three of you were born, and in your *mamacita's* wardrobe. As they are all marked with the names of those who have merited the angels' generosity, it shouldn't take their owners very long to locate them."

This was the cue for a noisy scraping of chair legs on the brick floor and for the eager tumble to begin. Though they knew more or less what the packages were likely to contain—candies, cookies, religious medals, toys—the fascination of the weekly game never diminished. "What may *I* receive from the good angels this time?" "Have I really deserved a gift this week?" And then for those who had—joy. While oh, the remorse of those who, very stupidly, had not! Theirs the role of onlookers while the others exclaimed excitedly over their beautiful prizes. What a price to pay for their sorry errors of self-will, a few moments of heedless naughtiness! But already brave, new resolutions were taking form. After all, another week wasn't so *terribly* long!

From the beginning, the house watched over so carefully by Don Miguel and blessed by the all-encompassing love of Doña Josefa stood in a self-sufficient solidarity against the outer world —its storms and its vicissitudes. . . .

As for Miguelito's small disgraces, after the "white horse episode" they were never again born of stubbornness. It was just that sometimes his keen sense of the absurd or his agile imagination betrayed him into impulsive acts whose unforeseen results occasionally fell heavily on one or more of the family. But the alacrity with which he willingly admitted his fault and his total lack of malice usually extricated him from the "jams" that might not have dissolved so easily for a personality less winning or a character less kind. And above all he could not bear the thought of hurting his mother's feelings. One day he overheard her say in some anxiety, "Can it be that we have another Augustine on our hands?"

"Well, that is my name, *Mamá,*" he observed quietly, somewhat startling the gentle Josefa.

III

MIMICRY, MISCHIEF, MUSIC—AND OBEDIENCE

WHEN his father's mining interests dictated the Pros' removal to Monterrey, Miguel was six years old. By this time his wiry frame gave no evidence whatsoever of the punishment inflicted by his infant ills, nor any constitutional weakness. The boy was constantly in motion, physically and mentally. Nothing eluded his agile attention. Life was filled with wonders for the deep, dark eyes which were so huge, for all the downsweep of the lids toward the outer corners. We do not know the regional origins of Miguel Agustín's Spanish ancestors, but his eyes were certainly those of the south, Andalucía or Murcia.

Below a finely formed skull, his face was long and strong. The high, full forehead, expressive brows, the well-proportioned nose, and generous mouth, separated by a long upper lip, were nicely balanced by the deep, firmly cut chin. At this period his features were rather oversized, but only the prominent, somewhat protruding ears might be accused of having detracted from his handsomeness.

In view of the declarations that the child's characteristic mood was jovial and fun-loving, it is surprising to find his boyhood photographs consistently reflecting a sober, almost pensive expression. Perhaps México's turn-of-the-century photographers were adamant in demanding dignity of the subjects they were recording for posterity. Or it might have been that, even this early, Miguelito did have some insight into life's serious realities —indications of which arose to the surface only when his natural restlessness was forced to hold still for the black-shrouded old cameras and their operators' "birdies." However it was, the likenesses show the face above the high-necked serge jacket embellished by a double row of brass buttons as that of an attractive, appealing child.

Upon their arrival in the northern industrial city, the Pros went first to the home of Don Miguel's brother, the *jefe* or manager of Monterrey's telegraph office. As seven or eight guests imposed a strain upon the domestic accommodations of their uncle, Miguelito was assigned sleeping quarters in the room containing the telegraphers' keys and paraphernalia. The whole process of talking by electricity proved a new enchantment. On rainy afternoons the little boy was glad to remain indoors to watch the workings of the magic apparatus which sent messages to the distant ends of the earth faster than his flexible tongue could waggle. However, he soon decided that it was not so pleasing a method as nature's provision for human communication. "No, I'll never be a telegrapher," he declared to his sisters. "They only speak with signals. I'd much rather *really talk* with everybody!" [1]

And soon his preoccupation switched to another interest. Don Miguel had taken the house next door to that of Nuevo León's Governor, General Bernado Reyes, who later was to be Dias' Minister of War. At eight o'clock each morning the General's troop flamboyantly presented itself before his gate to give the salute. The trumpet blasts and the rolling of the military drums set Miguelito half crazy with delight and veered his play-acting instincts into a new channel. He warned Concepción that she must forthwith transform herself into a Sister of Charity since he was now a valiant soldier who would have urgent need of her ministrations upon the field of battle. He was, he said, fated to receive frightful wounds while gallantly capturing the enemy's flag. The good Sister must fly to his aid to support his suffering head and

[1] Pulido, p. 15.

wash the blood from his wounds *until* a still more devastating blast would make a tragic end of them both. This grim drama required considerable rehearsal before their "tear jerker" had been brought to perfection for the edification of the little sisters. Though merely a passing diversion, one is struck by the poignant analogy between this child's play and the destiny of the daring young man who, after having "conquested the standard of the enemy" so heroically, would one day fulfill just such a role in a real-life finale.

But now it was time for school. Miguel was enrolled in the private establishment of the Señoritas Sánchez. Even so, fun and a boy's personal investigations still came first—most decidedly. Awakening one morning to find Monterrey asparkle beneath the only snow he had ever seen at close range, Miguelito was overwhelmed by a desire to see how the trains would look enveloped in glistening white coats as they came puffing into the Monterrey Railway Station. He fairly ached to witness this marvel, but was not betrayed into mentioning it at the breakfast table. He recognized the uselessness of seeking his routine-respecting parents' permission for any such schoolday digression as he contemplated.

At the accustomed hour he left his house, apparently headed for his classes. Playing hooky in México is by no means the casual procedure it might appear to our independent young North Americans. This is because the smaller children are conducted to and from school by trusted family retainers. Miguel's only chance lay in prevailing upon his escort to consent to an unprecedented irregularity. Either this particular *mozo* was exceptionally vulnerable to his little master's blandishments, or himself exceptionally young. For, after but a half-hearted struggle, he surrendered to the lad's suggestion that they dedicate this morning's study to research at the *Estación de Ferrocarriles!* Miguelito could spell out his letters for the Profesoras Sánchez any day, but how often could they hope to see Monterrey's trains come lurching and screeching into the big sheds, splendid in their brand-new snow mantles? Would it not be *instructive*—as well as delightful—to inspect the results of the night-long contest with icy-fingered winter, which must have turned those clanging, prodigious black monsters, the engines, into dazzling visions of blinding white? This was the argument that, triumphing over the servant's better judgment, set their feet on the short cut to the railway station.

Miguel was not disappointed. His adventure proved every bit as thrilling as he anticipated. When the servant finally tore him away from his winter-glamorized trains to deposit him at the school, the child called a general conference to give his classmates the benefit of his fascinating observations during the hours which had seen *them* bent over their slates and primers. The aftermath was hardly the unmixed joy which the enterprising heir of the Pro family might have preferred, but such reprobation as his shocking "informality" netted him from his irate teachers failed to dampen his ardor. At the supper table he told his story all over again. Don Miguel encouraged his children's reports on the day's doings over supper; and this one appears not to have been badly received. Of course it is possible that Don Miguel at least partially agreed with his son's theories upon the comparative merits of so rare an experience and one more humdrum morning of first-year reading exercises. But even had it incurred another punishment at home, Miguel could not have contained his thrilling story. He was too used to sharing his delights with Concepción and María de la Luz, who were so vastly intrigued that they begged permission to go view such a wonder for themselves— the very next time that snow might fall upon Monterrey.

About this time Josefa was preparing for the Corpus Christi procession to be celebrated at Monterrey's famed Iglesia del Roble. Well in advance she ordered the making of a generous supply of great wax candles to be expertly worked and adorned with elaborate designs. Miguelito watched all this activity with his habitual interest and, when the holy day [2] dawned, he rather nonchalantly claimed one of the candles (which proved to be considerably longer than himself), as well as his own place in the much-discussed procession. Even though she was aware that chil-

[2] Corpus Christi is a day of obligation in México.

dren were not expected to participate in this particular event, Josefa consented to take him along.

The fact that he was the only child in the procession in no wise caused Miguel any embarrassment. His volatile spirits leaped to such heights of exhilaration before the drama and beauty of the ceremony that he was soon asking his mother to tell him where he could find processions like this "that would never, never come to an end." And even before this one had terminated, his glowing face had attracted the attention of the parish priest who requested Josefa to send him her son as an acolyte. But this proposal was precisely what it took to break the spell for Miguel. He was almost frantic in his demands for his *mamá's* promise that she would refuse to permit such a thing. His biographer Pulido comments: "I do not know why he combatted [the idea of undertaking] this office"; [3] and apparently it either did not occur to anyone to seek an explanation of this aversion or else the little boy was successful in eluding his questioners. We know he was not shy; and since thousands of Mexican lads quite as young as he counted it an honor to serve as altar boys, there should have been nothing unfamiliar or alarming in the idea.

Might this son of Josefa Juárez, this grandnephew of old Fray Crisóstomo Gómez, have somehow sensed that drawing so near to his Lord on the altar might be tantamount to setting off in his bright young heart the opening detonation of a spiritual explosion? If this is an acceptable guess, it would suggest that, for all his natural intrepidity, there lurked an intimation of life's power to present at least *one* adventure before which Miguel Agustín might well experience the brush of fear.

After rejecting the invitation to undertake the duties of an acolyte at the Iglesia del Roble, Miguelito found himself more than pleased to present himself at the same church to shoulder the obligations of a "godfather." [4] It was a situation that incor-

[3] *Ibid.,* p. 16.
[4] In Spanish-descended countries the term *"padrino"* is interchangeably used for the godfather of Baptism, the sponsor of Confirmation, and that required for the First Communion.

porated a number of novelties. In the first place, without having
made his own First Communion, he was sponsoring the First
Communion of another. In the second, his godchild was three
times his age! He was a nineteen-year-old former shepherd who
had found his way into the Pro domicile as a servant. His name
was Abraham and he was, according to Father Pulido, "an excellent *muchacho.*" Perhaps the circumstances of his early surroundings—the vast, lightly populated northern sheep ranges—
had deprived Abraham of the opportunity to make his First
Communion from the customary age (six to eight years in México) onward.

Following the ceremony, Miguel solicitously escorted Abraham
back to the house and the festive breakfast. This was set out in
the main patio where Miguelito took his place beside Abraham
at the delicacy-heaped board smiling benignly upon his "spiritual
protégé." According to custom, it would never again be "Abraham" and "Young Master Miguel" between these two, but always *"Abijado*—Godson" and *"Padrino*—Godfather."

"Do take another cup of chocolate, *Ahijado!* And a piece of
this exquisite papaya. You mustn't be shy!"

"A thousand thanks, *Padrino.*"

Abraham accepted these attentions in the simple dignity born
of full confidence that on this day of days it was his due from the
house which commanded his faithful service. Following the
breakfast and his small godfather's brief speech of congratulation upon Abraham's new promotion in Christian status, came
verses and music rendered by Miguelito and his sisters. And then,
the obligations of the house having been meticulously dispatched, the little boy could, in all propriety, put his request.

"*Ahijado,* we all know that you sing enchanting songs and
have a fine voice. Will you not make us the favor to sing for us?"

"*Muchas gracias, Padrino.* It is kind of you to say so. But know
that my songs are merely *las pastorales* sung by the shepherds of
my land. They are rude and humble compositions, really not
worthy."

"*Vaya, Ahijado!* They are splendid songs. Whether sad or gay, they move the heart equally. Even *mi mamacita* says this . . . and that there is no harm whatsoever in their words. She says you may teach my sisters and me to sing them if only you are willing. Teach us to sing your *pastorales,* my godson, *por favor!*"

This was pleading from the lad's heart and no mere courtesy. Abraham could "distinguish" these differences, so he replied kindly, "With much pleasure, little godfather. *Pues,* if the estimable Doña Josefa has given us this permission, I shall certainly do it. Which of my poor little *pastorales* would you care to hear first?"

Miguelito and his sisters had soon mastered Abraham's full repertoire of "little *pastorales.*" And the boy's expertness in rendering them exactly in the voice and manner of Abraham never failed to evoke the laughter of his parents.

Not only the novel and comic brought his facile imagination into play. The pathetic and the weird made claims upon his sensitivity. He experienced tremendous woe in considering the fate of the unfortunates who peopled the Monterrey insane asylum, an institution the Pros passed on their regular Sunday-afternoon walks about the Alameda. He could never bring himself to include these poor insane whose vacant eyes sought his through the barred windows of the *manicomio* or asylum among his impersonations. Rather, night after night, he made their plight the subject of his longest prayers.

About the time of his discovery of tragedy, Miguel was in the process of perfecting a new diversion for his sisters. This was the brain-teasing game he called "*Nada*—Nothing." Just before supper the children would gather in the drawing room to give *Nada* the concentration it certainly demanded. Following a period of highly charged silence dedicated to an examination of what it was that constituted Nothing, each would give his or her individual interpretation. Was it vacancy? Was it outer space? Could smoke, which you can't feel, or wind, which you can't see, be properly said to share the qualities, or lack of qualities, of Nothing?

The evening that Josefa first took note of the unnatural, tomb-like silence enveloping her roomful of children she demanded in some alarm to know what they thought they were doing. She was hardly reassured by the confused chorus that purported to set forth the object of *Nada.*

"*Válgame Dios!*" she exclaimed in annoyance. "Cease this dangerous stupidity at once and go play with your toys or at least games that have movement. Do you all wish to turn into *locos?*"

Miguelito heard this question with horror; and solemnly promised his mother that he would never again suggest or participate in another session of *Nada!*

It was fortunate that the Pro family was so large and so sufficient unto itself that the various removals imposed by Don Miguel's mining activities could be effected with few regrets. There were never many ties to be severed since, during these years, the family always moved in a body. For each of them their real home, rather than a house filled with intimate associations and possessions, was the great spirit of affection and co-operation within which they lived together, outside dependence upon places, people, or things. Thus, the only drawback attached to their now-projected return to Zacatecas was the fact that Don Miguel's new station (the Mineral de Concepción del Oro) might prove detrimental to the children's education. Doña Josefa admitted concern at the news that there were no acceptable schools in this isolated mining town. Even so, she rejected the thought of remaining in Monterrey. The little ones' schooling was of lesser moment than the daily counsels and protection of a good father. Furthermore, "she preferred that they all follow their *papá* so that she would not have to see his sadness in being deprived of his children."[5]

As for the little Pros, the mere thought of the new adventures and experiences which lay ahead of them in the wild mining country was sheer delight. All through the excitement of the packing and other preparations the air was thick with their childish plans. Miguel would become a "fantastic" horseman—or any-

[5] *Ibid.,* p. 17.

way learn how to ride a mule through Zacatecas' mineral-streaked mountains. He might even discover a new mine while out riding all by himself which would turn out to be the richest ever seen in America! The girls would become angels of mercy to the grateful miners who, as was well known, suffered strange and painful accidents at their hazardous labors. No poor, wounded miner would go unnursed after the appearance of their new manager's kindhearted and capable daughters. Perhaps it was a bit early for Josefina and Ana María to take an active part in such grown-up work, but María de la Luz and Concepción were big, strong girls of nine and ten years and certainly able to launch projects for the rehabilitation of Concepción del Oro!

Miguel was well past seven now and so brave and tireless that he could easily be a real *ayudante,* or assistant, to their overworked father, who often said that in spite of all his son's pranks he was a well-intentioned boy and fundamentally the most obedient of them all. And was not baby Edmundo already walking and giving promise of soon learning many other useful things with which to abet the ambitious schemes of his big brother and sisters? It would certainly be much more convenient to have two male actors for the charades and comedies with which they would fill the long evenings at Concepción del Oro.

In this mood of happy expectations the six little Pros and their parents set out for the rude mining center which was destined to be the place of their longest residence together. The year was 1898.

IV

MINER'S BOY

THE first problem posed by Concepción del Oro has a most familiar ring in modern ears. To the Pros, however, it was so new as to be a little absurd. This was the "housing problem," almost unknown to Mexicans of their class a half-century ago when nearly every boy's father was owner of his own big house, not to mention the many "second homes"—those of long lists of uncles, aunts, and more distant relatives which were always open to relatives for how ever extended the visits might be.

Don Miguel's profession was not conducive to a settled pattern of life. During his brief seven years, Miguelito had already known three homes in as many communities. But until now, there had never been a scarcity of houses available to a gentleman seeking shelter for his *hijos*. In Concepción del Oro there simply was not a single habitable residence either for rent or for sale! The new mine manager would have to build his own. Meanwhile, his only alternative was to engage a section of the pueblo's modest hotel.

This arrangement afforded the family sufficiently comfortable accommodations, but there were several drawbacks. First and foremost, in the eyes of the conscientious father, was the matter of their fellow guests. The types of transients encountered in a mining town were unlikely to be the best, or even acceptable, examples for carefully reared children. To reduce the risk of ob-

jectionable influences upon his little ones, Don Miguel prohibited their association with any of the guests. Only by special
permission might they so much as speak with these *pasajeros*
who, for the most part, were traveling salesmen, minor politicians, theatrical roadshow or carnival personnel, and, occasionally,
a company of second- or third-rate bullfighters. The actors and,
above all, the *toreros*—coming and going between the hotel and
the bullring in their brilliant costumes—could hardly fail to
arouse excitement in color-loving young hearts, and particularly
in that of an imaginative boy who was himself a "born performer."

Upon one occasion the appearance of the popular Compañía
Infantil de Toreros provided a very heavy temptation for Miguelito. The very thought of the dramatic tales of peril and glory
which these dashing young "celebrities" would be sure to tell
him constituted a threat to his customary obedience. However, he
limited his contact with the Compañía to the minutes spent in
passing from the Pro quarters to the hotel dining room. They
sufficed, nevertheless, to give the bright-eyed little fellow a certain acquaintance with this most ubiquitous and fascinating of
Hispano-American spectacles (which incorporates all the elements of high drama and sport as well as the most perfect skill
and daring).

Despite his lively interest, the glamor and rewards of bullfighting did not awaken in Miguel even a passing ambition for
such a career. His interest was quite satisfied by make-believe. He
would catch up a cape and stick and, imitating the footwork and
postures of the *toreros,* name each pass of their most famous
figures or plays as he reproduced it for his wide-eyed and admir-
ing sisters—*"un pase de pitón a rabo," "una veronica," "un vola-
pié"*—quite as any little North American fan might explain the
high points of *his* national game—"a hit," "a strike," "a home
run," and so on.

Then, when the Compañía Infantil, or other visiting con-
tingents, continued on their way, leaving Concepción del Oro to
its own devices, Miguel's attention would revert to the normal

aspects of the life centering about the big mine. Sometimes when he found himself thinking of the interminable wanderings of the rootless young *toreros* who, wherever they went, achieved no more than a passing acclaim from more solid folk, he pitied the loneliness and the futility he had sensed in them even while their boisterous boasts and mirth had imbued a country hotel with an illusion of gaiety and a self-sufficient sophistication. It wasn't happiness, he decided, that filled the heart of the professional performer as he exhibited and re-exhibited his little repertoire for the approval of only casually interested strangers. Although Miguel could not have expressed it then, he understood that, beneath the self-conscious charm and talent by which these people earned their little hours of adulation and their daily bread, there lay a hidden kernel that was a hard and selfish obsession—vanity. There was an element of grimness in their elaborate efforts to capture the applause and the pennies of these rude miners and the equally simple tradesmen who composed their audiences.

No, it could not be happiness—which is love—that made a business of what should be disinterested play; as it was not love that the entertainers evoked in the composite heart of "their public." They supplied momentary diversion for the men who labored long hours for small pay far underground in the damp galleries, but that was all. None of it was the joy one knew when, safe in the heart of one's own dear family, one created merriment with spontaneous little offerings—the charades, impersonations, verses, and songs shared in the sweet intimacy of affection and respect.

Miguelito Pro only felt all these things. Years were to pass before he would put them into words, but he had already begun to distinguish between the real and the false—which was perhaps the single advantage that accrued from this initial period of hotel living at Concepción del Oro.

The Day of St. Joseph (San José), the name saint of their mother, little Josefina, and the still smaller brother José Edmundo, was chosen by Miguelito, Concepción, and María de la

Luz for making their First Communion, received from the hands of their pastor, Padre Mateo Correa. This was the same Father Correa who was to achieve martyrdom during the opening terror of the Calles persecution. But in 1898 the savagery and wasteful agony that lay ahead for all Mexican Christians (i.e., ninety-five per cent of *all* Mexicans) had not yet been intimated. Such attacks upon Church property and prerogatives as had, now and then, been attempted by certain self-styled patriots had usually been attended by some pretense of legality. There had been "steals" and occasional sanctions in an effort to justify them, but total barbarism had not yet lifted its head in México. And so neither the good pastor nor the new little communicant, Miguel Pro, as they faced each other across the altar rail of Concepción del Oro's parish church, had any presentiment that their names would one day be linked in glory for the reverence of their countrymen.

At this time, that his older children might attend a Holy Week mission, Don Miguel broke all precedents by entrusting them to the hands of outsiders. The friends who had so fully won his confidence were the Pérez, a family residing in Mazapil, a town some thirteen miles away from Concepción del Oro. Two Jesuits, Fathers González and Maya, who were to conduct the mission, had stopped, en route to their station, at the mine to visit Don Miguel and invite him to bring the little Pros to attend it. As it was impossible for Miguelito's father to leave his work just then, he promised to send the older children who could stay with his friends, the Pérez. Meanwhile, he impressed upon his son a sense of responsibility for his sisters' safety on this short trip.

This was a new role for Miguel, but one he was determined to dispatch with honor. The servants who were to accompany them to Mazapil had no sooner hoisted the little girls into their saddles on the burros which had been carefully selected for their gentleness, than the boy began to launch warnings and instructions right and left.

"Look out there! Be sure to hold on tightly, my sisters! Don't give these animals a chance to throw you off!"

As the little cavalcade moved slowly along the unpaved streets of the town and into the narrow trail which wound off toward the hills and into the mountain passes which would bring them to Mazapil before sundown, the stimulating novelty of the adventure served to increase Miguelito's diligence. Casting sharp glances at the girls' burros to assure himself that their easy-going appearance was not a blind for some secretly planned perfidy, some act of sudden violence against the "little ladies" he was pledged to protect at all cost, he forgot to keep his own mount under observation. In a moment when he was bending a critical eye upon María de la Luz' posture in the saddle, disgrace befell the young cavalier himself. Only imagine the shame of finding oneself, the leader, victim of the single accident of the whole journey! Although his poor beast had committed no greater offense than to lower its head to nibble the tempting young herbs sprouting along the trail over which they were moving so slowly, Miguel lost his balance, then his seat, and rolled over the animal's neck to meet the ground with a thud.

This was ignominy! How could he ever re-establish his dignity in the eyes of the little girls he had been practically bullying in his role of male protector? As he lay sprawled upon the stony trail, remembrance flashed over him of how, while they were still in Monterrey, they had loyally supported his ambition to become a "fantastic" horseman. Fortunately, inspiration came. Instead of scrambling to his feet in confusion, wretchedly rubbing his bruises, he remained where he was on the ground, deliberately stretched forth a grubby hand, and plucked a bunch of the coarse mountain grass that was, luckily, growing within reach. With this prize in hand, he arose and announced with an air of satisfaction:

"I just wanted to cut this fodder for my burro to eat when we get up among the peaks where there will likely be no herbs whatever."

His small anatomy was covered with scratches and bruises and they hurt a lot, but he knew he must not let on about *that,* if he expected to "get by" with his face-saving dissimulation.

They found Mazapil aswarm with people who had come in from the outlying ranches and hunting lodges to celebrate the Holy Week and to attend the mission in the parish church that reared lofty spires above the plaza. During the Holy Friday procession the crowd was so dense that one moved about the church environs with difficulty. And in this milling throng the hospitable Pérez suddenly discovered that Miguel Agustín had managed to get himself lost. Concerned for what might have befallen him and their responsibility to their esteemed friend, Don Miguel Pro, they began a frantic search for their lively young guest. Their efforts were rewarded when Miguelito was located standing alongside Padre Maya in the presbytery where he was preaching to a large crowd of the faithful. Unnoticed in the press of listeners, the youngster was busily engaged in pulling the threads, one by one, from the fringe of the Padre's sash!

Pulido tells us that many years later, when Miguelito had become his country's beloved "Padre Pro," he was to say in remembrance of this scene of his childhood, "How *I* would glory in being able to preach to so many—even though that blessing were to leave my sash in ribbons!" [1]

On the return trip from Mazapil the little pilgrims missed serious trouble by a narrow margin. An inattentive servant mistook the route and permitted the burros to stray off along a trail leading to an abandoned mine. Before this error had been discovered and rectified, many hours were consumed by wanderings through a dangerous, uninhabited wilderness of jagged hills and canyons, so that the anxiously awaited homecoming of the exhausted and excited children was alarmingly late. This mishap determined Don Miguel to ban, at least for a time, any further mountain excursions, a fact greatly distressing to his offspring. Their first trip had stimulated an enthusiasm to repeat this form of adventure at frequent intervals.

Before long, however, study was making such inroads upon the waking hours of Miguel and his sisters that there would have been little time for excursions, in any case. Their father now set-

[1] Pulido, p. 19.

tled the second serious problem presented by life at the mine—
his children's primary education. Despite his heavy schedule, Don
Miguel would be their *profesor!* He allotted two hours, from 5
to 7 P.M., in which to hear recitations of the lessons he had assigned for each day. From breakfast until the four-o'clock Mexican dinner the children's whole time must be dedicated to their
books—a schedule whose fulfillment Josefa was charged to su-
pervise. Miguelito, by no means a studious boy, nevertheless good-
naturedly adjusted himself to his father's inflexible dictum that
there was to be no slightest nonsense about the study. Every
day, immediately following *comida,* he must be prepared to
give a good account of himself. There was no use trying to avoid
this "discipline of the lessons" on ordinary days, though festival
days were exempt, glory be!

Don Miguel's authority and his son's obedience soon resulted in
the lad's ability to write very well, to read "with facility and understanding," and to express himself fluently. For the rest, his
extraordinary memory rendered it easy for him to make satisfactory recitations, at least, even in subjects which interested him
but slightly or, alas, not at all.

Many of Miguelito's evenings were spent in another study
which was really dedicated. But this was quite a different matter.
This was music—which the boy did not regard as work. He had
learned "to dominate" the guitar and mandolin with very little
effort. Now the big project was a *típica* or string orchestra. He
was the player-director who organized the programs and re-
hearsed the four sisters until their quintet was capable of giving
a respectable and even spirited account of itself. It did not take
long for them to bring honor upon the house of Pro. Hardly was
the family established in its home before the orchestra had become a highlight of all its fiestas: the saints' days, birthdays, and
other anniversaries that, in México, would be simply unthinkable
without music. As these special celebrations automatically demanded the preparation of thirty or more "concerts" annually,
there could have been few evenings, indeed, when the Pro *sala*
was not resonant with melody and rhythm. And it was soon seen

that Miguelito, the impresario and artist, could be quite as adamant as Don Miguel, the *profesor!*

On the red-letter dates requiring an expression of joy and thanksgiving through music, the children could revel in the novelty of arising and retiring at all hours. Father Pulido (who had much of this data firsthand from Don Miguel and Ana María less than twenty years ago) says that during these celebrations the little Pros frequently performed from daybreak until midnight. This testifies not only to their industry but to the excellence of its results. The most affectionate and indulgent parents in the world could not have borne any such protracted periods of inexpertly rendered music.

The sixth of March was one of the most important of the family festivals since it was the wedding anniversary of Don Miguel and Doña Josefa. It opened just before dawn with the orchestra's offering of the *mañanitas* [2] to their beloved parents. Thereafter, the morning advanced to the accompaniment of every form of felicitation. Each of the children had prepared a gift for *mamá* and *papá,* both of which must be presented with appropriate speeches expressing the donor's love and respect. Miguel Agustín, who had already commenced to write verses, liked to give his presents this form. He would recite his odes or read them from the flourish-filled manuscripts he had dedicated to his proud parents. The joy which pervaded their intimate celebrations often brimmed over in the emotion and sentiment that, for Mexicans, is always inextricably mixed with tears.

Don Miguel was the indisputable authority in this growing family. Doña Josefa, its heart and the tenderest of mothers, was, first of all, her husband's loyal, co-operative helpmeet. The children of these two were all unusually intelligent and responsive. Rather than viewing their father's firm, almost rigorous, discipline as a cause for resentment or rebellion, they accepted it as their security. Confident in his love and respecting his obvious justice, they never found a reason to question his teaching that

[2] Early-morning serenade of a person whose special anniversary it is.

filial obedience is one of the most desirable and necessary of the
virtues.

This is not to say that their behavior was always perfect. They
were lively, imaginative children and they unquestionably had
their moments of thoughtlessness and selfishness; and others
which saw distressing collisions of temperaments, interests, and
egos. But these were precisely the *desgracias* that they depended
upon their father's authority to disentangle.

In their mother they, and especially Miguelito, found the sum
of all that was best in the whole world. A single tear in Josefa's
eye reduced her eldest son to quicker contrition than all his father's logic, reproval, or punishment. But Josefa's were never the
easy tears which some mothers substitute for character and the
correction that incurs greater patience. In fact, the requirements
that this exemplary woman placed upon her little ones for their
development frequently exceeded those of her husband.

For example, it was Doña Josefa who initiated the procedure
whereby each Saturday Miguel, Concepción, and Luz were now
put to work in their father's office to assist with the weekly payroll. As the miners queued up for their salaries, the children
checked the cash disbursed and the receipts. This innovation was
so far from being Don Miguel's origination that he had at first
opposed his wife's suggestion. His miners were extremely rough
fellows whose ordinary speech was filled with profanity—and
worse. Strange and violent quarrels were likely to blaze up between these men when their recriminations rapidly stooped to
the most offensive insults. Could the Pros, who had been so careful to avoid the bad influence of the hotel guests, permit their
children to be thrown in contact with the crude *muchachos* at the
mine?

To this logic, Josefa only smiled. She felt considerably more
confidence in the innate decency of Don Miguel's "boys" than
he evinced. She believed that the very presence of their manager's
gentle little daughters would serve as a restraining influence.
Surely, the miners' respect for innocence would cause them to
reserve their vulgarities, postpone their altercations until they

were beyond earshot of the children. Such an improvement would make things easier for the manager, and meanwhile, the youngsters, besides assisting their father, would be gaining valuable experience.

Not without serious qualms, Don Miguel finally agreed to try out the idea. Everything turned out almost exactly as Josefa had predicted. The men, up from their hard labor in the depths of Zacatecas' rich-veined earth, intent only upon claiming their due and commencing their week-end sprees, did indeed restrain their explosions until, pay in pocket, they had quit the mine premises where two demure "little ladies" had smiled at them sweetly while taking their thumbprints for the payroll receipts.

And that high-spirited *chico,* their manager's namesake—there was a manly kid—as friendly as anyone might hope to find! Who would deny it? Didn't he bring them drinking water in his own hand to cool their dusty throats while they waited their turns at the pay table? More, he was just as likely to distribute all his own candies and cookies among them to see their grins as they gobbled the sweets down in their healthy workingmen's hunger. Sometimes at his triumphant cry, *"Adiós, muchachos,* I'm a miner now too!" they would forget their hurry to get on down to the *cantina* and, tossing him onto their shoulders, respond to his special affection for them with ear-splitting *"Vivas!"* He was all right, that son of their *Jefe!*

At this time Miguelito's name for himself was *"el barreterillo* —the little miner." Throughout his life he would find many occasions to refer to himself as *"el pobre barretero*—the poor miner."

V

"MI PADRE DIOS"

DON MIGUEL'S labors and cares were increasing by the month. There were now eight little ones requiring provision in his home. The mine, too, was supplying new problems. It was no longer merely a matter of keeping the output up to company requirements without making unjust demands on his crews. His own relations with both elements were satisfactory, but one felt the new and unsettling tensions that were taking form. And if trouble lay ahead, one thing was sure—the manager would be standing squarely in the middle! Also, his success in bringing the operation to full efficiency had greatly increased the production with a resultant matching increase in his paper work. The time had arrived when Miguelito's father could no longer spare two hours daily from the work to fulfill the duties of teacher to his children.

Therefore, when a Señorita Garza who possessed the proper qualifications and credentials arrived at Concepción del Oro, she was employed to teach the little Pros. The *Señorita* was the very first Mexican Protestant whom Miguel and his sisters had ever met. But, having accepted her assignment under Don Miguel's condition that she avoid all reference to religion, she meticulously complied with her promise. Doña Josefa, watching quietly on the side lines, was soon content that the new teacher merited full confidence. The association developed into friendship, and the Señorita Garza was frequently invited to take her meals with the family.

On one such occasion Miguel's mischievous humor asserted itself in a rather unusual way. He insisted on saying the mealtime grace, a privilege which, by custom, devolved upon the youngest child at table. As he anticipated, the teacher made the responses only in the "Our Father," and maintained silence during the "Hail Mary." He pronounced the "Amen" and then observed: "You see how only our Faith is complete, *Señorita?* And without love for the most holy Virgin, how much value the rest loses!" There was no reply. As their son was by no means a pietist, Don Miguel and Doña Josefa were as startled as Señorita Garza must have been.

Her successor was Don Adolfo Ruíz, a resident of Concepción del Oro, who taught the Pro children until Don Miguel was fortunate enough to secure the tutorial services of Rebeca Rubio, a lady reputed to be one of Zacatecas' most distinguished educators. Under her guidance, Miguel's studies were advanced as far as they might profitably be pursued at home. Whereupon Don Miguel decided that he must be sent away to school.

If this necessary move pained his parents, induced rivers of tears among his sisters whose entire life pivoted upon their brother's projects and companionship, it surely fell just as heavily upon him. Not only had the girls and the little brother been his only comrades, but they had cheerfully conceded his leadership in everything. It was always *his* game and *his* plan that were undertaken with so much enthusiasm. None had ever shown him opposition or jealousy. Without their shared delights—the concerts, comedies, recitations and, perhaps most greatly cherished of all, the sisters' total approval of Miguelito Pro—what meaning would life hold for him? Study was no attraction, merely a duty performed in obedience to the kindest of parents. That Miguel completely overlooked the benefits of school friendships was not surprising. During the three years since their arrival at Concepción del Oro he had made no outside friends because there were no boys at the mine whom Don Miguel considered suitable associates for his son.

Miguel did endeavor to accept this dreaded, rapidly approaching ordeal with resignation. His father must know best. Even so, it would be exile, pure and simple!

But first there would be the long vacation and he determined to improve its possibilities to the utmost. As a reward for his good showing in the Profesora Rubio's final examinations he had received a much-coveted little jackass. The handsome, skittish creature was as yet unbroken to the bit, but its young master was confident that its high spirit was exactly what he required to develop the horsemanship he so greatly longed to attain. The single drawback lay in Don Miguel's order that, until the jackass could be gentled, his son's rides must be accompanied by a servant who would walk beside the animal's head to hold the halter and lead it by a length of rope attached to his own saddle—whenever the father was unable to go along.

Miguelito knew it would be most ungracious to complain in the face of his gratitude for the gift, but how *could* he submit to presenting such a sorry figure? To be ridiculously towed through town by a servant! And the contrast between the really good lines of his small mount and his father's big, fat mare—even that might provoke the smiles, possibly the jeers, of the spectators. Either procedure was insupportable.

One morning after Don Miguel had left for the mine, Miguel explained all this to his attentive *mamacita,* imploring her to give him a chance to prove that he could manage the pretty little animal. He would have to do this someday, so why not today? He wanted so very much to ride his jackass *alone,* although if she insisted, the servant could follow at a suitable distance—and he would solemnly promise not to go far from home.

Despite her endless concern for the children's safety, Joséfa frequently demonstrated her conviction that doing is learning for the young. She also believed that individual powers should not be too severely restricted even when certain risks were involved.

So now, though with some misgivings, she agreed to Miguel's experiment.

Almost giddy with delight, the boy invited his sisters and Edmundo to witness his proud "take-off." Their admiration as they watched their brother ride off in triumph only increased his pride—just a few minutes before he was to be powerfully reminded of the old adage which tells us exactly what pride precedes. For he had hardly passed beyond sight of the house when the uneasy jackass promptly ran away with him and, heading directly toward the brink of a deep arroyo, tossed him cleanly over the edge. At the very bottom of the ravine, Miguel made his landing—squarely upon his head!

Luckily, some of his friends—the miners—happened to be in the vicinity of the accident. They hastened to pick up the senseless boy and, carrying him to a nearby hut, managed to revive him and bind up his injuries. The servant delegated to look after him had evidently taken the qualification, "at a suitable distance," too literally, for he did not show up in time to prevent Miguelito from resuming his saddle. The miners unanimously approved of his stout declaration, "It mustn't be said that I was frightened!"

And thus it was that he arrived home in independence—even though the head he held so high was swathed in bandages and his clothing was in ribbons. The ineffectual servant tried to base his defense upon a complaint of his own. He hadn't overtaken Miguelito even on the return ride because the *niño* had kept the now obedient little jackass at a brisk trot. The grim-faced boy was at last on his way to becoming a *caballero!*

The aftermath took two painful forms. From Don Miguel he received a severe scolding; and the distressed Josefa met him with the tears he could hardly bear. To the former, he submitted in respectful silence. For his *mamacita's* woe he offered his customary consolation. He hugged her and called her "his dearest Doña Pepecita" [1] as he begged her to understand how it was that this

[1] *"Pepe"* and *"Pepa"* are, respectively, the intimate, or nicknames, for José and Josefa. *"Pepecita"* means "little Pepa."

time he had simply *had* "to dominate that disgraceful animal."
But she would see that he would never, never risk worrying her
so greatly in the future!

It was his mother's brother, Don Florentino Juárez, who made
what seemed the best suggestion about Miguelito's schooling.
Don Florentino lived in México City where, as no one would
deny, the schools were the country's very best. Wouldn't it be
better all around if his sister and her husband were to send their
young son to him? Then, instead of being thrust abruptly into
the impersonal life of the dormitory, Miguel Agustín could enter
one of the best academies as a day scholar. It would be less strange
for the lad if after his classes he could return each evening to
affection and a normal home. His parents' concern would be
eased by the assurance that his welfare was in the hands of a
loving uncle and aunt. For the rest, Don Florentino imagined
that Don Miguel would likely agree with his own opinion that
the Colegio de San José was the best selection in a school.

Josefa found this plan very consoling. Despite the great distance between the capital and Concepción del Oro, there would
be no terror in Miguelito's absence if she knew him to be with
Florentino. Moreover, it would be cheering to have him attending a school that had been placed under the patronage of her
own beloved San José. Surely the wonderful saint who had protected *El Niño Jesús* would look out for the small son of his
loyal devotee! Her husband approved and especially liked the
idea that his boy would profit by the finest instruction available
in México. A man can be proud of doing the best by his sons in
these matters.

This unexpected turn of events also took some of the sting
out of Miguel's reluctance to go anywhere at all away from his
beloved family, his entrancing activities, and his already quite
friendly little jackass. He remembered his Tío Florentino, if but
vaguely, and relatives can never be strangers to Mexicans. The
intimate family talk includes them all, those far away as well as

those close at hand. Mexicans never permit time or distance to separate them from their own.

Thus it was settled in that winter of 1901, about the time of his tenth birthday (which would have preceded the opening of México's official school year, February first, by little more than a fortnight). With a few days to spare, Miguelito was put aboard the train that would double north to Saltillo to make connections with the southbound mainliner for the capital. He was in the care of a merchant acquaintance of the Pros, an *Árabe*,[2] "but a person to be trusted," who happened to be making the same journey. The whole family, including infants and servants, saw him off in the customary confused jumble of gallant little jokes, solemn parental counsels, and the reiterated reminders of the detailed messages to be delivered to his aunt and uncle. And of course all this was intermingled with the little chokes and the ready tears ever attending such emotional events as the departure of a cherished son and brother for a distant point. What else? There were no pretenses or reticences lurking within families like these Pros.

But when the small train had whistled the clan out of its narrow aisles and chuffed off with Miguelito and their friend, "the Arab," on its fine, glistening rails, the little fellow began to feel that the sorrow of parting might be the prelude to a rather interesting adventure, after all. His zest in everything that presented itself was too keen to permit depression to hang like a curtain between the eager eyes and the much there was to see wherever he directed them. It was the first journey he had made at an age in which the details are graven upon the memory to remain a part of a boy's conscious experience and understanding.

Long before the transfer at Saltillo, his spirits had picked up to normal; and when they had settled down on the rattan seats which would do little to cushion the long ride to their final destination, Miguel knew that he wasn't going to be bored for a

[2] México's numerous class of Syrian tradesmen are commonly, though erroneously, called "Arabs."

single moment. Right there beside him were unreeling fascinating views of a rapidly changing terrain as their stout-hearted engine wound them out of the stark mineral mountains into the deep, green, highland valleys of San Luis Potosí. Then, just as magically, this fertile black soil of San Luis gave place to the tawny cattle ranges of Guanajuato; and these to the lush and fragrant haciendas of Querétaro. Coming into the City of Querétaro, he glimpsed the emerald knoll called the Hill of the Bells where the ill-fated Emperor Maximiliano gallantly faced a firing squad of the nation which had so determinedly rejected his sincere if sadly mistaken intentions toward it. All this had taken place when *papá* and *mamá* were just about his age! A moment more and he saw the beautiful rose-tinted walls of the magnificent old churches, convents, and monasteries, masterpieces of the great Tresguerras who had transformed Querétaro into one of their country's rarest architectural jewels. And, on the opposite side of this enchanting city, the superb arches of its celebrated aqueduct cut their soft pink tracery into the fathomless blue sky. The cadenced arches reminded Miguel Agustín of a poem, a sonnet in stone.

Strange and intriguing people kept boarding the train at the various stops. Minutes before they bustled cheerfully into the aisles beside him with their air of self-satisfaction in the knowledge that they were of the fortunate few who would always possess the means to cut fine figures in their little world, he had watched them picking their way, somewhat daintily but patiently, too, across the untidy, Indian-jammed platforms. The platform crowds were largely composed of the vendors who, almost before the engine had jerked to a stop, were pressing against the sides of the little cars, thrusting their laden trays aloft for the inspection of the fine gentry who traveled so easily above wheels and rails—up and down *la patria* wherever their fancy might lead. Then, let them spend a few of their *pesitos* right here in Huichapan or Actopan, and then their extravagance would be a little luck to all! The wheedling clamor set up by the vendors, however, was couched in no such undiplomatic phrases. In their way they were very gifted traders.

One might have purchased almost anything from these importunate platform peddlers. There were serapes from Saltillo, gold and silver filigree from Zacatecas, semi-precious stones from Guanajuato's mysterious hills, Tehuacán's onyx and sombreros. There was Puebla's elegant candied fruit and jugs of Celaya's glossy, cloyingly sweet confection called *cajeta*. Miguelito peered into the big baskets of fresh fruit, fried chicken, and all manner of Mexican delicacies that were lifted so temptingly before his window. Was it possible that these vendors could sense how hungry he was, right through the glass?

José, the trustworthy "Arab," had, with very un-Mexican bluntness, declined to patronize any of the railway restaurants during meal-stops. Instead, he had uncovered a lunch basket packed high with a variety of *tortas* or sandwiches made of a pale wheat substance soaked in oil and spiced with sesame. This appalling mess, he proclaimed with satisfaction, was known as *malhajas*— very nourishing and particularly good for the digestion on long train rides. Miguel must try one! Two or three could never hurt a healthy boy like him! So, though his small stomach turned over nervously at the mere sight of the concoction, Miguelito did try one. The first bite left him faint with nausea, and he diffidently returned the *torta* to the basket. José shrugged indifferently at such finicality and proceeded to put away his *malhajas* with ghoulish gusto.

Now as Miguelito had given his money to the merchant for safekeeping, his only alternative to watching this revolting scene was to stare into the food vendors' entrancing baskets which put his mouth to watering miserably. Finally, however, the engine gave a little screech and pulled them past all the beautiful trays of *tacos* and *tamales*. At last the sated "Arab" mopped his mouth with a huge red kerchief and promptly sagged into a doze. Thanking both the Virgin and San José for this great favor, Miguelito rose stealthily and poked about the cluttered rack above their seat until he located the immense box of sweets which his mother had charged him to give to her sister-in-law. These toothsome confections consisted of candied almonds and walnuts deliciously held together by puffs of smartly beaten egg white dashed with vanilla. The famished boy fell upon the sweets feverishly and had managed to finish off half of his good aunt's present when he was startled by the drowsy José's disapproving question: "What are you doing with this package your mother ordered you to deliver to your relatives, *niño?*"

Miguel met the man's eye bravely, a speculative expression in his own brown gaze. "It is only that I was so anxious, Señor, for you to try the kind of *malhajas* that are made by my mother and sisters—whenever you might wake up," he replied smoothly. He insisted that the merchant must "take just one little fruit of the almond"—after which it was Miguel's turn to eat another. This routine became a game and thus it was that two greedy males cleaned up the entire contents of the gift box without further ado. At least, as Miguelito explained later, it wasn't a fast day!

Arriving at the capital, he was soon installed in Uncle Florentino's fine home and inscribed at the Colegio de San José, so everything seemed most promising. However, the wonder city, famed the world over for its hospitality, again failed to treat Miguelito Pro with kindness. Within a few short weeks he fell seriously ill, for the first time since his infancy.

This, said the doctors, was a difficult ailment to diagnose definitely, though it clearly centered in the stomach. They prescribed various treatments, but it was soon seen that he was failing to respond and his worried uncle decided the lad's parents should make their own judgment of his condition. Reluctant to frighten them, Don Florentino composed a careful letter saying that, as Miguel Agustín was still not strong enough to attend his classes at the school with regularity, they might prefer to have a look at him. They knew well enough how wrong the doctors usually are, but if they could arrange to come to the capital they could see for their own satisfaction how he appeared to them. At the same time, the trip would make possible the happiness of their presence at the baptism of his own new baby boy.

So Miguel's father and mother hurried down to México City where they were by no means reassured to see the thin little face he lifted joyously for their kisses. They determined then and there that, immediately after the baptism of tiny Alfredo Juárez, their son would return with them to Concepción del Oro. . . .

The fresh air, country food, and his happiness in being back "in the center of everything" once more soon settled Miguelito's troublesome little stomach and put the color and roundness back in his cheeks. By year's end he seemed quite himself. And this again brought up the old problem—school. Don Miguel had no thought of returning the boy to México City. A school in Saltillo, or even Monterrey, would be more convenient to reach in an emergency and, of course, a less expensive journey.

It was now that someone told him about Saltillo's Colegio Acuña. It was a new foundation, but highly recommended by responsible persons. Here in the mining country one could not be a stickler for tradition in the same degree that was only natural for the inhabitants of the capital or those who had clung to the other centers of the nation's culture. The circumstances imposed by the careers of those who were developing México's vast mineral resources bound them to semi-primitive areas which still had cause to rejoice for any establishments which contributed to the enrichment of life. Furthermore, the Colegio Acuña's location was ideal because, although Saltillo is the capital of another state (Coahuila), it is nearer Concepción del Oro [3] than any other city or, more realistically, any sizable town. All these considerations decided Don Miguel to take his son to Saltillo where, if he found the school all that was claimed for it, Miguel would be enrolled as a boarder.

The boy himself could unearth no reasonable objection to a routine that was accepted custom for all the better-class provincial families. He knew, too, that a great sorrow lay in the heart of his mother just now over the loss of the tiny twin girls, Amalia and Amelia, whose deaths were the first among Josefa's children.

[3] Situated almost upon the Zacatecas–Coahuila boundary line.

Moreover, she was preparing to welcome another little newcomer at about this time. Her only "big boy" could not permit complaints of his to complicate life for his "dearest Doña Pepecita." He did his utmost to keep this latest farewell as light and cheerful as it could be made.

The Colegio Acuña boasted a fine plant and, after looking it over with his characteristic thoroughness, his father decided it was the place for Miguelito. The boy would have to adjust to an unfamiliar ambient and companions, but it was to be hoped that some of these might become his good friends during the ensuing ten months. He would develop independence and benefit by experience with outsiders. All this, with a regular course of study, would prepare him for a fitting and useful future. Before leaving him in the hands of the optimistic headmaster, Don Miguel explained these points to the solemn-faced eleven-year-old who loyally promised to do his best. There was a final embrace; and then his wise and wonderful *papá* was gone! As the Director had taken himself off to permit them their farewell in privacy, Miguelito was alone in the big room, which shone so much with its new paint and about which there still hung a slight odor of varnish.

It wasn't very much fun, but he'd get through this stiff-seeming start somehow. It ought to be almost suppertime, though he hadn't heard a bell. He had passed through the dining hall with his father on the tour of inspection, and believed he could find it again. A lonely little boy who did not recognize the tightness pulling at his chest as a manifestation of nervousness slid out of the dusk which had begun to envelop the parlor and down the staircase toward the dining hall.

He found the big room already full of youngsters who were allaying healthy appetites with appalling enthusiasm. However, they suspended operation on their plates to greet his entrance with what seemed to Miguel Agustín as unnecessary rudeness.

"Hurrah!" they chorused loudly, "here comes our miner!"

Miguel attempted a smile, only partially successful. Why should he mind if they wanted to dub him "our miner"? Hadn't

he always insisted proudly that he was just that, a *barreterillo?*
It was only the tone to which he could take offense. It seemed to
imply that being a miner was somehow ridiculous. But maybe
they didn't mean it like that. He slipped into an empty place at
the nearest table and sat patiently waiting to be served.

When a *mozo* carelessly slammed a huge portion of *barbacoa*[4]
before him, he politely asked that it be taken away, explaining
that he took only bread and chocolate at supper. He saw nothing
remarkable in his preference, but it brought another roar from
the pack.

"Hurrah!" came a hateful yelp. "We were mistaken,
muchachos. It seems that this new one is a friar, after all!"

Although Miguel appeared to be concentrating on his chocolate, he did not see the thick coating of scum on the top, the
result of the milk not having been properly boiled. The first
swallow left his mouth encircled by the brown *nata.* Another
wicked hoot from his persecutors! Poor Miguelito had never
been so affronted in his life. When he had escaped at last to his
rigid little cot and darkness, he wept for some minutes in humiliation. He was sure that his father would not condone such
execrable manners as everyone displayed in this place, but he
decided that to report the matter would be unmanly.

Things had not improved by Sunday. And that morning he
observed that no one appeared to be preparing for Mass. He
waited a little before expressing his desire to set out for the parish
church. He did not care to wait until midday Mass. To his
astonishment he was coldly informed of a fact which had been
carefully concealed from Don Miguel: the Colegio Acuña was a
Protestant foundation! Although the Director had assured his
father that complete liberty of religious belief and practice were
guaranteed the pupils, Miguelito was now prohibited from going
to Mass. He would attend church services, however, as it was
obligatory for all the boys to present themselves at the Protestant
chapel.

An exceedingly indignant Miguel complied with the order,

[4] Barbecued meat customarily shredded and reheated by frying.

but this, he *knew*, would never be tolerated by his father. The same afternoon he put it all into a letter to Concepción del Oro, which, oddly enough, failed to reach its destination. To his great surprise no mention whatever of his forced attendance at Protestant religious exercises was made in subsequent letters from home.

Several Sundays dragged by in this manner. Miguelito was confused and miserable. Finally, on his own responsibility, he rebelled. Something had gone wrong somewhere. He knew his devout parents could not be indifferent to a matter like this. He flatly informed the Director that he would not enter the chapel again.

The headmaster met this defiance by locking the boy up all alone inside the school while the student body and the teachers attended chapel. And this became the regular routine.

On what was destined to be the last of these bitter, boring Sundays, Miguelito was wandering sadly about when his music-conscious ear caught the strains of a military band. Perhaps if he hurried to the gate he might catch a glimpse of it! He could not see the band from the gate, but, happening to look up, he noticed that by some oversight the padlock was unfastened. He had only to stand on tiptoe and stretch his arms a bit to slide the heavy bar aside and make good his escape from this hateful prison. Why not? He had done nothing wrong to be caged in like this each blessed Sunday morning.

Then he reconsidered. Might not such an action raise a general scandal that would bring criticism upon the beloved parents who had placed him here? If so, the idea was no good. Not for the world would he be the cause of embarrassment to his father and mother—though he certainly didn't believe that God wanted him in any such place as this. It was a difficult problem, truly.

While he was hesitating, he noticed the family across the street—returning home from Mass, no doubt. His impulsive call attracted their attention. Two small daughters were sent over to see what this boy wanted. He thanked them for coming and asked to speak with their mother.

The good *señora* came immediately. Miguel unburdened his afflicted heart and begged her to write his home so that he might be sure his parents actually understood what sort of school the Colegio Acuña was. The pious lady was horrified and assured him that the letter would be on its way within the hour.

And this is how Don Miguel and his wife first came to hear of a situation that was to evoke their indignation and put the father aboard the first train for Saltillo. Declining to pass so much as a word with the Colegio's deceitful Director, he simply bustled Miguelito off the premises forever. Together they paid a visit to the kind mother who had served them so well, to offer her their heartfelt thanks.

Oh, the joy of Miguelito's reappearance on his own doorsill in Concepción del Oro! After he had ecstatically hugged each member of the family several times and they had all cried a little, he turned to Josefa and observed sagely, "This is how *mi Padre Dios* pulls us out of the very worst straits."

"God, my Father," would henceforth be his favorite designation for Divine Providence.

VI

A BOY GROWS UP

THE compassionate heart of Josefa Juárez could not be bounded by the needs of her growing family. In the past sixteen years she had borne ten babies [1] and lost two, had suffered and prayed over the illnesses and heartaches of them all while ceaselessly fulfilling the countless duties of a wife and mother; but this fragile-looking lady still found time for many acts of mercy in behalf of the poor miners' families comprising Concepción del Oro's majority population. She well understood the mounting restlessness and rebelliousness of the workers who incited the unpleasant incidents that plagued Don Miguel. The truth was that, no matter how hard they worked, the miners could not earn enough to maintain their families in reasonable decency. Worst of all was the tragedy that overtook them in illness. The good mother who had hovered over so many sickbeds in her own home could not help but be touched to see that, before contagions and those other debilities induced by insufficient diet, these people were heartrendingly powerless.

None of this was chargeable to her husband. He was not an owner, merely one of the company's more valued workers. The best he could do for his men was to see that they received justice under the existing laws and prevailing practices and as much

[1] Alfredo and Humberto had both been born by 1903.

50

work as the mine could support. His wife knew that from his own pocket he was always as charitable to his unfortunate workers as he could afford to be. There were no extravagances permitted the Pro family. But the expense of clothing, feeding, and educating so many little ones very nearly consumed his mining engineer's salary.

It was true that the miners were exceedingly ignorant, gross, and, frequently, obstreperous. The general complaint that they were ungrateful and bound to squander whatever one might be able to spare them on drink and other equally stupid, if less obnoxious, diversions, did indeed have a basis in fact. But Doña Josefa was not one of those who, after admitting the realism of all this, could then forget the whole unpleasant subject. The miners were ignorant, gross, and drunken because they were given very little opportunity to be anything else. When or by what means these things could be improved was beyond her conjecture. But it was clear enough that something had to be done for their wives and children; and especially for their sick.

From the beginning this good lady had maintained close contact with the miners' families through visits on which she was accompanied by one or more of the older children. She hoped that after witnessing the misery, want, the positive degradation of these fellow human beings, her children would understand the need for her gifts of food, medicine, and clothing; would develop their own charitable instincts.

A busy, rather mischievous boy just entering upon adolescence might seem an unlikely companion for such visits. But this was not the case with Miguelito. He had long since "adopted" the miners whom he liked to call "my *predilectos.*" His father and, before that, his grandfather had linked their lives with the mines and thus the Pros had always been fully conscious of the miners' problems and tribulations. How many times had not Miguel, by his own election, shot down into the depths of the earth far below the warm sunshine and the invigorating air of Zacatecas, to tour the long galleries and greet his "brother *barreteros*" as they toiled in the dead, musty subterranean world to extract from it the riches they could not hope to share? Oh, yes, he knew what gave rise to their almost chronic "disgusts" with a system from which it seemed that all their physical prowess, all their anger, could never free them.

No more than Josefa did he know how a nation's social evils might be cured. But, also like Josefa, he understood the plain duty of all Christians to make every possible individual sacrifice for the suffering underprivileged while being sure to guard good humor, the loving attitude and, above all, to work for peace with justice. We do not know how he judged the system which permitted the misery he saw all about him, but it is sure that he could not have had a presentiment of the tragedy in which it was to result—the blundering violence that would, for so many long years of unmitigated agony, ineptly butcher his poor fatherland, until it would seem incontestable that the "doctors" were more deadly than the disease. But that there were answers for all of earth's woes which every man of good will (even a lad like himself) were obligated to apply in their personal spheres by easing sorrow, poverty, and pain whenever encountered, Miguel Agustín knew perfectly well. He knew, too, that there was no novelty here—since the answers were already nineteen hundred years old. And so it was his delight to serve the miners by becoming the messenger who delivered his mother's gifts to their poor households.

Doña Josefa's charitable activities and dreams finally crystallized in a project of great import to Concepción del Oro, the foundation of a hospital for the free care of its poor. Don Miguel's assent had been somewhat reluctantly conceded—his wider experience warned him that opposition might arise to involve his family in unpleasantness and threaten the tranquillity of their home. Such considerations, however, in no way dampened his wife's enthusiasm or the high glee of her kindhearted children who were already doing everything they could to assist in the realization of their wonderful *mamacita's* wonderful plan.

In short order a license was forthcoming from the *Presidente*

Municipal or Mayor; the unpaid services of the town's three physicians were pledged; and she had the promise of Dr. Ramos, who owned Concepción del Oro's leading apothecary shop, to contribute the required medicines. A suitable building was the next acquisition of the indefatigable Doña Josefa, and then the funds to pay for the workmen and materials to turn two large rooms into convenient and pleasant wards where her poor patients would make happy recoveries. This money she secured through personal solicitation of the more prosperous citizens. But the labors and anxieties of all the organization and execution were hers alone.

Once the carpenters and the masons finished the alterations, she attacked the days'-long toil of the cleaning, furnishing, and equipping of her little hospital. The evenings, indeed far into the nights, she devoted to sorting supplies and linens, and listing the items to be checked with the doctors. She knew that many of her cases would be mine-accident casualties; and she dared not overlook anything that the generous medicos might require for emergency operations. In common with nearly all gentlewomen of her time and place she commanded considerable knowledge of practical nursing, but as she had never received specialized training in this branch she deemed it needful to examine such medical books and journals as she might be able to obtain. Altogether it was a colossal undertaking for a woman whose entire experience had been acquired in her own home, and that a home which, save for six short years, had always stood in a provincial town of no more than three to five thousand inhabitants.

As she worked on toward the opening of the institution, which would be known as the Hospital de San José, she refused to be discouraged by the noticeably widespread indifference, skepticism, and even, in some cases, the ridicule of her fellow townspeople. Was this from resentment at being reminded of their own faults in charity to these poor by whom they had always been surrounded? Or might it have been jealousy that a plain housewife had been granted the heroism that "exceeds the call of duty"?

Whatever it was, very few of the ladies came forward with offers of assistance; and some of them did not even bother to wish her well.

Josefa did not mind. She was consumed by that joy which comes only from the confidence that one is making a valuable contribution to those who suffer in this life. And she had her helpers right in her own house, the excited and co-operative children who were the badge of her successful motherhood. Concepción was already almost grown up by Mexican standards. By the date of the hospital's inauguration, St. Joseph's Day, 1904, she was past sixteen. María de la Luz was but slightly younger, and Miguel Agustín's thirteenth birthday was more than two months past. He was Doña Josefa's right-hand man in everything. The older girls made sure that their home would run smoothly for the comfort of Don Miguel and the little ones. Josefina and Ana María were old enough to hem linens and roll bandages. Even Edmundo could fetch and carry, to save extra steps for the weary mother. Only Alfredo and Humberto were babies still, and with so many loving, willing hands to serve them, they missed no necessary attention. The sacrifices made by Josefa Juárez to bear a large family were now clearing many obstacles from the field of her continuing sacrifices for others.

So when all this effort culminated in the dedication of San José, a very real triumph was written into the annals of the Pro-Juárez clan. This function, attended by the Mayor, several members of the City Council, and other local celebrities, was enlivened by the town band, the inevitable speeches, the recitation of a poem and, as the closing number, a selection rendered by the *Típica Pro* under the able baton of Miguel Agustín.

Doña Josefa had long been an associate of the St. Vincent de Paul Society which sent San José its first patients. One of these was a crippled woman, rescued from a remote mountain cave where she had subsisted for eight years on such scraps of bread as she was able to beg whenever she could manage to drag herself to the town. Others were an aged, totally helpless man; a tuberculous old woman; a small boy injured in a mine accident. After these came others from all sides.

During its year-and-a-half existence the Hospital de San José provided the sick-poor with medical attention and asylum. A free dispensary served those not requiring hospitalization. There seemed no reason why it would not continue its splendid service to the community for many years.

But times were now changing rapidly in a land where a long, long chapter was drawing to a close. If it was true that some of that chapter's pages had been blotched by injustice—and it was —at least they carried a complete text: the dreams and beliefs, as well as the achievements, of a great people throughout nearly half-a-hundred years. And all these pages, the glorious and the shameful, the brilliant and the stupid, were still intact, bound firmly into place in the tome of this people's history. No one had yet disowned the book, nor begun to rip out the pages, though there were fingers itching to do just that—as a prelude to writing the succeeding chapter. This nation and this race, said the fingers' owners, must be made over in the image of other nations and other races of men!

Some of the rebels, motivated by compassion for the down-trodden, who, as things stood, had little opportunity to rise, may only have intended to change an outmoded political order. But the fact remains that their planning and execution could hardly have been worse. Their first tragic error was to overlook the principal reason for the strength of the opposition. Old Don Porfirio Díaz and his *Científicos* were tyrants in many ways, but they had been shrewd enough not to attack the basic beliefs, in short, the deep religious faith, of their subjects. This, precisely, was what had preserved the adhesion of millions who were by no means in full approval of the dictatorship. If the Revolution were not led by idealists (and the idealists are both few and notably impractical), it would be made by ruthless opportunists bent upon using it as a vehicle for their own selfish ends. Ruthless men with nothing to lose, neither property nor reputation, are likely to stoop to anything in the pursuit of power. Unfortunately, México, one of the world's devoutest Christian nations, was also well supplied with such men.

Toward the end of 1905, when such elements were already jockeying for key positions in the land, Concepción del Oro welcomed a new *Presidente Municipal*. One of this functionary's first decrees was aimed at the so-called exclusiveness of the Hospital de San José. No more could its services be devoted to the town derelicts and its poorest families. It must receive all classes of mining personnel without regard for individual creeds, or lack of them. To make sure of this point, the Mayor denied the patients' right to receive the Last Sacraments at San José.

Josefa was desolated to see the ruin of her idea. The whole purpose of her effort had been to succor both the bodies and the souls of the poorest and the totally abandoned. She had given them her best and her best had been a very fine work. Meanwhile, she had suffered over the deathbed of her little Alfredo, and given birth to her eleventh and last baby, Roberto. In the face of all this public and personal upheaval Don Miguel ordered his family's immediate withdrawal from the hospital. The fourteen-year-old Miguel, deeply pained by his mother's sorrow, sought to comfort her with the promise: "When I'm a little older, I'll make a hospital for all your poor people, *Mamacita!*"

By this time the boy had successfully completed his grammar-school courses but, with so many complications, it had been impossible to determine upon a career for him or the means of training him for one of the professions. Such plans had been postponed pending the day that would see Don Miguel's withdrawal from the company. Things had become so bad at the mine owing to the workers' increasing fury that the manager at last gave ear to his family's pleading that he abandon so dangerous a post. This would, they hoped, result in their removal to other parts where Miguel could complete his education.

But Don Miguel's resignation had no sooner taken effect than he was appointed Agent of the National Department of Commerce, Division of Mines, an important charge which would keep him stationed at Concepción del Oro. The agency was flooded with work for which he would require assistants. Miguel, therefore, entered his father's office where he was assigned the task of reviewing all the *expedientes* or case histories of the mine litigations, and put in charge of the files. His outstanding qualification for so responsible a position was his exceptional memory. The legal actions then in process or pending were numerous and exceedingly complicated. But it took this lad, not yet fifteen years old, no time to memorize them all with all their technical ramifications. It was only necessary to mention any individual case for him to state its classification and file number without any need to refer to the record.

Life was not unrelieved labor and care for the Pro family, however. With its growth, both in number and ages, the members became closer and more companionable. As is usual with Mexican families, the activities of one were the interests of all. Miguel, long a diligent collector of geological specimens, had acquired a very respectable little museum. Nothing gave Edmundo and the girls more delight than to contribute unusual items they picked up on their gay invasions of the mountains and canyons surrounding the Mineral. Holidays favorable to family picnics were improved for jaunts which provided high pleasure for all. The parents and a cavalcade of bubbling youngsters mounted on burros or mules made tours in many directions and returned home the richer, not only in geological items, but in new treasures for their storehouse of priceless memories.

Sometimes they ventured to lonely mines, abandoned because they had been worked out. Occasionally a mine still holding promise would be guarded by a caretaker and his family, living in splendid isolation amidst the high silences of jagged peaks and precipices. Such a custodianship was exercised at the Sensitiva (a mine that had been Don Miguel's discovery) by a man named Hilario. At Hilario's dwelling, perched loftily in the Temeroso Range, the young Pros experienced one of their most noteworthy adventures.

They had savored the delights of a ride through the pine-scented, appetite-sharpening mountain air toward the succulent ranch dinner they knew to be awaiting them at Hilario's snug little cottage. It was a perfect picnic or *día de campo* and, when they had finished their merry feast, Miguel and the girls were in the mood for some intrepid exploit. The caretaker's eldest son, a lad about the age of Miguel, proposed the examination of a certain abandoned mine in the vicinity. So they trooped off together in high spirits. It was a real scramble over jutting boulders and wicked crevices to the mysterious black hole which formed the mouth of La Luz—The Light! Peering into the challenge of this ominous perforation, they heard their young guide's suggestive comment:

"One gets down by a stairway."

A stairway? They glanced at one another speculatively. The "stairway" turned out to be no more than a vertical thick beam of wood with side notches for footholds, but Hilario's son had already lighted his miner's lantern and, with his next words, the big adventure was under way.

"Hang on tightly now—don't lose your footing!"

One by one these children and grandchildren of miners commenced the descent into the unknown, eager young feet feeling cautiously for the crude notchings upon which the lantern's beams flickered so weakly.

When the long drop had been successfully negotiated, what a strange world met their blinking eyes! They were amazed to find herbs growing way down here in the thick night of the old cavern. Perhaps this was because of the little stream of water gurgling through it. And the mine was not uninhabited. Before this resented invasion small animals scurried to cover too swiftly for identification. Were those light hissings the angry protests of vipers? The girls drew closer to Miguel. But, following the lantern's dim glow, they forgot danger in the enchantments revealed by a series of caves that were a forest of wondrous crystal stalactite and stalagmite formations between which were splashed great mosaics in blue, Nile-green, and rose. It was a fantasy fairyland of richly gleaming tints and glistening sparkles that reflected the beams of their puny light for their astonishment.

Suddenly, without the slightest warning, their lantern made one convulsive splutter and—went out. Their first reaction was merely intense disappointment in the loss of their new-found magic. But when it was revealed that Hilario's son was unprovided with matches against this emergency, they began to deplore the termination of their explorations less than the long, tortuous route which must be recovered without the aid of sight if they were ever to escape from this ironically named mine. "La Luz," indeed! There wasn't a glimmer of light anywhere! The girls were terrified; and certainly no one was feeling very valiant unless it might be their young escort. At any rate, Hilario's son coolheadedly attached the rope he always carried on his person to the youngest girl and they started slowly feeling their way back toward the stairway which was not even a respectable ladder.

The mine was so deep that the dim patch of gray glimpsed when they finally stood huddled beneath the entrance was wholly inadequate to disclose the notches which, once they commenced the ascent, would be all that stood between them and a tumble to brutal death. For this risky business it seemed best to place the smallest girl first. Perhaps she could manage to keep one foot moving up the notches and the other on the shoulder of Concepción who would follow immediately behind. Last of the Pro children on the ladder, Miguel must make sure to keep one hand and arm free at all times to guard against sudden slips or missteps above. The adventure was no longer an unadulterated pleasure. In the fulsome language of Father Pulido, they spent "minutes of mortal anguish, though, in the end, they came out on the earth's surface without even knowing how [they had done it]!" [2]

Meanwhile Don Miguel and the faithful Hilario were searching everywhere for the missing children. And we are assured that when the worried men finally found the returning adven-

[2] Pulido, p. 30.

turers, the situation "was something very serious." Only when it was established that the pale-faced youngsters had returned without a scratch did the atmosphere lighten. Then the emboldened Miguel offered his *papá* the stalactite pieces he had carried up in his pockets. Don Miguel thanked him gravely, but warned him that they might easily have made "specimens" of themselves through this particular bit of audacity.

The diversions and social life of the Pros were not invariably restricted to the family. Several engineers had lately brought their families to live at Concepción del Oro, and the attorneys who guided the litigations of the mining interests were rather constant visitors. The Pros received invitations to the parties and entertainments which had begun to enliven the small community. Occasionally they offered the hospitality of their own home to the men with whom Don Miguel must work closely settling the claims and counter-claims that passed through his office.

One cold, rainy evening during the Christmas *pastorelas*,[3] Miguel mounted the stairs to their family living quarters above the office to say that their father had invited a number of gentlemen to supper. After a conference of several hours' duration, they found themselves at nine o'clock, with "their heads full of '*disgustos*' and their stomachs quite empty."[4] The tired young secretary was prepared for the alarm this announcement would occasion among his sisters for he knew that their mother, being indisposed, had taken to her bed, and that the servants had the evening off to attend the festivities. It had been an exhausting day for everyone and he took pity on the girls in their consternation at being caught totally unprepared to do their father justice before his guests.

"*Vaya, muchachas*, stop worrying," he told them. "You need only to set the table. You may leave the supper to me but I don't want any supervision or suggestions, so just stay out of the kitchen!"

[3] The commemoration of the shepherds who followed the Christmas star.
[4] *Ibid.*, p. 32.

Then, snatching up his raincoat, he started for the door, adding that he'd be gone only a few moments in quest of some necessary items—and that their mother must not be worried by any word of what was taking place. The girls had hardly completed the preparation of the table when the door opened again on their father and his guests. Conscious of the empty kitchen, they were suffused with embarrassment. Almost on the instant, however, Miguel reappeared accompanied by a crew of *mozos* from the Chinese restaurant laden with a complete meal for the refreshment of the visitors. Miguel's sisters were filled with admiration not only by his resourcefulness, but to observe that he proceeded to pay for all this from his own pocket!

In the office, Miguel Agustín was already filling a man's shoes. He was learning to take responsibility, too, for domestic problems. He had stood as godfather to baby brother Roberto, a charge he took very seriously.

On the social side he was beginning to be in great demand among the little community's hostesses. He wholeheartedly enjoyed many of the functions and his undeniable popularity with the girls of Concepción del Oro. But he could not overcome his detestation for dancing. When it was absolutely necessary for him to engage in this activity, he invariably chose one of his sisters as partner. In order to lighten the obvious disappointment of the young ladies, he took the pains to write them mollifying, since exceedingly flattering, verses.

Toward his family he maintained the playful and tender attitude that had distinguished his childhood, only now this contribution to their happiness was more consciously offered. He sympathized with Josefa's sorrow over the deaths of her babies and the failure of her great dream of a hospital for her sick-poor. He also appreciated that Don Miguel's life was growing ever more complicated and difficult, for it was now impossible to doubt that their beloved country was facing ominous days. Altogether, there was real need for his efforts to cheer his dear ones. Miguel Agustín, at sixteen, had already achieved the awareness of a man.

VII

"MI AMIGO"

DON MIGUEL'S worries sometimes took the form of self-reproach. By now his eldest son's training for the professional career that is the ceaseless concern of Mexican parents for their boys should have been well advanced. Instead of this, Miguel Agustín faced a completely undefined future. Although he was his father's right arm in the Agent's Office, the youth had given no indication of planning to identify himself with the mines on a definite basis. He had demonstrated an efficiency really astonishing in one so young and his cheerfulness was unfailing, but his heart was not in it. Despite his affection and compassion for the miners, mining, itself, or, for that matter, commercial enterprise of any sort simply did not appeal to him. The good account he was giving of himself now was merely a repetition of the filial devotion he had long ago shown in facing those days of his bleakest memories—in the México City and Saltillo schools.

It was really too bad about Miguel Agustín, thought Don Miguel, that illness and his own errors of judgment had ended the boy's formal education almost before it had gotten under way. And later—well, the difficulties of their isolated living here in Concepción del Oro were understandable. But if he had seen himself forced to neglect the education of his eldest son, this must not form a precedent for a like mismanagement in the cases of the younger brothers. It was high time for Edmundo to be placed in a good school; even Josefina and Ana María should be benefited by a few terms of instruction outside the home.

So Don Miguel decided to send his family to Saltillo, where Doña Josefa could make a home for them while Edmundo and the girls attended their classes as day scholars. This would guard against any such unsatisfactory experiences as had dogged Miguelito's school days. To attain this good for his children he would have to deprive himself of his happy home life as well as Miguel's services, for the boy must go along in the role of the "man of the family." It was unthinkable that a lady and her young daughters should find themselves entirely unprotected in a strange "city."

There were innumerable consultations between father, mother, and son on this project. Neither Josefa nor Miguel wished to see the poor man left all alone, but in the end Don Miguel's judgment of what would be for the best good of the greatest number prevailed. Miguel Agustín need not entirely abandon his work for his father. The *expedientes* could be mailed to him for reviewing and indexing. Don Miguel would visit his family each week end; and on his Sunday-night returns to Concepción del Oro carry the lad's work back with him. This, then, was the framework of the life they soon took up. It was to endure for two years.

The children's sadness at the separation from their father for five days each week was their only strong regret in this departure from Concepción del Oro. During their nine years' residence at the Mineral, the Pros had never cultivated any intimate associations. They found much that was exciting and delightful in this larger town where they were soon comfortably settled. The object of the transference, the children's schooling, was also quickly arranged to everyone's satisfaction.

It was therefore a great blow when Josefina, eldest of the three for whose benefit they had come to Saltillo, fell desperately ill. Then indeed did Doña Josefa have cause to thank Heaven that her Miguelito was by her side to aid her in this terrifying misfortune. But, even so, they could not save Josefina. Her death at thirteen years was the worst blow the Pros had yet been called upon to sustain.

Miguel did his best to make things a little better for his sorrowing mother, his three remaining sisters, and the three small brothers. He had soon become a second father to the young children whose respect he commanded as readily as he had always commanded his sisters' co-operation in the games and schemes of his early childhood. And through all the time of this transition he never failed to keep abreast of Don Miguel's case histories. His father had only to write an inquiry on the most involved litigation to find a complete summation and an intelligent analysis awaiting his next week-end arrival at Saltillo.

As the sorrow over the loss of their sister softened a little, Miguel resumed their musical evenings, became the inspiring genius of their play once more; and again turned his attention to the little jokes which were usually good for a general chuckle. On his own account, he may have commenced to know loneliness about this time. As a small boy, he had never missed his lack of outside friends. But as a youth, he now doubtless felt the need of a special confidante because one day he suddenly announced to Concepción: "You will have to be *mi amigo,* since I have none." Inasmuch as he used the masculine form of the noun, "friend—*amigo,*" he obviously meant that he had chosen this eldest sister for his particular companion—the one among them whom he had selected to share his whole confidence and most personal thoughts. And henceforth it was to be so, for these two now drew closer than ever before. They went everywhere together, and the understanding Concepción came to know all his dreams and all his perplexities. A thing which was less agreeable, she also occasionally saw herself the object of his most spirited pranks—which were likely to prove decidedly embarrassing.

One never-to-be-forgotten afternoon the two were out walking, "giving turns" about the plaza in the traditional small-town *paseo* of México. Miguel had proposed this diversion pretending an intense interest in a rumor that some pretty girls were new arrivals in Saltillo. Perhaps they would present themselves in the plaza where he might be able to make his own estimate of their highly-rated charms! But they saw no lovely strangers and when Concepción finally tired of trying to keep up with her brother's enthusiasm, she suggested that it was time to go home. Miguel agreed cheerfully, but as they headed into one of the streets giving onto the plaza he suddenly halted before an imposing residence remarking that he wished to make a call.

Having not the remotest idea who might be the occupants of the strange house, Concepción experienced a sharp premonition and started to protest. Too late! Her brother had already dropped the heavy brass knocker in a clatter against the thick, hard wood of the portal. She looked at him in a sickening panic. What in the world could he be up to? Miguel's impish grin was transformed into an ingratiating smile as he turned from his sister to greet the master of the house who opened the door to them personally. The gentleman was considerably perplexed to see the completely unknown pair standing on his doorsill, but he could do nothing less than return Miguel's elaborately courteous greeting by inviting the visitors into the drawing room.

Concepción was in an agony of suspense. This terrible Miguel! What could he be thinking of? And then he opened the most ridiculous conversation she had ever listened to.

"A thousand pardons, *Señor,* but my sister was so enchanted by this image of the Virgin which she glimpsed as we were passing your window that she implored me to ask if it might not be possible to purchase it. I would like very much to gratify her dream—that is, if you will be so amiable as to sell it to us."

Concepción turned a deep scarlet. She had not, of course, even seen an image. However, turning her head now toward the corner indicated by the glances of her preposterous brother and their amazed host, she barely prevented herself from gasping as she looked upon a statue of the Virgin that was the most ridiculously overdressed and most tasteless representation she had ever seen. Her impulse was to giggle hysterically. As she fought valiantly to maintain her poise, she heard the troubled owner of this atrocious "work of art" apologetically explaining that, inasmuch as the image was a family heirloom, he felt he could hardly part with it, that is, for less than five hundred pesos.

And then Miguel was thanking the man profusely and averring that nothing remained but to advise his parents of such a remarkable opportunity. He placed himself and his sister at this stranger's orders in everything and supplied their "address," street and number, both invented so rapidly and smoothly that there was not the slightest break in the flow of his extravagant rhetoric. He now arose, bid their new friend—probably the most flabbergasted man in Saltillo—an effusive *adiós,* and ushered his furiously humiliated sister into the street. Before she could utter a word, he remarked casually that, after such a fine rest, they might as well return to the plaza to see whether the pretty visitors had meanwhile made their appearance.

Concepción had no intention of taking this very heavy joke lying down. "And exactly *what* do you think *papá* will have to say about such goings on?" she demanded severely.

"What do you mean *papá?* Aren't we *amigos?* Just you keep perfectly quiet now and come along with me. I'll buy you an ice cream."

Miguel himself, however, related the whole incident to their mother and with so sharp a mimicry of both their host and Concepción's horrified reaction that Josefa was totally disarmed. After her first spontaneous outburst of merriment, she could hardly undertake to mete out the reprobation which her annoyed daughter was convinced Miguel had well merited.

Another day while his *amigo* was taking a very formal leave of some callers, *señoritas* belonging to Saltillo's best society, at the doorway of the Pro domicile, Miguel happened to sail past on his bicycle. Greatly to the surprise of the elegant young ladies, their friend's customarily courteous brother ignored their salutations until he had reached the corner of the block. There, he turned and bowed to them with a great show of gallantry. Next he was seen to address a few words to a street vendor who bore an enormous basket upon his head. The peddler made a beeline for the Pro house while Miguel nosed his wheel around the corner out of view.

Nonplused by this inexplicable routine, the young ladies returned their attention to their farewells, but suddenly became aware of the vendor standing before them proffering his basket which was piled high with *chicharrones,* a vulgar preparation made by toasting the thick, dried skin of the pig.

"That young man ordered me to deliver my *chicharrones* as a gift to his sister, the young lady standing among you who is so exceptionally fond of them," he stated confidently.

This astonishing message caused some most unladylike chortling at poor Concepción's expense. Her protests that this was merely another of Miguel Agustín's stupid jokes did little to repair the damage to her injured pride.

This time, even Josefa was irritated, and when Miguel finally put in an appearance he was spared from neither side.

"Oh, my dearest *Mamacita,* don't you see?" he answered the parental scolding. "I only did it to deflate their silly pretensions. They were surprised into a laugh and had to drop their stupid affectations." However, as he hugged his mother affectionately, he promised to keep his humor under better control henceforth— or at least to avoid hurting the feelings of his *amigo.*

He frequently did try to restrain himself, though his delight in the more preposterous practical joke would never lessen. This same sense of humor it was which would one day serve him so well against the vicissitudes of a life in which many would have found occasion for little besides bitterness for, most fortunately, Miguel Pro was also quite able to laugh at himself.

VIII

PREVIEW OF TROUBLE

DON MIGUEL'S salary, while adequate to meet the needs of his family and provide the background against which it enjoyed many of the good things of life, left small latitude for the luxuries. It is unlikely that he ever built up any reserves worthy of mention. But these hard facts, as they might be termed today, had never appeared very important to the Pros, who understood that the best security of Christian families is achieved through the unselfish co-operation of its numbers. Nor did their lack of wealth deter their generosity in offering to the poor such spare pesos as were occasionally heard clinking together at the bottom of the family purse.

Let us see just what the youngsters of this sizable household contributed toward its general welfare and happiness. At this time (1907), the seven surviving children ranged from two to nineteen years of age. Loosely, they fell into two groups. Concepción, María de la Luz, Miguel Agustín, and Ana María were in their teens. As they had all been well-trained, these four were equipped to offer and, for the same reason, did gladly lend intelligent assistance throughout the domestic organization—which was considerably more complex than today's middle-salaried home. For the middle salary in México did not imply the informal, much less an impromptu, middle-class pattern of life. The home was not regarded as a living area for a group of persons having little more than its blood relationship and a mailing address in common; nor as a retreat from the taxing strains of each individual's outside interests. It was a world in itself whose smallest detail was of the utmost mutual concern. It had to function as an independent, self-sufficient entity—and every minute of the day.

A primary task of the Pro daughters was the clothing of the family. They must select materials, design, and make all the apparel required by themselves, their mother, and the smaller children, as well as repair that of the entire family, and the household linens. Concepción and María de la Luz also watched the markets for bargains, kept a strict listing of the larder and housekeeping supplies, planned menus for which they did much of the baking and other cooking. When there was illness, they helped with the nursing. All they knew of these useful activities they had been taught by Josefa. Now they were teaching the same things to the single younger sister who was left to them.

Miguel saw to it that the house was kept in a state of repair and co-operated in the supervision of the little boys. He escorted his mother and sisters wherever they had occasion to go outside the home and, as we know, had been his father's efficient business aide since the age of fourteen.

Young Edmundo's approximately eight or nine years qualified him for the younger group, but he was not thereby excused from many small jobs he could handle outside school hours. The little fellows, Humberto and Roberto—now four and two, respectively —were too small to afford him much in the way of companionship, but Mexican boys, at any age, are notably attached to their infant brothers and sisters, whom they find a constant source of amusement and delight. In any case, Edmundo's was an enviable position in the family. As the connecting link between Josefa's two sets of *hijos,* he was doubly privileged. Looked up to by the infants, his was the valuable experience of a "big brother"; and at the same time, he enjoyed the solicitude of three older sisters and a "big brother" of his own.

By birth, breeding, and living standards, these people were gentlefolk—which is why they could scarcely avoid living up Don Miguel's earnings year after year. What, precisely, were these standards?

Private schools were requisite for all the children. Such government (public) schools as there were did not rate with the majority of *escuelas particulares*. México's most esteemed and most numerous schools were Catholic institutions—which, however, asked but small tuition of day scholars.

The house was necessarily large, since it must shelter and afford the suitable privacy for children of widely divergent ages. There must be abundant, flavorful meals. Although these were at least partially prepared by the two elder daughters, one of the servants was certainly designated by the title of cook. She it was who cleaned the fowls and vegetables and made the dozens upon dozens of *tortillas* consumed daily, in the time-honored, infinitely patient technique by which the corn-meal dough called *masa* was hand-patted to that smooth, thin roundness approved by fastidious housewives. She also washed dishes, scrubbing the huge copper kettles which collected so much soot over the smouldering charcoal fires of the open braziers to a glowing burnish that would not "give her shame" when she saw them hanging massed on her kitchen wall.

The servants were not a luxury. For the heavy work in these old houses they were a necessity. They were employable for very little more than their food, lodging, and the materials which kept them decently clad. They required cash for little more than the gay bouquets they could never forego as gifts on the saints' days of their relatives, their *comadres,* and *compadres,*[1] for the graves of the dear departed on the Day of the Dead (All Souls'), or for the collection boxes before the altars of Our Lady of Guadalupe. If they fell ill, their employers looked after them and bought the needed medicines. Their long terms of service to the same household were all the security they needed and so all it occurred

[1] Godmothers and godfathers with respect to one another.

to them to ask. On the whole, they were kindly treated; always, we may be sure, by the considerate, warmhearted Pros. In this house, as in many others, there was an easy courtesy and mutual concern running between the servitors and the family which, oftener than not, developed into affectionate friendship. From parlor to the kitchen joys and sorrows were things for sharing —down to the last detail.

Besides the cook and the little Pros' *nana* (a mother's helper rather than a nurse or governess) there was a sturdy brown woman (likely to have an infant or two of her own playing in the sun-flooded kitchen patio) who kept the house gleaming. Her life was devoted to an incessant scrubbing of the tile or brick floors, the polishing of windows and woodwork. Between times she might lend a hand with the laundry, which was assigned to one of her relatives or *comadres*. Such co-operation made welcome opportunities for the amusing gossip and shared humor so dear to the gregarious "little people" of their country.

So what was lacking for the general comfort and well-being in such a home? Nothing really important. Naturally, it boasted no labor-saving devices to make a bagatelle of the housekeeping, but had these been available, the suspicious little *criadas* or maids would not have known how to operate them, nor wanted any part of learning. They would have insisted on following the traditional methods—which produced just about as good results as does the machinery regarded as indispensable by so many modern housekeepers. The cleansing of floors, clothing, and bedding by hand in cold water was by no means a light process, but the soap was strong and so were the dusky arms which wielded it in the rhythmic motions that were a joy to watch. The vital point, as any *Indita* can prove by long quotations from her foremothers, is that cold water does not bring on premature rheumatics—which "result from plunging the hands and arms into that which has been heated." Moreover, as eager as the servants otherwise were to please their *patronas*, they were adamant in setting their own tempos, certain protection against the perils of overexertion. So much for the kindly folk who served the Pros faithfully and undemandingly, as their kind still serve countless thousands of Mexican homes in our own day.

What were the other advantages and deprivations enjoyed or sustained by this family? Certainly there were no installments to be met on radios and television sets. And if it may seem absurd to mention items then non-existent, it is merely to suggest that at any time such contrivances would have been superfluous to the Pros, as well they might be to our families, were they large enough and sufficiently companionable to achieve their private "live" orchestras for home music at any hour; to supply the elements for mounting their own theatricals.

Apart from their talent for making music and fun, the Pros believed that an important reason for having learned to read was that thereafter they *might* read. And so their home contained books, veritable revelations of wonder, to set young minds pondering and young hearts dreaming mightily about this vast world—its history, biographies, its singing poetry, and the proud science which had made their modern age so fascinating a time to find oneself alive.

These young folk did not pass all their hours under their own roof. Whenever the stirring street sounds, muffled but not entirely obliterated by the thick, iron-studded doors rising between their jealously guarded privacy and the humming town, seemed more than usually attractive, they had only to step over their threshold to plunge into the picturesque pageant flowing from that eternal fountain of animation and color—the plaza.

The leisurely but exciting early evening *paseo* was an institution. Circling round and round the plaza, the girls of Saltillo, flanked by their intimates, formed one continuous procession, advancing at a matched pace in the same direction. Each pretty *señorita* took pains to cover, by animated participation in the chatter, her lively interest in the lads who might be casting ardent glances upon herself as the boys' line passed and repassed that of the girls, counterclockwise. No one was fooled by this elaborate indirection. Although to have fallen out of line for converse with members of the opposite sex would have been tantamount to creating a scandal, gay greetings were exchanged with acquaintances—one's brothers' friends, naturally—and vivacious smiles were flashed upon many, sometimes even toward attractive youths to whom one hadn't been formally introduced—*as yet.*

So if, in 1907, Saltillo boasted no movie palaces to supply synthetic romance by the linear foot, there was real romance aplenty, and this but intensified by the guards which wisdom and tradition had thrown about it since, also by wise tradition, the walls had been left transparent. A girl whose charms had smitten the heart on these unhurried strolls beneath the strains of the sentimental old waltzes floating from the municipal bandstand could also, in time, be met. (One of her various brothers was sure to be a contemporary.) Soon, if all went smoothly, a fellow would be her welcome caller, and then her serious *pretendiente.* What did it matter that "dating," as we know it, was tabu? For all the careful chaperonage, they would come to know each other well. Their mutual attraction had brought him to her house. Once inside, it was easy to judge the gifts and disposition of the intended. If she was loyal to her family, an obedient daughter, she would be a loyal and obedient wife. If her background was good, she would know how to give her children a well-ordered home. If she had a kind tongue in her head for the menials, she would almost surely never become a nag. What more did anyone need to know about the one who would go through life by one's side?

But, although the *paseo* was one of the delights of the Pro youngsters, none of them had found a personal romance. They joined the lighthearted throng to greet their friends and listen to the music, but always together. It was another advantage in their number. Doña Josefa, largely occupied with the supervision of her home, her baby boys, her religious observance and charities, could know that wherever her carefully instructed adolescents went, they were looking after one another.

Her decision to send Miguel back to Concepción del Oro was, then, a real hardship. Without him life would be restricted for the sisters; much less lively for the boys. But her husband had been struggling alone for two years in the midst of ever more unfavorable conditions. No one doubted now that the miners' restlessness was building toward serious trouble. To visit his family, Don Miguel had made a hundred round trips on the cramped, dirty little trains plying between the Mineral and Saltillo, but how long would this exhausting schedule be possible? The day the miners launched a real riot, the duties of the government agent would nail him to the center of trouble; while a disturbance of any magnitude was nearly sure to disrupt the transportation. Even if no such disaster impended—which God grant it would not—it was only right that Don Miguel now be given the full-time aid and company of his son.

So Miguel Agustín went back to the Agent's Office, leaving the orchestra, the charades, and the gaiety of the *paseos* he had enjoyed so hugely. He carried his father the consoling news that with the opening of the long vacations the others would also be returning. His mother believed that in such troublous times they should all be together. If to Miguel the vacations still seemed very far away and if he sorely missed his "dearest Doña Pepecita" and his *amigo,* he bore his loneliness in silence, dutifully attacking the work which had never been much to his taste.

Since the unoccupied evenings in their empty house constituted the most dolorous problem of all, this rather unstudious youth suddenly decided to devote them to the mastery of English and French. He fell to work on these subjects with avidity and discovered that his retentive memory served him excellently in the study of languages.

And then—the saints be praised!—the whole family was home once more, reunited with its beloved menfolk. If this was a boon to the tired father, it was delirious delight for the brother. Now there would be music again, music unending. There would be great laughter—and the pranks that, for Miguel Agustín, invariably exploded dull care and depression.

His mischief, however, never took the form of outright disobedience to his parents' commands. They knew him worthy of their trust and occasionally he was permitted to escort the girls to some local entertainment. It was on one of these evenings that Miguel was to marvel at the *positive* merit that lay in obedience. He and Concepción were returning from a play, picking their way along the tracks of the little mine railway, when they noted the rapid approach of some cars loaded with molten metal from the furnaces. Recalling their father's injunctions against permitting themselves to pass anywhere in the vicinity of these dangerous carriers, Miguel automatically bustled his sister, not only off the right-of-way, but deep into an adjacent field. They stood there watching the dramatic glow of the red-hot cargo streaking through the night. Suddenly they were shocked to see a heavy shower of fire splattered across the spot where they would have been standing had they merely stepped off the tracks for the cars' passing. One of the cauldrons filled with searing liquid metal had chosen that exact place to tip over!

After a grinding of brakes, the drowsy driver leaped from his seat to readjust the equipment—only to lose his footing and plunge headfirst into a pool of fearsome, flaring death. The fellow's agonized screams brought Miguel at a run to see if he might not extricate him, but it was quite useless. There was no way to reach him; already his head and torso were charcoal. Brother and sister hastened for help but long before their return with the others the driver was dead. After that first false step, no one could have saved him. This gruesome tragedy made a profound impression on the youth who repeatedly cited it in proof that even a small carelessness in obedience would have earned a like fate for his sister and himself.

This was only a normal reaction and, indeed, all of Miguel's responses to the experiences of these days can be so termed. For he was an average chap, well disciplined enough in important things while, in matters of lesser significance, inclined to be whimsical, or, as some said, almost incorrigibly impulsive. If his obedience and devotion to family strike us as rather notable, in his day and place they were not remarkable. Indeed it is quite possible that his intermittent mischief attracted more comment than did his everyday solid characteristics.

His Mexican and Spanish biographers do not emphasize his
personal piety in relating the anecdotes that highlighted these
years. But it would be a mistake to overlook the fact that he had
always been accustomed to receive Communion each First Friday
as matter-of-factly as he habitually fulfilled his religious obligations. In such a family, it could hardly have been otherwise. The
Pros' day-by-day living was conducted in an atmosphere condi-
tioned by the doctrines and devotions of its Faith. None of them
found in these dear, familiar observances any sense of burden or
melancholy whatsoever. Thus the evening gathering of her
youngsters and servants with Doña Josefa for the recitation of the
Rosary for the souls of their dead was an honor happily anticipated rather than dreaded in boredom or reluctance. It would
no more have occurred to Miguelito to consider any of this irk-
some than it would have occurred to him to regard it as indicative
of exceptional virtue. He looked to his Faith as the source of
consolation, beauty, and love. If constancy to it was also a duty,
it was the rewarding duty of those greatly privileged to be born
into a felicitous society unlimited by lines of race or geography—
one that would endure eternally. For all these convictions, there
was nothing sanctimonious about this boy; nor was he aware,
even in the slightest degree, of the spiritual heights that he had
been born to scale.

On the contrary, when he occasionally indulged in foibles
which were rather sure to be disapproved by his parents, they
were concealed in the immemorial manner of youth. Cigarettes
were just coming into fashion and Miguel had discovered their
attractions. His sisters were aware of this development, but they,
too, carefully avoided any mention of the subject before Don
Miguel and Doña Josefa.

The denouement came about during one of Miguel's more ir-
ritating afternoons. A pile of new *expedientes* towered on his
desk. Small hope of getting through it before another day's mail
swept in a fresh load of the things. Was business more than half
litigation? Surely there must be a pleasanter way to gain a liveli-
hood!

At this unlikely moment one of the sisters burst into the office from the upper-floor living quarters and launched into a breathless tale of woe. Her favorite canary had escaped and was now perched high on the *azotea* or flat roof. If someone—Miguel, of course—didn't come to the rescue, her beautiful pet was lost forever!

Miguel was in anything but an heroic mood. Leave his work in a mess like this to go crawling across the roof after a pesky bird? Nothing doing!

The next voice to be lifted was Don Miguel's. "Go along and attend to your sister!"

Thrusting his pen over his ear with a savage jab, the boy gave vent to his exasperation. "These women live only to torment us. I could hang them all!"

Don Miguel arose abruptly and so did his son—all the way to the *azotea!* As he passed a knot of anxious sisters on the stairs, he was glowering, but once on the pleasantly sun-swept roof, his bad temper evaporated. He commenced to stalk the tiny bundle of bright feathers with a boyish interest in the contest.

The family, watching from the patio, heard him call for a towel. This was produced, rolled into a ball, and tossed roofward. And then it happened! As Miguel leaned over the roof edge to catch it, a shower of cigarettes was released from his pocket precisely over the head of his father. The youth's consternation was not lessened by the involuntary giggles which escaped his silly sisters. His face turned a flaming red quite apparent from the ground below.

Slithering about the roof after the canary, he did some fast thinking; and when, the enmeshed bird safely in hand, he descended to face the music, it was seen that a cranky brother had been transformed into the most amiable and innocent creature imaginable.

In Don Miguel's hand were the telltale cigarettes, but his impassive expression gave no hint of his reaction. His question, addressed to the wary Miguel, was equally noncommittal. "These . . . er . . . objects. What might they be?"

"Those objects? Ah . . . only a sample of a new brand of fine cigarettes, *Papá,* that I picked up for you in the *tienda.*"

"*Muchas gracias,*" said Don Miguel gravely as he tucked the "sample" into his pocket.

Dinner that day was more than ordinarily enlivened by Miguel's sprightly anecdotes. Over the coffee, however, their father produced the hopefully forgotten cigarettes, suggesting, "Well, now, suppose we just try these *cigarros exquisitos* provided by my son."

But somehow Miguel was not in the mood for smoking and it was most convenient to recall the mountain of neglected work on his desk. The girls, too, suddenly discovered urgent errands, a claim which in the case of the canary's mistress turned out to be quite accurate. She was summarily dispatched to replace the lost smokes, incontestably sacrificed in her interests. Her cheerful compliance completed the revision of her brother's harsh opinion of women and, that same evening, he presented the girls with an outsized box of most "magnificent" cookies!

Some very real excitement now fell upon humdrum Concepción del Oro. Over the two-day Independence fiesta (September 15–16), the long-dreaded riot broke loose. Exploding in the cry, "Exploiters!" the miners' disgust with the owners brought a mob down upon the Agencia de Minería in the middle of the night. The rioters' object was the destruction of the property titles in the official files entrusted to Don Miguel, which he had taken the precaution of transferring to his private quarters. However, as these adjoined the office, there was small margin for comfort.

As the first rocks and gunshots broke the agency's windows, Don Miguel prepared to go forth and face the infuriated workers. He knew the crowd must include some of his former *muchachos*—and this impulse suggests his confidence in their regard for himself. But his wife and daughters pleaded fervently against the taking of so great a chance. The violence had been sparked by the holiday celebration and the mob was obviously drunk.

Someone might discharge a pistol before Don Miguel could utter a syllable. The frustration of failing to locate the files had run the feeling still higher. Would he permit himself to be killed or injured uselessly?

In the end their logic prevailed, and Don Miguel remained inside listening in mounting concern to the destruction being wrought below to the accompaniment of the alcohol-induced bravado in the yells. A shout came for "Miguel *chico!*—young Miguel!" who was known to be in charge of the *expedientes*. Determined to maintain a playful note for the reassurance of Doña Josefa and the girls, the youth exclaimed, "Only hear how I am acclaimed! Poor me—to be hated so roundly! Know, impious folk come to rob us of our sleep, that I'm really quite innocent!" Then he reached for his guitar and undertook a counter-demonstration with a lusty rendition of his most rollicking ballads. When ordered to be quiet, he went to the dining room for a tray-load of sweets with which to regale his sisters. Nothing could be done about this grim storm outside, but he knew it was important to keep the morale high.

It was a relief when the marauders, to judge by the waning commotion, began to move off. Watching through cracks in the shutters, Miguel reported that the malcontents had turned into an adjacent street; and later, that they were working off their resentment in an assault upon the Protestant chapel. These new depredations only augmented the rage of the mob, and it soon came boiling back to Don Miguel.

The Pro women prayed to the Virgin for liberation from this danger while father and son shoved the massive dining table against the door and prepared to defend their home. Suddenly, at the very instant when a new attack was hurled upon the premises, the pounding of horses' hoofs broke through the yells, crashes, and shots! The *Rurales!* It was the famed and fearsome *Guardia Civil,* old Don Porfirio Díaz' legendary guarantee of the "order" that had been the long-time boast of the proprietors (so many of whom, alas, were North Americans). The magnificently equipped *Rurales* galloped upon and literally over the unfortunate demonstrators. Horrified, Miguel observed the ruthless decimation of the rioters under the blazing guns and cried in consternation, "Oh, the poor things are being killed like dogs! May God in His mercy pardon all of them!"

And thus the disturbance ended abruptly, albeit in circumstances more anguished than Don Miguel and his son could believe warranted. They had too long and deeply sympathized with the sufferings of these men who went down into the earth to labor long hours for a totally inadequate recompense, to be able to harbor resentment. Furthermore, as they well knew, this sort of thing, the pyramiding of violence, was no solution. This one riot had been put down, and they thanked God for their delivery, but nothing had been settled. Might Heaven aid them all—the miserable miners as well as the family Pro Juárez!

The following morning they began to fulfill the vows they had all undertaken at the height of the danger. Miguel's promise, it seems, turned out to be a considerably larger order than he had realized. This was to forego a *novia* (a special girl friend or sweetheart) for a full year. "Pardon me, Lord," he was heard to say later, "I didn't know what I was doing!"

LAST DAYS AT CONCEPCIÓN

SOMETHING exceedingly strange was happening to Miguel Agustín, a change which fell upon his affectionate family like a blight, destroying the ease which had always reigned among them. It was not only that his jocular and loquacious disposition had suffered transformation into an unfamiliar mood of chronic impatience and taciturnity, though that in itself was hard enough to bear. His distracted loved ones were forced to recognize an inexplicable cooling in his attitude toward the Faith. Indubitably, he was now bored by the devotions he had loved all his life. What might have worked this change remained a mystery, but if its effects afflicted the entire household, for Josefa Juárez the situation amounted to heartbreak.

As she fastened the last stitch in the chalice veil she had embroidered for the Church, Doña Josefa was praying for the wisdom to save her boy as well as his good influence upon his brothers and sisters. If she might only be granted this blessing, she would not ask to know the whys and wherefores lying behind Miguelito's present spiritual disturbance. Its causes could forever remain a secret between God and the youngster if He would but show her how to overcome their frightening results.

She blinked against the pressure of tears as she wearily folded the needlework into a neat little square. Then she summoned her daughters. "One of you will please wrap this up carefully and tell Miguel Agustín to take it to the *padre cura* for me."

There was a moment's silence during which one of them took the mother's offering. "You mean Miguel's to deliver it to the church personally, *Mamá?*"

"Precisely." The brevity of the reply discouraged comment. As Josefa arose and left the room, the girls looked at one another uneasily. None of them found this errand to her liking, but there was nothing for it; one of them was stuck with the job of facing Miguel's certain ire. Perhaps the risk was accepted by the *amigo* who had for so long been his favorite companion, though it may well have been the unselfish, wide-eyed Luz who resembled him so markedly. Whoever it was evoked the reaction they had all anticipated.

"So I'm to hustle right down to the rectory with an altar orna-ment, of all things? Am I the friar's servant—or what?" he snorted disgustedly as he fiddled with the small parcel.

"What in the world is wrong with you, Miguel? *Mamá* is go-ing to hear you!" expostulated his agitated sister.

"All right, all right, I'll go," he snapped, "but I tell you this: I only do so because it's *Mamá* who orders it!"

Had he again been preserved by his ingrained obedience? It might seem so. For upon his arrival at the rectory, the dis-gruntled youth was surprised out of his sulks to encounter some visiting Jesuits, one of whom had been the Pros' very special friend in Saltillo. Fathers Gordoa, Pautard, and Martínez were en route to the Hacienda San Tiburcio to conduct a mission. They invited Miguel to go along with them, an idea which, for some unaccountable reason, he found pleasing. He asked the priests to accompany him home to obtain his father's permission.

His return to the house with the priests and his obvious high spirits were only less amazing to the family than his jubilant affirmation, "I'm going on a trip with *los frailes curas!*" And when, two days later, clad in a dashing *baquero* suit, he did take off astride a spirited mare, the greatly heartened household was moved almost to tears to hear the old-time gusto in his cry, "*Adiós!* And now—on to the mission with *los curas!*"

Happiest of all over this seeming return to normalcy was Josefa who, after raising her heart in thanksgiving, startled everyone by announcing with conviction, "Oh yes, this *muchacho* will be a Saint Augustine!"

But how to account for what had gone before? Only too soon would the affair be clarified for his mother. The first envelope to arrive from San Tiburcio, though addressed to her, contained a note Miguel had written to a Protestant girl of their acquaintance —whom no one had remotely suspected of being his *novia!* The exact contents of this missive are not recorded, but the implications were clear enough to cause Josefa intense suffering. The other side of this embarrasing, but most fortunate, accident was that the young lady in question received the letter meant for his mother. An exceedingly penitent son had detailed the first day of a mission so inspiring that it had touched his heart deeply. Now he was preparing to make his confession and receive Communion. His decision to return to the Sacraments had already filled his spirit with peace and gratitude. He asked Josefa's pardon for his recent indifference and the deplorable faults that had sprung from his interior confusion.

This affecting expression was indignantly forwarded to Doña Josefa by the disgusted *señorita,* along with Miguel's earlier letters and gifts to her. There should have been real consolation for his mother in Miguel's change of heart. Nevertheless, the revelation of so elaborate a deception under her own roof caused the poor woman to fall ill. She returned both letters to the hacienda —not to her son, but to Padre Martínez, upon whom it devolved to inform the youth of the awkwardness precipitated by this mishap.

Miguel was horrified to learn just what his folly had cost his beloved Doña Pepecita. He passed an entire night on his knees in the sanctuary, blaming himself bitterly for having brought suffering upon her in a cause which, as he had already recognized, was wholly unjustified. Long later he declared that on this, his *noche triste,* he would have infinitely preferred being buried alive to facing his family after the exposure of his stupid deceit. As he had suspected from the beginning, his entanglement in this foolish romance had not sprung from any deep affection for the girl, but from pride. He had committed himself in a moment of bravado and then when he had realized the extent of his error, he had been simply too inexperienced to know how to withdraw. His irritation with his ineptitude and deception was what had given rise to the nervousness and agitation that had turned him into a rebellious son and quarrelsome brother. He knew in his heart that only some such disgrace as this could have guided him out of the labyrinth.

His relief at having made his peace with Heaven, his conscience, and his mother (he never did achieve the courage to write Don Miguel), sent his spirits soaring again. Once more he felt the old urge to frolic—even mischief. It was so very fine to be rid of the burden of guilt that he could not wait for the mission to terminate before involving himself in one of his characteristic pranks. The joke he played on the *frailes* was harmless enough, but that they did not let it perturb them speaks well for their own sense of humor.

Secretly garbing himself in a soutane belonging to one of the missionaries, Miguel sallied forth for his own little "preaching excursion" about the neighboring *ranchos.* The innocent countryfolk accepted him as the genuine article, listened respectfully to the sympathetic and appealingly youthful "padre," "covered his hands with kisses and filled his pockets with cigarettes, eggs, and fresh cheeses," [1] until the real priests caught up with him. As Miguel had apparently made a fair job of his preaching, they contented themselves in carrying him off to the hacienda and deflating his frisky spirit by relieving him of his contributions.

The homecoming to Concepción del Oro was not difficult, after all. Josefa's exceptional understanding of her son's temperament smoothed his path back to happiness with the whole family. The

[1] Pulido, p. 45.

only untoward incident to mar the joy of his restoration to them was the shower of stones with which some resentful Protestants of the Mineral met his arrival. He escaped without injury and, though the unkind gesture alarmed his parents, he refused to be annoyed or to worry over a possible repetition of any such evidence of ill-will.

"Don't give it a thought," he admonished them cheerfully. "All that is important now is that I've learned that the only real love for me lies in my own family." He had stated a fact that would continue to be true. Miguel Agustín Pro would never experience a profound love for any girl. Upon one occasion he was heard to declare that usually he had found "their heads very empty and their hearts equally hollow."

In his eighteenth year, Miguel was left in complete charge of the agency while his father attended an engineers' convention in Zacatecas, the state capital. Don Miguel had taken Concepción along on this trip to give her the opportunity of renewing her acquaintance with Guadalupe, her birthplace, and with the relatives and friends still residing in that section. But he returned alone. His eldest daughter had been received with much love by the Pro and Juárez connections who had pleaded that she be permitted to remain for a good, long visit in Guadalupe. He had been pleased to allow her to stay. And very soon after his return to the Mineral he surprised Miguel and María de la Luz by presenting them with their own tickets to Zacatecas. He wished them to share their sister's vacation, following which they could all come home together.

The youngsters were overjoyed. They anticipated nothing but delight in their native pueblo among people quite different from the population surrounding the mines. They would be staying in the fine house of their father's great friend, Don Luis Flores, and there would be visits and expeditions in all directions. It seemed too wonderful to be true.

They were not disappointed, for they were given a royal welcome by the Flores and were showered with invitations to all the community's best homes. Everywhere they noted the great respect and affection that these families had preserved for their good parents. For the first time since their infancy the young Pros found themselves surrounded by a circle of gay contemporaries who had been reared as carefully as themselves—and several of these fine youngsters soon became their fast friends.

One of the first places they were taken to see was the famed old Convento de Guadalupe where their distinguished greatuncle, Fray Juan Crisóstomo Gómez, lay buried. There, too, they found the mummified body of their mother's former confessor, Padre Galván. They heard how, after death, this holy man's hair and nails had continued to grow and now, as he looked upon the mummy's long, thick beard, Miguel was inclined to credit this story. He touched the eyes and hands with reverence and grew sentimental contemplating the latter which had so many times absolved the dearest lady on earth. Father Galván's casket was uncovered. When Miguel took note of the dust that had accumulated on the face, he wiped it clean before following his sisters and companions from the crypt and up the ancient stairs for an inspection of the archives which were being opened to them as a very special courtesy.

To think that these priceless records dated from the days of the Venerable Antonio Margil de Jesús, that missionary without peer in the history of their country! Miguel became engrossed in the registry of favors and miracles granted through the long line of holy men who had been stationed at, or had visited, the Apostolic College. Nothing had ever thrilled him more than the knowledge that he had been born on a spot where such spiritual titans had labored and sacrificed everything of this world for love of God and His poor Indian children. In the end, Concepción and Luz had to drag him away from the archives for the remainder of the day's program. Were the girls surprised to see this unexpected preoccupation with long-dead ages and men on the part of their naturally lighthearted and, as they sometimes accused, light-minded, brother? *They* were the ones whom Miguel frequently chided for unnecessary seriousness. Somehow he seemed out of character prowling about these musty old corridors and poring over crumbling tomes, wide-eyed and reverent.

But the girls' biggest surprise was yet to come. When they had finally dislodged him and were conducting him back to their friends—who were so nobly endeavoring to conceal their impatience over the long delay—Miguel commented casually, "Do you know what I'd like best? To be one of these saints who eat and sleep, enjoy their little frolics—and then work so many miracles!"

But he wasn't "mooning" about saints the day he promised to fight a bull at El Club Violeta's fiesta. Several of the lads belonging to this social group had gaily undertaken to do the same, including the Flores son nearest Miguel's age, his special friend. In view of the fact that the youth of America's Spanish-descended countries are enthusiastic *aficionados* of bullfighting, it is not surprising that many boys of even the best society submit themselves in amateur contests to this formidable test of skill and courage.

When they learned of this project, Concepción and María de la Luz were aghast. What did their brother know about bullfighting, for goodness' sake? He must be crazy! If this adventure resulted in a serious injury, what would their parents think of them for having countenanced any such rashness? They descended upon Miguel like twin tornadoes, positively prohibiting his participation in this foolishness. In vain did he plead that it was too late to withdraw. He had agreed to fight a bull. If he backed out now, he would be guyed unmercifully and perhaps really be scorned as a coward. Was that what they wanted? The girls were callously unimpressed. "If you disobey us in this," they told him portentously, "you'll see soon enough that Our Lord won't help you!"

Again those fatal words—"obey," "disobey"! Were they to pursue him everywhere? And yet—there was magic in them; good magic in one; in the other, evil. Had he already intuitively sensed that his life might have been destined for the "total obedience"? Presumably not. But he gave in, accepting the fact that in the absence of his parents his older sisters represented authority. But it would have demanded far less bravery to face the most ferocious *toro* in the ring than the ridicule of one's friends in the street.

The eagerly-awaited day of the fiesta dawned in brilliance. The sun was a great golden platter slipping lazily across an infinity of azure. It warmed Zacatecas' highland breezes and glinted down upon the dazzling hues and embellishments of the *torero* costumes which had turned the plaza into a magnificent stage. Out of each approaching street merrymakers were swarming into the central square, the physical heart of Guadalupe. In a degree only possible to Latins this day was dedicated—to seeing and being seen, to flattering and being flattered and, most of all, to rejoicing and lighthearted romancing. On such a day it was imperative to be gay with all the others. And so, though Miguel would assuredly have preferred skipping the whole celebration and certainly the bullfight, it could not be done. Calling on all the fortitude at his command, he went along to the plaza with the others knowing that for him alone this fiesta was an ordeal. His premonitions were justified. The moment it was noted that he had failed to appear in the glorious array of a *torero,* eyebrows were lifted and the questions commenced.

"No, I'm not fighting today because I don't wish to offend my sisters. They are older than I and it was their right to decide." This candor required considerable courage in itself, but no one took account of that. He was ridiculed cruelly. The boys in the billiard parlor which he forced himself to enter were the most obnoxious of all. At one point Miguel found himself clinging desperately to a table with both hands to prevent himself from striking the most insulting of his tormentors.

But he would not be vanquished and, in the afternoon, still giving no evidence of his inner misery, he escorted his sisters to the bull ring. The very first thing that happened was the severe goring of his chum—the rashly intrepid Flores boy—by the young bull he had selected to meet for the *corrida's* opening event! Hastily charging some of his friends to look after Concepción and María de la Luz, Miguel hurried to the aid of the injured youth. The hurt was critical and required immediate surgery. Moreover, it was now revealed that the unlucky *torero* suffered from a weak heart which would prevent the administering of an anesthetic. Miguel offered to support the poor chap while the doctor operated. The procedure was excruciating and young Flores, who was enduring the agony with clenched teeth, suddenly sank them into Miguel's arm with such force that he bit a fair-sized piece of flesh out of it. At the conclusion of the operation, therefore, the surgeon had to turn his attention to repairing the results of this last mishap. Miguel spent the rest of the day at his friend's bedside, doubtless cogitating the wisdom of his sisters' opposition to his own ridiculous daring in agreeing to fight a bull. . . .

The Zacatecas vacation produced no other dramatic incidents, though it extended itself through three full months. Nor did Miguel's thoughts return to dwell upon the saints who had inspired his enthusiasm during that first visit to the monastery. There was too much going on, too many pleasures devised by their hospitable hosts for the young Pros' entertainment. Miguel, who had rarely given his wearing apparel a second thought, now discovered undreamed-of satisfaction in the accumulation of a natty wardrobe. He carried this indulgence to such an extreme that twice he spent funds forwarded by his father for their return trip on augmenting it.

Finally, Don Miguel's patience ran out and he wrote Don Luis that he desired his children's immediate return to the Mineral. When this was made known, Miguel accepted the situation cheerfully, although he regretted having to say *Adiós* to his native *tierra,* which he preferred to any section he had ever known, and to the friends who had shown his sisters and himself so much hospitality and warmth of heart.

Their arrival at Concepción del Oro took place in February,

1909. As Miguel handed the girls off the rickety little train, his heart sank. He had forgotten how sad a spot the town really was! After the mellow charm of Guadalupe, the stirring scenes of Zacatecas, the excitement of the parties, and the congenial companionship of fellows his own age, he was aware of something almost ominously tragic in this glimpse of the straggling streets and bleakly ugly buildings spreading before him. Must he actually accept a place like this as his home—for always? What sort of future could he possibly expect this bedraggled community to offer him? He sighed with discouragement, but then, in one of those quick lifts of the spirit typical of his temperament, he smiled.

"It's in God's hands," he said aloud, and suddenly was knowing how blessed a thing it was that he would, in a matter of minutes, be reunited once more with those he loved most dearly in all the world.

Don Miguel had a special reason for ordering his elder children home. He had decided to send the family off to Saltillo again, this time in the cause of the little boys' education. Even Roberto was now of school age. Miguel Agustín, who must again assume the role of head of the family, saw a bit shamefacedly that his dread of restriction to the Mineral had been wasted. Moreover, this time his father had secured a house for his family in a very superior section of the northern city, immediately adjacent to the Jesuit Colegio de San Juan Nepocumeno.

Doña Josefa and her little brood had scarcely settled themselves in this delightful location before they were courteously welcomed into the pleasant life of the fine families comprising the select quarter. Although their new neighbors were conservative and notably devout people who were accustomed to receive Communion daily, there were frequent fiestas of the simpler sort, *tertulias* (private musicales or reading recitals), and picnics to be enjoyed together. The whole group was pervaded by a cordial spirit of mutual help and sharing in everything affecting their homes. Josefa was deeply grateful for such an improvement in her children's background. And for the trio so recently returned from Guadalupe it was a happy surprise.

Not long after their establishment in this favorable environment came the dramatic appearance of the Halley comet. Alerted by the advance notices, Miguel set himself to watch for the phenomenon. He awoke the house with triumphant cries the instant he spotted the trail of fire against the rich night skies above Saltillo. He insisted that one and all accompany him in climbing the steep street of the Cerro to a vantage point where he would "give them a class in astronomy." Only the sisters and Edmundo, the latter but half-awake, took him up on this invitation.

Miguel's excitement before this nocturnal wonder was not satisfied by merely banishing the sleep of his immediate family. Rendering his merriest and noisiest songs, he proceeded to arouse the entire neighborhood. One by one touseled heads and faces blurred by incomprehension popped into view from behind window frames. Startled from deep slumber, many of the owners of the heads and faces imagined that the commotion emanated from a *gallo,* the early-hour serenade by which enamored Mexican youths reveal the seriousness of their latest affections to the highly flattered subjects. Doubtless some neighbors who would not have stirred from their blankets to honor "Mr. Halley's celestial wonder" felt impelled to identify the principals in a new earthly—and very local—romance. The mischievous young Pro bowed to his sleepy audience and observed with mock solemnity, "How very gratifying that, as I pass along absorbed in contemplation of the blue heavens I shall one day inhabit, there are so many to give me a suitably attentive reception."

But at three o'clock, when the great comet achieved perfect visibility, its beauty produced an emotion in this youth which could not be diluted by irony, comedy—or anything else. *"Viva mi Padre Dios,* the Worker of things so lovely!" he exclaimed. Then, a note of defiance creeping into his excited shout, "Just wait, little stars—or big—until you see how I shall outdo you in leaving my trail across the heavens. Isn't that true, *muchachos?"* This strange proclamation he followed by cries of *"Sí, sí, sí!"* (in imitation of the clowns who advertised shows in the streets of the towns about to be privileged by presentations of "spectacular" performances).

On the fourth *"sí!"* a night watchman appeared out of the darkness to quiet this unseemly uproar. But Miguel only laid hold of the *sereno's* arm and urged more loudly still, "Come on, neighbor: just contemplate that which has appeared over your head and see if you can insist upon quiet. Isn't that true, *muchachos? Sí, sí, sí!"* And his yells were now running upscale in a most alarming crescendo.

"Be silent!" implored the harassed watchman in desperation. "Do you want to awaken the whole town?"

"I think I do," came the airy reply. "We're peaceful folk but, at the moment, very happy. And we think it only just to give them all a happy awakening!" He flung his hat into the air and commenced the recitation of a rigmarole of verses, by way of conclusively proving his point.

There was nothing to be done with him, since herding a group of well-born youngsters to jail would be unthinkable, so the watchman admitted defeat—for the moment. The following day, however, he lodged a complaint with Doña Josefa. Standing modestly on the side lines during this painful interview, Miguel promised himself revenge for the affront. At the height of the discussion he contrived, without being observed, to attach a long cord to the man's lantern. Then he slipped from the room with the string's free end in hand. The flabbergasted gendarme caught a flash of his indispensable equipment as it slid out of sight around the doorjamb and forgot his complaint to pursue it. The street chase which ensued was not rendered less mortifying by the fact that the amused spectators made no effort to control their glee.

The whole of this second two-year period in Saltillo proved exceptionally enlivening. Did it occur to the Pros that their almost uninterrupted gaiety might be an advance compensation for the

strains and sorrows which could lie ahead in times like these—
of mounting political tensions? Did they take account of the fact
that the older children were rapidly approaching maturity, that
there would soon be inevitable separations? Probably not. They
were simply grateful that life was growing fuller and happier
all the while. For the Pros everything was still intact. But oh,
they would remember these days, these wonderful months of
1909 and 1910; take strength in the knowledge that, in God's
goodness, heart-free joy such as this is, at times, possible of
realization.

María de la Luz and Ana María were taking lessons in an art
which is most popular with Mexican women and girls. They
were learning to fashion flowers from wax. Their teacher, who
came to the house to give their classes, was a spectacularly pious
lady of middle age. Sometimes she seemed more determined to
save their souls than to impart her skill in artificial flower making. No sooner had she given them a few brief instructions than
she would produce a book of spiritual reading and promptly
commence pouring its contents over her pupils in a high-pitched
and otherwise uncultivated voice. It was as though she meant to
compensate for her lack of talent with the vigor of her rendition.
As their fingers and minds went on with the intricate business of
reproducing rose and poinsettia petals, the girls managed to miss
much of the enlightenment so unattractively directed their way.

Confident of the merit of the literature which moved her own
emotions so forcefully, as well as of her intentions, the *señorita
profesora* believed her persistence nothing less than her Christian
duty. Moreover, she harbored dreams of even bigger things. She
had set her heart upon bringing Miguel and Concepción within
range of her ringing tones. But alas, this light-minded pair seemed
diabolically clever in blocking their spiritual development. They
frankly preferred not to interrupt their custom of devoting the
maestra's class hour to practicing their music, a portion of which
the good woman had identified as downright "profane," i.e., pop-

ular. With what Miguel called "consummate insensibility," she
kept pressing her inescapable arguments for Concepción and her
brother to attend the readings.

Miguel contained his irritation as long as he believed courtesy
demanded, but finally he persuaded himself that since self-will
is a character defect, it might be his duty to enlighten the mis-
guided lady.

"*Bueno*," he responded to the teacher's hundredth urging that
he bring his *amigo* to class. "Today we shall accept your kind
invitation. But as the weather is very cold right now, you must
permit me to kneel where I choose for the devotions. And there
is one other condition. After giving us the pleasure of your reading, you must remain to take supper with us; *si no, no y no!*" [2]

The poor woman was so overcome with delight at her success
that she was willing to promise anything. As they approached the
classroom, Miguel and Concepción heard her triumphant boast
to their sisters, "We have conquered them at last!"

They saw at once that the preparations for this occasion had
been very special. The *maestra* had ordered her pupils to lay
aside their manual work (the single reason for her presence in
the house). She thought that, inasmuch as Miguel had indicated
that he would kneel for the spiritual reading, the others could do
no less. One by one they took their places while their brother
now innocently marched to the sofa and knelt upon that. The
girls suppressed their amusement at the absurd picture he presented, perched there with the springs moving under each slight
shifting of his weight. But the reader was oblivious to this undercurrent and, after clearing her throat self-consciously, she commenced in a voice made hollow by solemnity: "From Chapter
such-and-such of *The Imitation of Christ.*"

Miguel emitted a profound sigh, exactly the encouragement
the lady needed. In her project of reforming a hardened young
sinner (Miguel) she judged this manifestation to be cause for
optimism. Thereupon, with more fervor than ever but certainly
no more skill, she literally flung herself upon her subject. From

[2] "If not, nothing doing."

this start, the repetition at frequent intervals of the sighs from the sofa was matched by the mounting emotion of the teacher's rendition. Now and then she cast a furtive glance in Miguel's direction, which is how she happened to catch his surreptitious dab at a wholly imaginary tear. At this positive evidence of a response far greater than she had dared hope, the poor soul let herself go completely. The strident tones became comically tremulous.

Between this ridiculous exaggeration and Miguel Agustín's shenanigans the sisters were soon biting their lips to control their mirth. Their brother was not so absorbed in his own performance that he failed to keep their reactions under observation. Seeing that at any moment one of them might explode into laughter and ruin everything, he deemed it time to hurry the scene to a climax. Of a sudden he startled them half senseless by pitching off the sofa across a fragile table which shattered noisily as it splintered beneath his weight where he thudded upon the floor in a "dead faint."

"*Jesús, Jesús!* The young man is having an attack!" shrieked the horrified teacher who had never dreamed that any gifts of hers might produce such dramatic contrition. Nervously imploring the young ladies to bring water, to get their brother off the floor, to call aid or, at any rate, to do *something,* she began to fly about the room wringing her hands in the utmost distress.

One of the girls approached the prostrate clown and whispered in his ear, "I should have expected something like this. Miguel Agustín, you are positively shameless!"

Another appeared with a glass of water which she thrust none too gently to the lips of her slowly "reviving" brother. Miguel weakly permitted a sip of the water to be jostled into his mouth. Then, savoring it critically, he abruptly sat up. "But this is impossibly insipid!" he protested in righteous indignation. "Put some sugar in it, please."

By this time the befuddled *profesora* should have been entertaining certain suspicions, but she accepted the youth's apologies for having become so unduly *"emocionado"* by her reading. She also remained for supper as she had agreed to do. Miguel's sensational recovery permitted him to hasten into the kitchen where he fell to work with both energy and imagination to prepare a "stupendous" chili sauce for the meal. At table in his office of head of the family, he served the hapless lady so generously with his radical concoction that she was, quite literally, reduced to tears.

The girls were inclined to feel that this final attention carried matters altogether too far. But, after the red-eyed *profesora* had bid them all adieu, their brother asserted aggressively, "A tear for a tear. Just so did she make me shed them over her execrable reading of Kempis!"

But when he saw the strong disapproval on his mother's face, he was humbled into an admission that his own performance was perhaps in comparably poor taste. Whereupon he promised—as he always promised—to make every effort to mend his ways. Not the least of Miguel Agustín's talents, as his sisters frequently noted, was his ability to pacify Doña Pepecita following the most preposterous pranks.

SEPARATION—
END OF INDECISION

THE closely-knit Pro family had to be aware that, soon now, they must be prepared to face the changes inherent in the older children's approaching maturity. Miguel was nineteen and a half; the two elder girls had entered their twenties. All were standing upon the very threshold of the future they had so long anticipated.

Had María de la Luz given any advance warning that she wished to be a nun? It would appear not, for Miguel sustained a shock when, at the beginning of August, 1910, this attractive, talented, and kindest-hearted of sisters effected the family's first breach by leaving Saltillo to enter a convent in Aguascalientes. His personal reaction to this impressive event was the deepest sadness he had ever known. The Pros' second daughter was sorely missed by them all, but Miguel Agustín was the hardest hit by the vacancy she left behind her.

Was this because he was less capable of the supernatural joy which surely balanced her parents' sense of private loss? Or was it partly frustration in having somehow been left behind, an awkward, uncertain youth still without prospects or even the vaguest plans for his own future? If a quiet slip of a girl had found the answer to personal fulfillment, what was the matter with him? It was well enough to play at being proxy head of the house, to be the leader in all the family fun and many of its domestic activities, but where, after all, was he *going?* The next thing he knew Edmundo, and then Humberto, would be forging ahead to their own individual goals; and he would find himself without a justifying function even in the home.

Or was this profound depression, which everyone accepted as his stunning sorrow over the loss of Luz, a considerably more complicated matter than met the eye? In brief, had Miguel already sensed the pull of the great destiny marked out for him without, as yet, being able to recognize it?

For the moment he threw himself headlong into his music. He drove the remaining members of the Típica Pro ruthlessly in a heartbreaking attempt to fill the gap María de la Luz' desertion had left in the orchestra. She had been his best performer and, he told himself in desperation, the aggregation could not hope to compensate for so lamentable a loss. He never complained openly of his bitter disappointment after each of the concerts by which he tried to lift their loneliness, for he knew how greatly his parents, too, felt their daughter's absence and, ironically, never more than on these occasions to which she had once made such a fine contribution. It was only Concepción, who, following a performance particularly displeasing to him, heard him mutter through clenched teeth, *"Caramba!* How great Heaven must be that it has to be purchased at such a price!"

Exactly six months after her departure the family received the invitation to attend María de la Luz' reception of the habit. Excitement ran high as the clan boarded the train at Saltillo. They would have to change connections at San Luis Potosí the following morning. It would be First Friday, and before the departure of the Aguascalientes train, they planned to attend Mass to offer their customary First Friday Communions for the new little Sister.

But as they chugged south through the night across the long state of San Luis Potosí, Miguel, too tense with conflicting emotions for sleep, absent-mindedly began to dispatch a box of chocolates. His consternation at discovering that it was past midnight was so great that he awoke the entire family to deplore this mishap. Among them all, he alone would be unable to receive Communion.

Upon arriving at their hotel in Aguascalientes, they found it swarming and noisy with a company of bullfighters, reason enough for the good Sisters to offer the Pro daughters the hospitality of the convent for the duration of their stay in the city. This invitation was gratefully accepted over Miguel's strong objection. He explained that he did not wish to be deprived of his sisters' company while seeing the sights of fascinating, unknown Aguascalientes. Later, he would admit that the true reason for his opposition was a mighty fear that somehow this stay with the nuns might give rise to religious aspirations in the hearts of one or both of his "remaining" sisters. Although he was overruled on this point, he decided to do something about the situation. Within two days he presented himself at the convent gate saying he had orders to "call for those of my sisters who are not nuns," inasmuch as the Pros were preparing to entertain a party of friends in their quarters. When Concepción and Ana María were once more in his care, strolling the streets and becoming acquainted with the city, he told them that the "order" had been issued by *"mi Padre Dios"* which did not mean, however, that their earthly parents wouldn't be delighted to embrace their daughters once again.

But his precaution came too late. Concepción had already made up her mind. Before two more days had passed she and Doña Josefa were on their way to León on some mysterious business known only to themselves. This unaccompanied side trip filled Miguel with dire—and justified—premonitions. They had gone to make the necessary arrangements for the girl's entrance in the same Order and house that had received María de la Luz! [1]

When Miguel knew definitely that he must also watch his *amigo* disappear forever behind convent doors, he threw himself on his bed and sobbed unrestrainedly. Later, somewhat calmed, he asked Concepción to take a last walk with him. As soon as

[1] Presumably the motherhouse of the Order was located in León.

they were alone, he begged her to tell him *what it was* that impelled her to abandon her loved ones in so precipitate a fashion, especially after having seen what Luz' going had done to them all.

"The will of God," she told him gently.

"Well, then, there's no more to be said," he replied sadly. "But what is His will for me? May I learn it soon! Pray that I may, sister!". . .

The following morning (February 12, 1911) little Humberto made his First Communion in the Chapel of the Colegio de la Inmaculada. María de la Luz, who had been his godmother at Baptism, was again his sponsor. At the breakfast, the Pros' last all together, Miguel, overwhelmed by emotion, asked the two who had pledged themselves to religion, "Why shouldn't *I* do the same thing?" When he saw that the only reply was the smile they shared, the words which tumbled from his overflowing heart indicated that he was, at least momentarily, moved in that direction: "If what I'm feeling now is a divine vocation, that's exactly the way it will turn out!"

This was the first time in his twenty years that Miguel Agustín Pro had ever made reference to the possibility of a personal vocation.

That same day Concepción accompanied her sister back to the convent. The next morning the others set out upon their return trip to Saltillo. Although before leaving Miguel had asked the Mother Superior for the prayers of the community in behalf of his own future, his depression had assumed unprecedented proportions.

At home once more, he found himself the eldest of the children —but oh! how gladly he would have exchanged this distinction for a return of the old, happy life when they had all been together! The two who had been closest to him in age, interests, and sympathy were gone forever and there was no recourse but to try to rejoice that they, at least, were pursuing their dreams along—he recognized this—the highest possible path of life. At the moment, however, everything was lost in the pain of his loneliness and a grinding worry that accompanied him relentlessly: What was he going to do with his own life?

Doña Josefa wrote her convent daughters that there had been a great change in Miguel Agustín. Their formerly gay and playful brother had returned to Saltillo reserved and pensive. Forgotten were the jokes and pranks which had always seemed to be almost an obsession. Trying as these had sometimes been, his mother would be glad to see a restoration of Miguel's old-time enthusiasm for the embarrassing practical jokes she was beginning to believe had passed into family history.

At Easter the girls were encouraged to receive evidence that his spirit had, to some extent, lightened. He had sent them, by way of an Easter gift, a little magazine of his own composition. This periodical entitled, *De Todo un Poco* (A Little of Everything), contained a collection of skits, verses, and quips. He had copied some of the material from a book which, since early childhood, he had been compiling under the title *Libro de las Injurias*. They recognized the verse appearing on the first page of the present as one he had written at the age of seven:

> *"Beneath a green palm*
> *a sad coyote sat,*
> *whose sighing song said,*
> *'Drop down dates!'"* [2]

Had this gesture been a final effort to recapture the charm of their merry, irresponsible youth together? Did it carry a touch of defiance because he had been deprived of the dearest-loved among his sisters and brothers? Or was the nonsense with which he filled these pages for their amusement meant to assure these companions of his innocent childhood that he was recovering his self-possession; was commencing to see light at the end of his dark night of loneliness and sorrow?

[2] *"Debajo de una verde palma*
estaba un triste coyote,
y en su cantido decía,
suspirando: '¡Abajo dátiles!'"
(Reprinted by Pulido, p. 56.)

It was August before he told his parents of his decision. With the permission and blessing of Doña Josefa and Don Miguel he would, without further loss of time, seek acceptance by the Society of Jesus.

It had not been so simple as the bare statement might make it appear. The inner struggles which had finally led this youth to recognize his vocation may only be surmised. But sometime during the summer, before his parents had any intimation of his intention, Miguel had held a preliminary conversation with their close friend, the Jesuit Father Mir, who had thereupon recommended him to Padre Gabriel Morfín, rector of the Colegio de San Juan Nepocumeno. As this celebrated Mexican establishment was right next door to the Pros' residence, Father Morfín must have been acquainted with the family, his neighbors for more than two years. Although pleased and touched by the news that young Pro wished to enter the Society, the rector knew his duty to test the applicant. Should Miguel's temperament prove too impatient for the career he was contemplating, the time to find it out was now, before he was accepted as a novice.

The young aspirant, who knew very little of these needs for prudence, arrived at the Colegio to keep his appointment with Padre Morfín punctually and in rather high spirits. Knocking upon the rector's door, he heard the welcome response from the other side, "*Adelante*—Come in," in a state of understandable excitement. Bracing himself for the all-important interview which should set his feet upon a path of service to mankind (in how great a contrast to his present uselessness in the world!), Miguel drew a deep breath, turned the knob, and entered the study. He greeted the priest with the most respectful phrases at his command. It was a bit of a letdown to discover Father Morfín settled deeply into a rocking chair engrossed in his newspaper which he gave no indication of laying aside. Without even offering Miguel Agustín the courtesy of a seat, the Jesuit went right on perusing the news.

Considerably affronted and uncertain as to what he should do in a circumstance so strange and disappointing, the youth felt himself coloring with embarrassment as he stood shifting from one foot to the other. Could there have been some misunderstanding? Even so, how could the man just sit there rudely ignoring a visitor he had summoned and then bidden to enter his room? From his first reaction of surprise and dismay the volatile Miguel felt his choler rising until his resentment had reached such a pitch that, as he would admit later, he had to restrain a stupendous urge to tip the complacent rector right out of his rocker. Nevertheless, he could be stubborn, too, and so for a full half-hour he doggedly continued to stand "nailed to the floor," not once taking his eyes from the face of the padre. At length, when the latter was satisfied that Miguel was not to be rebuffed into retiring in disgust, he glanced up and said blandly, "It is best that you come back tomorrow, my son, since, as you see, I'm rather occupied today."

"*Muy bien, Padre,* good afternoon!" replied the insulted applicant, succeeding in a valiant effort not to choke on his fury.

While he was making his way toward the gate in a perfect blaze of humiliation and frustration, Miguel encountered Father Pichard, another member of the Society, who chose this unlikely moment to tease: "Pro, my boy, you are a *chato*—a pugnose!"

This gratuitous sally did nothing to lessen Miguel's irritation and he experienced "a violent longing to transform the clerical wit into a pugnose himself," but once more he achieved the needful control and merely responded edgily, "Yes, Father, with regard to my nose, I'm a *chato,* as you see; but whether my head is also snub, you'll hardly be in a position to judge without a more careful examination."

Padre Pichard met this sarcasm with hilarity; then opined that the ensuing day ought to suffice to make that part of the situation plain.

Understandably, Miguel returned home in a state of nerves. By nature a communicative boy, it was almost more than he could manage to refrain from telling his mother all about his chagrin at the uncalled-for treatment to which he had been subjected by her friends, "those excellent and holy men," next door. But forcing himself to silence, he proceeded directly to the privacy of his own room. There, he threw his aching bones full length on the bed and attempted to sort out his agitated thoughts. No youth with a heart full of dreams and plans for a lifework so inspiring could find it easy to see his first serious effort to offer himself met by such cavalier treatment as he had just been accorded.

He asked himself if this cold-shouldering had not been the rector's way of spurning his desire to enter the Society. Had his capabilities and merits been prejudged too meager to qualify him for that erudite company? Following so deliberate a slight, was he really *expected* to return to the Colegio for a serious interview? On the other hand, if he didn't persevere, might they not deem him a coward or, at the least, a fellow whose convictions were too weak to overcome a single discouraging snub? In the end, he knew that, for better or worse, he would go back, if only because he recognized that his heart would give him no rest until, after revealing its sincere desire, the Jesuits made it abundantly clear that they simply did not want him.

The next afternoon merely developed a variation of his first attempt to talk with Padre Morfín. This time the rector was engaged in writing what appeared to be an interminable document. Again Miguel was left standing miserably in the center of the room, a repetition of humiliation which again soon had him grinding his teeth with rage. He could scarcely breathe without sputtering. Meanwhile, the silence was so intense that the scritch-scratching pen amounted to a loud noise. The sound annoyed Miguel acutely as the minutes dragged into a period considerably longer than he had suffered on the preceding day. And when, with a satisfied flourish, Father Morfín finally signed his protracted missive and pushed back his chair, it was but to remark exasperatingly, "Well, young man, you had best return another time—tomorrow, say, inasmuch as you can see for yourself that today I'm even busier than I was yesterday."

Miguel, who had been endeavoring to pass the time rehearsing the impressive little discourse with which to meet Padre Morfín's "What may I do for you, my son?" now angrily told himself that *never again* would he be such an idiot as to enter this inhospitable study. But when, outside once more, he came upon a group of religious, all of whom were complaining loudly and bitterly of their lot, the almost insurmountable difficulties and hardships of life in the Order, he began to do some wondering. Surely this was a very odd way for men of God to be speaking—and before a young layman! Then, with the coincidental appearance of the "amusing" Father Pichard who forthwith launched into a banter even broader than his previous baiting had been, the light finally broke upon Miguel Pro. He understood that this mortifying behavior was a deliberate policy devised to test his patience and perseverance.

It was such a relief to recognize that they did not consider him presumptuous in seeking to join his life with theirs that his heart lifted marvelously. Gladly, he conceded them this inning. But they would soon see how he would match them, point by point. Play-acting had ever been the forte of Miguelito Pro; and he undertook this game with such good will and aplomb that Padre Morfín was speedily satisfied that his young prospect was truly endowed with the long-sufferance, persistence, and humor so essential to a successful priest.

Still Miguel delayed communicating his plans to the family, though they may have suspected what was in the wind. As reticent as their son, however, Doña Josefa and Don Miguel avoided all reference to his repeated visits to the Colegio. When once he did volunteer the information that he was engaged upon "a little piece of business with the Jesuit padres," they smiled in innocent sympathy.

This was how matters stood until suddenly Miguel fell seriously ill. As his high fever soared to delirium, he commenced to babble of his impending entrance into the Order; and even disclosed the hiding place (a small locker he had built into a corner of the patio) of his correspondence with Fathers Mir and Ipiña, the Jesuit Provincial for México. These letters provided conclusive proof that their sick boy had not only already been accepted, but had been offered every facilitation by the Society. And as soon as he was convalescent Miguel soberly explained everything and asked his beloved parents' permission to leave them for "the service of *Jesucristo*."

He encountered no opposition. By this time Doña Josefa and Don Miguel were both convinced of his vocation and, as in the cases of Luz and Concepción, they viewed this third sacrifice as well balanced by the assurance that God had found another of their children worthy of His service. The good father's only condition was that he accompany Miguel to the state of Michoacán to see him established in the novitiate of El Llano, both as a safeguard to his still delicate health and to have the honor of personally delivering him into the hands of the greatest of all Fathers.

Save for the heartbreak in parting from Josefa, the pain of the home farewells would have been considerably mitigated by the pleasure of a stopover at Aguascalientes to visit María de la Luz and Concepción. The rejoicing of these two at the decision of their favorite brother may well be imagined. But Miguel found it impossible to blot out the memory of his mother's face as she had valiantly bid him good-by. In mentioning this sorrow to his sisters, he broke down and wept "like the veriest *niño*." Needless to say, however, his grief did not cause him to falter in his determination to dedicate his life to religion; and, on August 10, 1911, he arrived at the Hacienda El Llano to commence his new life.

Pending his son's reception of the habit, Don Miguel was lodged in the novitiate, though he was not permitted to see or speak with Miguel, who had gone directly into a preparatory retreat. On Assumption Day he was clothed with the habit. After Mass, the generous gentleman and wise father who had thus witnessed the conclusion of his paternal responsibility in behalf of his first-born son embraced his boy once more—and took his solitary departure from El Llano.

XI

THE FUGITIVE

DURING the early months of this same year México had experienced the convulsion that had overthrown the dictatorship of Don Porfirio Díaz—the regime under which Miguel Pro had been born and passed his entire life. The seemingly invincible "Man of Iron," whose vast power, public achievements, and shrewd grasp of foreign diplomacy had long been internationally hailed as evidence of brilliant statesmanship, had finally succumbed to old age and the pressure of the exciting ideas of an unassuming theorist named Francisco I. Madero. Because this change—or some change—was undeniably overdue to the exploited classes of the nation, the approbation of the Mexican majority had gradually been won for this initial revolt, usually designated the Revolution of 1910.[1]

Despite the general disappointment that Madero's gifts for government were already proving decidedly slighter than his ability to state the case for his revolution in blood-stirring rhetoric, the Mexican citizens were, by and large, still loyal to the man who had intelligently articulated their aspirations and inspired their struggle toward freedom, individual opportunity, and the democratic political processes.

[1] The first sporadic skirmishes commenced toward the end of 1910, but the Revolution did not assume national proportions until the following year. Don Porfirio Díaz fell May 21, 1911.

From the record it would be difficult to ascertain just how much Miguel Agustín was personally affected by this significant experiment which, impulsed by a tidal wave of propaganda, had broken across his native land in a rough zigzag of violence. But, given his lifelong sympathy for the downtrodden, it is safe to assume his support of any undertaking dedicated to the alleviation of the misery of the underprivileged.

No more than other hundreds of thousands of his countrymen could Miguel have predicted the failure of the impractical and strangely remote little President to consolidate his original victory and bring his high-sounding theories (strongly influenced by a study of North American institutions and processes) to realization. So, while he must sometimes have wondered how the dismayingly inept new government expected to control the ruthless and, unfortunately, only semi-civilized forces unleashed to effect its rise to power, and while he surely deplored the religious vagaries of its leader, he doubtless esteemed Madero's generally conceded sincerity and certain of the contemplated reforms which should have been—but were not to be—swiftly effected, to the benefit of an emancipated people. At least there was no basic disagreement between the Christian ethic and the democratic premise which had been the basis of the rebellion. And, if revolutions are largely wrought by violent and greedy men, there was as yet no proof that the violent and greedy Mexicans who had participated in this one could not, in time, be restrained by the traditional Catholic concepts of their compatriots. Therefore, Miguel's entrance into religion took place against a background of national optimism and brave new social ideals that paralleled his own hopes and dreams.

The immediate concern of the new novice was to demonstrate his worthiness to be considered a follower of that magnificent soldier of Christ, St. Ignatius of Loyola. And now he was awestricken before the realization of how much must be mastered by his intellect as well as by his will. At times he asked himself how he dared seek a place in a company of men universally celebrated for the scope of its erudition and experience—he, a poorly prepared fellow past twenty who had not even completed his secondary education. But if his facile memory would just get him by in his courses, he would try to compensate for his mediocre intellectual powers by working for greater perfection of soul. How did one go about attaining this greatly desired end? Miguel knew the answer: by prayer. One had only to pray hard enough, with the proper disposition, to obtain this victory which is denied to no man. So, while he did study diligently, he prayed even more. His classmates and professors began to call him "the *hermano* who is convinced that God wants him to be a saint."

Meanwhile, Miguel Pro never lost his enjoyment of the little joke, the apt imitation, and simple play. According to Father Adolfo Pulido [2] who was a novice with him at El Llano: "From the very first time that I spoke with him in the novitiate, I was struck by his good humor and, even more, by the abundant inventiveness of the wit which he possessed in a degree that I have never seen equaled in any other person I have known. This was not a coarse wit, but rather one of that intelligence which accompanies a genius for mimicry and which bubbled spontaneously from his lips to make him an irreplaceable companion for diverting recreation and an indispensable actor for the Christmas festivities, literary society events, and entertainments with which we were wont to make the life of our houses of formation agreeable.

"But everyone who had occasion for close contact with him soon took note that there were two Pros in one piece: the one who played and the one who prayed; the one who joked, smiled, and sang, and the one of sensitive abnegation and long-suffering silence. I was not the only one to observe how the fluent Pro turned himself into a Carthusian for the annual eight days of [spiritual] Exercises and that he probably spent more time in the chapel than any other while being scrupulously exact in all his devotions, commencing with the matutinal meditation. I recall how once, while we were novices, after having eaten together at the second table, I invited him to take some recreation.

[2] Quoted by Bernardo Portas, S.J., *Vida del Padre Pro, S.J.*, p. 16.

He replied half seriously and half in fun, 'I can't or I may lose my vocation.'

" 'I don't understand,' I answered him.

" 'If I don't take my siesta now, I shall be sleepy at prayers, and if I don't pray well, I shall have to leave the Society,' he explained."

And Father Bernardo Portas adds: "He who laughed at all the world, commencing with himself, took the things of God more seriously than some would ever have suspected." It is quite possible that this testimony which applied to Miguel Pro the Jesuit novice, might have been true of Miguel the youth of the Saltillo *paseo,* or Miguel the "miner" at the Mineral. If so, we may find here the secret of more than one of the puzzling transitions of his earlier days.

The last cited biographer goes so far as to attribute the contrasting impulsions found in Miguel Pro to a "dual nature": "He who is unable to comprehend that in the same man there may well be such a dualism will never succeed in understanding the moral and religious physiognomy of our brother Pro." [3] Though his gaiety might frequently, or even habitually, cover his depth of spiritual recognition and piety, there was no fundamental cleavage between these two sides of his make-up.

There would be, nevertheless, many trials and much secret anguish for Miguel Agustín before he had succeeded in bringing his sensitivity to criticism and his tendency to proud flashes of resentment before reprehension to ideal humility. In all this, it was his undeviating practice of prayer that worked the change in his temperament which, to him, seemed a miracle in itself.

Padre Manuel Santiago, his novice master, has related many incidents which illustrate Miguel's rapid advance in self-domination. At one period Father Santiago appointed the novice Pro *distributario* of the orders and messages from the superiors to the students. After a month or so during which he discharged this duty to everyone's satisfaction, a slight defect in the youth's per-

[3] *Ibid.,* p. 17.

formance was utilized by the *maestro de novicios* to prove his disposition toward authority. The scene took place in Miguel's cell and was very painful. After a censuring so harsh as to be disproportionate to its cause, Padre Santiago abruptly relieved the novice of his post and then, in seeming indignation, stamped out of the little room.

Less than a half hour later Miguel presented himself before the novice master to ask pardon for his error in so honest a humility that Father Santiago was completely undone.

On another occasion, the test to which he was subjected by the same man was probably even harder to meet. During the first visit to El Llano by His Excellency Bishop Mora, Padre Santiago ordered the embarrassed novice: "Go ahead and tell some of your funny stories for the diversion of *El Ilustrísimo!*" Miguel was aghast. What would the prelate *think* of a would-be Jesuit whose head was crammed with such stupid nonsense?

Father Portas, also a novice at that time, was present and witnesses that, after a moment of indecision during which he turned red with shame, Miguel Agustín told one of his absurdest yarns. "I shall never forget the deep impression which his self-vanquishment made upon me." [4]

His obedience and humility received their reward, for the Jesuit superiors acknowledged their satisfaction with the spiritual progress of Miguel Pro and on August 15, 1913, he was permitted to take the vows by which he became a professed member of the illustrious Society of Jesus.

Before this long-anticipated milestone had been reached at tranquil El Llano, the outside world had been plunged into a turmoil almost indescribably devastating and complicated. From the beginning, President Madero had been beset by sporadic rebellions led by *caudillos* in various parts of the country. Although he had been able, with the aid of loyal General Ángeles, to put down the earliest of these, plot had followed upon plot, treachery

[4] *Ibid.,* p. 18.

upon treachery. Such presumptuous egoists as Pascual Orozco, Victoriano Huerta, Félix Díaz, Bernardo Reyes, Manuel Mondragón (and alas, the United States Ambassador, Henry Lane Wilson), either battled one another or combined to dictate the destiny of a now brigand-riddled land. Even those outright highwaymen and assassins, Emiliano Zapata and Pancho Villa, were again on the loose, wreaking terror through their ragtag mobs of insurrection.

Then, even after Madero had resigned his office, he had been vilely murdered. This crime (committed on the night of February 22, 1913) was followed by the news that Victoriano Huerta had snatched the executive power. This served as excuse for the next real revolution, that of General Venustiano Carranza, Governor of Coahuila, who had long been an active figure upon México's bloody political stage. Utilizing Huerta's most capable and ruthless enemies, Carranza now plunged the nation into her most tragic chapter thus far, on the pretext that only his pet Plan of Guadalupe could return it to "constitutional normalcy."

As one author sums up the chaos:

"Gradually the Anti-Huerta groups assumed the character of three columns. Obregón established his military ascendency in Sonora and the west. Francisco Villa terrorized Chihuahua and the center. Pablo González remained as commander of the northeast, in Nuevo León and Tamaulipas. . . . In the beginning the most sensational victories of the so-called Constitutionalists were not those of Carranza, but of Francisco (Pancho) Villa, a cattle rustler who had fought with Madero at Ciudad Júarez. . . . Gathering a bandit army of Indian cowboys in Chihuahua, he drove the federal troops from the rural regions. . . . The unspeakable depredations and crimes of these bolsheviks hardly harmonized with the loftier slogans of the revolution. . . . At first Carranza's troops were fairly moderate, but the eventual character of the movement began to reveal itself. At Durango, churches were profaned; and in the Carmelite convent, nuns were raped. At Guadalajara, horses were stabled in the seminary; libraries and churches were sacked, priests and religious were subjected to every indignity, and atrocious sacrileges were committed." [5]

The foregoing lines carry us slightly ahead of our story, inasmuch as Guadalajara had not yet fallen, but we may well ask how the Jesuit seminary at El Llano managed to remain tranquil in the face of the tempest that was raging toward it out of the north. The reason was that the superiors in this remote corner of Michoacán had determined to wait for reliably verified reports before making plans or permitting the disturbance of their students. Lurid rumors had filled the air for two years, but violence had not yet engulfed their corner of the country. Perhaps it would be spared indefinitely. They believed that their best service lay in remaining faithful to their posts where they were forming men of peace. They would depend upon their prelates to indicate the hour for the disruption of normal procedure.

So the newly professed Miguel Pro went on with his study of the humanities which he had commenced in the second year of his novitiate. Although he was no shining light in Latin and Greek, he was outstanding as a Castilian stylist. His writing, both verse and prose, revealed exceptional talent. He had a gift for rhyme and meter, and he was achieving the prose technique which would later attract favorable comment when his work appeared in the periodicals of several nations. In such activities and in the pursuit of his spiritual progress, he continued to live peacefully and happily at El Llano for the better part of another year.

But by May, 1914, there was no longer any possibility of overlooking the revolting atrocities perpetrated by forces which hesitated at nothing to gain their ends. The Society's Father Luis Benítez had just arrived at El Llano after a hazardous escape from the horror of Durango. As soon as the superiors heard his report on his perilous odyssey, they were forced to agree with his dire prediction that the clergy and the religious, from the ecclesiastical authority right down to the most helpless parish priests, were marked men. There was so little room for choice between the leaders now in the field and they were so rapidly losing the sup-

[5] James A. Magner, *Men of México*, pp. 495–96.

port of every decent element in the country that, from here out, it would have to be open war upon virtue and, thus, upon religion. The impoverishment and decimation of the manpower of the Church were already well advanced. There was nothing to be gained by longer delaying the preparation of the seminarians for the tragedy that lay ahead.

It was a fine spring afternoon when Miguel and his fellow students listened to Father Benítez' appalling story as they sat upon the cool grass carpet that spread beyond the foot of the wide orchard and on down to the eucalyptus-lined canal over which they could see the light-drenched pastures running away from El Llano to the distant hills. Was it possible that each day was bringing closer to this delight men who would deliberately deface its exquisite beauty with the lifeblood of their compatriots? This wonderful land had been Christian for nearly four hundred years; had been created by Christians (since the pre-Conquest tribes had never, even in the loosest sense, constituted a nation). The old missionary friars, men with the same inspiration, hopes, and good will which animated these youths of El Llano had, with their own hands, sown and cultivated this rich earth, as well as the spiritual ground into which they had dropped the seeds of the Faith. These were the processes which had created all that their followers, twenty generations of every color and class, had recognized as "México." What grotesque accident of history was this that could turn so much loving labor and beauty into a holocaust?

Before the month's end, Saltillo, too, had fallen—into the hands of the terrible Villa. Miguel soon heard that the good priests at San Juan Nepocumeno had not been so fortunate as Father Benítez. The half-mad bandit had first demanded that the Jesuits there hand him the impossible sum of one million pesos. Then, in rage at their failure to comply, he ordered their torture by mutilation before having them thrown into a cattle car for conduct by drunken guards to the American border. This heart-stopping intelligence brought the awful reality closer to Miguel Agustín than anything he had so far heard. And when, on July 8,

Guadalajara fell before Carranza, he knew there was no longer room for the slightest hope that any might be spared. Yet suddenly his spirit was infused with a sort of elation. Would it not be a very special blessing, a magnificent destiny, to suffer persecution in the cause of justice?

The situation prevailing about the nearby town of Zamora was already very precarious. During the early weeks of that summer of 1914 several formerly insignificant bandit groups had begun to swell through acquisitions from the vicinity's very lowest elements, poor devils who were daily becoming bolder as they saw a chance to cover their individual crimes in the general confusion. The depredations of these gangs had soon paralyzed the life of the outlying pueblos. They disrupted the local rail service between Yurécuaro and Los Reyes, incited disorders and violences in the streets of Zamora. The Carrancistas now fell in full force to oppress the community with insatiable demands upon the clergy and the more prosperous, or reputedly more prosperous, families.

On this occasion the federal forces managed to repulse the invaders. The Carrancistas fled to La Piedad, there to await reinforcements which soon appeared under the command of General Joaquín Amaro. Zamora was recaptured.

But despite everything, at El Llano all was still proceeding more or less as usual—with the students in the midst of year-end examinations. The community, moreover, was preparing to observe the centenary of the restoration of the Society of Jesus. On August 7 it would be just one hundred years since a papal bull had annulled the Brief of Suppression: *"Dominus ac Redemptor."* [6]

It would seem to have been an unpropitious moment for such a celebration, but the superiors adhered to the opinion that their best contribution to peace lay in sustaining the normalcy of the life of the house until the final hour. At any rate, the activity preparatory to this joyful commemoration (which seems to have been held a few days prior to the anniversary of the event it

[6] Portas, p. 23.

glorified) was the occasion of great happiness. Miguel, charged with the decorations, executed drawings and lettered inscriptions setting forth the history of the Order on the walls and columns of the patio. On the day of the fiesta, after a Solemn High Mass and special ceremonies in the public church, there was an afternoon procession through all the corridors of the house in honor of the Sacred Heart. This was followed by a literary and musical *academia* at which Miguel declaimed a famous composition describing the Society's foundation. Other works recited on this program were the prophetic: "Farewell to the Exiled Missionary" and "Maria, Mother of Exiles." After nightfall came a fireworks display. The contribution of Brother Pro toward the high spirits that prevailed throughout the celebration won the admiration of all.

The next morning matters took a sharp downturn with the report of the expulsion from Guadalajara of all priests and foreigners. Still worse was the decree suppressing the religious rights of the city's entire Catholic population which, as elsewhere throughout the nation, comprised 95 per cent of the inhabitants.

At one o'clock on the morning of August 5, the war finally came to El Llano with the appearance before the hacienda gate of twenty-two well-mounted Carrancistas who bristled with firearms. Two of the party broke into the gatekeeper's house and obliged him to open to their companions, who thereupon bore down upon the hacienda buildings in a whirlwind gallop, discharging their pistols in all directions. Hacking open the barred doors of the *hacendado's* residence, they proceeded to chop up the furniture, burn the account books, sever the telephone line, and destroy everything in their path.

When the first shots were heard in the seminary, Father González, the rector, and Brother Poza, a veteran of the Imperial War, stationed themselves at the church portal, prepared to offer their lives to prevent any profanation. Fortunately, the raiders did not attack the sacred precincts, but, after completing the ruin of the main house, took themselves off in the direction of Miraflores, an adjacent hacienda. Later that morning Miguel found a random bullet that had penetrated the wall into the sacristy; another was discovered in the rector's quarters.

This incident, together with the constant passage of armed parties around the property, completed the persuasion of Padre González to prepare for the worst. The library's finest books were packed and concealed; the most valuable chalices and altar ornaments were buried under the floor of a distant carpenter shop; the best paintings were secretly distributed among the families of Zamora. Ordinary secular street apparel was purchased for all the community. And during all these activities someone was constantly on guard in a tower overlooking the surrounding terrain.

As night fell upon El Llano, August 12, the community was ordered to gather in the chapel where the rector, after detailing the most recent developments and enumerating the precautions observed in their behalf, informed them that he saw himself forced to take the ultimate means for their preservation—dispersion. His seminarians must now go out to face their individual destinies which, God willing, might, at some not-too-distant date, bring them—or some of them—together again. Although they had been half-expecting some such move, the definite news was tragic. After high sacrifice, greater than most men ever offer, after long dedication and laborious efforts to prepare their souls and inform their minds for a life of service to God and man, this was dead end.

At daybreak on August 15, three years from the day upon which Miguel Agustín Pro had received the habit, in groups of two, three, and four men, the great exodus from El Llano began. Some headed for surrounding haciendas. Miguel and three companions made their way on foot to Zamora where, upon their arrival at three o'clock in the afternoon, they were tenderly received and thereafter sheltered for two weeks by the family of a brother in religion.

Meanwhile, the stanch little city was engulfed by terror. There were continuous attacks upon citizen property, innumerable torturings, sacrilegious acts and profanations. The cracking guns of the firing squads became too familiar to cause comment. The revolutionary chief in Zamora, not content with the mourning and desolation sown by his hordes throughout the countryside, personally undertook the brutal beating of a poor old priest to demonstrate in the presence of his troops "that the blood of a *cura* upon a man's hand will never wither it." The punishment of citizens presumed to be well-to-do who failed to meet this man's extortionate demands was suspension by the feet for hours of intense suffering.

This hideous state of affairs was not exceptional. Such acts were to be encountered all across the land, but in the remote, traditionally peaceful and devoutly Catholic sections such as Zamora, these infamous excesses seemed more appalling than in those places hardened by longer exposure to the brutalities some men will always be equal to perpetrating in the greed which it serves their purpose to call "patriotism."

Five days after Miguel's arrival in Zamora, the chief, who had commandeered the Bishop's Palace for his personal billet, ordered the assembly there of all the region's *sacerdotes*. (In *Carrancista* parlance the term *"sacerdote"* comprehended the entire scale of men pertaining to the Church, from its prelates down to the last sacristan or theological student.) Disobedience to this edict would bring wholesale raiding and serious castigations. Since it was soon seen that all who presented themselves at the Bishop's Palace received as bad treatment as those who were seized—incarceration, beatings, assignment to street-cleaning squads—there seemed to be no point in obeying the order. Miguel and his friends ardently prayed that they might soon receive instructions to flee Zamora, though they were loath to desert the local padres who, being well known, found it necessary to go into a hiding more rigorous than their own.

In behalf of two priests who had taken refuge in the open hills near the *cerro* known as "La Beata," Miguel and one of his companions undertook to supply food. On the twenty-fourth, after leaving a dinner in the rude lean-to which served the fugitive

Fathers as shelter, they evaded capture by a party of Carrancistas by a matter of mere seconds. The young Samaritans had no sooner commenced their return hike to Zamora than they heard the horsemen bearing down upon them. By the grace of God they managed to gain the cover of a thick growth of corn where they were forced to hide for more than an hour.

Each succeeding day drove the danger and the tension to a higher pitch. Thus the superiors who were still free to communicate with their religious ordered that only those with families in Zamora were to linger in that vicinity. Miguel and his group were told to set out at once for Guadalajara. Although conditions were no better there, they would be unknown in the larger city. Until safer arrangements could be made for them, the Jaliscan Jesuits and their partisans would make every effort in behalf of the youths.

Any project to leave Zamora was now exceedingly dangerous. The Carrancista guards holding the city's exits rigorously demanded passports bearing their *jefe's* signature. This was exactly the sort of challenge to his ingenuity and acting ability that appealed to Miguel Agustín. Deeming it the role most likely to deceive the soldiers, he assumed the garb and mannerisms of a peon. Who would be interested in a destitute and foolish-appearing rustic? A little stain for his face and hands would do for make-up since his eyes were as dark as any Indian's. Under a broad-brimmed sombrero pulled low on the forehead and muffled to the nose in a serape—the typical and logical means of protection against the chill of a rainy August evening—Miguel shuffled out of his friends' home prepared to match whatever astuteness the sentries might be able to muster with his talent for impersonation.

As it turned out, there was no real test, because at the gate he had selected for quitting Zamora the entire guard was unastutely snoring, so loudly that he slipped past without awakening anyone. The remainder of the night he spent in the open fields a safe distance from the town, awaiting the arrivals, one by one, of his companions. By dawn they were all together once more, setting out on a weary, worrisome trek to Negrete where, according to their instructions, they would board the Guadalajara train. The heavy seasonal rains had turned the roads into ankle-deep mire. They must not for a moment relax a sharp lookout for the armed parties which infested the entire area. There was no prospect of anything but discomfort and trouble on this long tramp that lay ahead, but they were young and, as they set their faces away from Zamora, their naturally high spirits, unlike their clothing, were only slightly dampened by the deluge that soon descended upon them with a vengeance.

It was on the second morning out that they suddenly glimpsed in the distance a long, straggling column of Carrancistas. As the boggy road prohibited a speedy return to the last village, the already-drenched wayfarers scrambled into the dripping thicket bordering the roadway where they were obliged to shiver through most of the day among the underbrush owing to the delay of the troops within view of their hiding place. This complication terminated, they continued their plodding, stumbling advance upon Negrete.

Miguel was the only one impersonating a peasant and, once aboard the train, he amused them all by elaborating the role. Assuming the attitude and duties of servant to the others, he juggled their skimpy hand luggage, waited upon them so obsequiously that at first they had all they could do to maintain their part of the act. But so expert was his impersonation that they soon found themselves actually forgetting that their *mozo* under the enormous sombrero was not the genuine article. They said later that somewhere along the line the identity of their classmate Pro became completely lost; that whatever may have been their fellow-travelers' estimate of the rest of the group, none entertained the slightest suspicion that this lowly manservant was, in reality, a fugitive Jesuit seminarian. Much less did anyone dream that his name was destined to become the most dramatically symbolic of the Revolution, the most revered and best-loved name of twentieth-century México.

It was September 2 when they chuffed into the Guadalajara station. They had achieved the first leg of an hegira that was to carry them half-a-world's distance from their beloved El Llano— and through long years of exile. Of Mexicans, no greater sacrifice could be demanded.

XII

TO SPAIN BY
WAY OF CALIFORNIA

PANCHO VILLA'S victory at Saltillo which had subjected the
Jesuits to such shocking brutality also spelled ruin for the Pros.
Don Miguel's long identification with the government as Agent
of the Department of Mines made him a marked man in the
Villistas' books. When they had swarmed down upon Saltillo
where he had joined his family, he was forced to flee for his life.
This left Doña Josefa, the three younger boys, and Ana María
without protection—not even knowing where Don Miguel was
or in what condition. And at once all their earthly possessions
were seized by the undisciplined rabble that comprised the in-
vading "army."

Convinced that it was exceedingly dangerous to remain in
Saltillo, the devoted mother contrived to take her children to
Guadalajara, presumably just before Jalisco's capital fell into the
hands of General Obregón. Lacking the resources to maintain
them suitably, she was reduced very soon to sheltering them all
in one miserable room of a wretched boardinghouse on the out-
skirts of town. Their only furniture consisted of two beds and
some chairs. These were the circumstances in which Miguel found
them upon his arrival in Guadalajara.

It nearly broke his heart. Although they had never been
wealthy, they had always enjoyed a comfortable, amply-supplied

home, the security provided by a capable, considerate father. (The single relic preserved from their former life was a fine painting of the Sacred Heart which Josefa had managed to carry from Saltillo.)

But this amazing woman, his mother, had not lost hope, because she had not lost faith. In the midst of the grimmest poverty and suffering over the unknown fate of her life's companion, her soul had attained a stature truly magnificent. No complaint had ever escaped her lips that her happy life had dissolved into an agony of chaotic uncertainty, deprivation, and unceasing concern for her children's daily bread. Roberto, Humberto, Edmundo (whose ages now ranged from nine to thirteen years), and Ana María were never to witness a sign of the sadness which dwelt in Josefa Juárez' courageous heart. It was as though she had vowed to compensate for her youngsters' material ruin by a wealth of tender love that would lift these distressing days to heights of spiritual sublimity which they must treasure all their days. And although their beloved country was drowning in a raging sea of shocking sights and incredible savagery, these four young people never found any reason to lose confidence in the All-Loving Providence, their mother's unfailing source of strength.

Enabled as never before to appreciate his mother's abnegation and spiritual attainment, Miguel Agustín dared not disturb this bit of perfection she had created from misery. In view of her loyal resignation to the will of God, how could he voice his consternation and sorrow at their helplessness? To recognize his own impotence to relieve the situation was to know an accession of pain. His vows had been taken and, although he would not, could not, have changed that glorious fact, it was heartsickening to realize that very soon he must leave them here in this deplorable hovel, unprotected against a future which seemed to hold little but ever-increasing hardship. Where *was* his father, his good, faithful, hard-working father who had so wisely sheltered and guided his own carefree youth? Why must these little brothers be deprived of the blessings he had been granted? The questioning eyes of Edmundo and Humberto, of his tenderly loved small godson,

Roberto, haunted him. Was it not only natural that they should now look to *him* for the answers? Would it not seem that he was abandoning them to an existence that had become an insoluble dilemma? Might God preserve them all—these friendly, sturdy boys, the sweet-faced Ana María and his heroic Doña Pepecita!

The grief he might not release in words found other ways of manifesting itself. He was attacked by excruciating, almost continuous headaches; and there was something very wrong with his stomach. These pains, too, he contrived to hide from Josefa, whose delight in these few weeks must not be marred. He gave her what companionship and happiness he could between the needful meetings with his three companions-in-escape who were now distributed among the homes of relatives or friends. Each day the four must do something together in approximation of the community living to which they were dedicated. It was a project just to hear Mass after the Obregonistas closed the churches on September 12. Outwitting the persecutors' vigilance became a sort of game—an arduous and dangerous game—as they sought out one residence, then another, where Mass was celebrated whenever possible. Taking care not to be seen too often in the proximity of any given home, or too often together, making use of varied countersigns which, it was hoped, might screen out the spies who could be the undoing of any faithful house, filled the mornings with excitement and suspense.

Later in the day these young men who never wavered in their vocations would reunite wherever it seemed safest and most convenient to discuss the most recent developments, conjecture upon the immediate future, and encourage one another against the ceaseless difficulties of this uncertain and perilous time. At these meetings Miguel never mentioned his poor state of health, nor his family's tribulations. As at home, he maintained a light spirit that readily expanded to rollicking gaiety when he reached for a guitar or mandolin to accompany the singing of old songs and new. These were almost invariably comic and, many of them, improvised couplets which, by calling up humorous happenings

in their life at El Llano, moved them in mirthful reminiscence to
a deeper awareness of their union.

Miguel Agustín was still irresistible when he set himself to
impersonation. He again undertook to enact skits, and even full
plays, for which he portrayed all the roles, drolly shooting his
gifted mimic's voice into an appealing treble or a shrill falsetto,
then dropping it into a rumbling basso to distinguish his characters. "It was impossible," writes Father Portas, "for anyone, no
matter how solemn by nature or however bowed down he might
be, to restrain his laughter in those unforgettable moments when
[Miguel] called upon all his ingenuity, only and exclusively to
inspirit his brothers." [1] But may we not take the liberty of be-
lieving that these deliberate contributions to morale, made by a
sick young man during that difficult September in Guadalajara,
were at least partially offered in tribute to his valiant little mother
who, surrounded by her defenseless children, was cheerfully enduring the greatest tragedy of a lifetime in the bare room she had
glorified with an image of the Sacred Heart?

Soon things improved considerably for the seminarians of the
Society who were scattered across the city. One of the Order's
priests who had taught in the novitiate arrived to guide them.
This solved their problems of Mass attendance, Communion, and
visits to the Blessed Sacrament; it also provided the harassed
young men with steadying counsel and encouragement. By the
end of the month they learned that railway service into the devas-
tated north had been partially re-established. Coincidentally with
this information came the telegraphed instructions ordering the
entire group to make its way immediately to Laredo on the
United States' border. Through this port of entry they were all
to leave their unhappy fatherland to accept the hospitality of their
North American brothers in religion.

At the meeting held to deliberate upon the manner in which
the departure and transference of so many might be handled least
conspicuously, it was decided that they would move in two

[1] Portas, p. 43.

groups. The first, composed of seven seminarians including Miguel Agustín, would withdraw from Guadalajara the following day, October 2.

Another farewell! Nothing in life had ever afflicted Miguel so sorely as his farewells to his loved ones. But none of the partings had been so grievous as this one. He felt as though this abandonment was almost too cruel to his mother. Nevertheless, her attitude of determined cheerfulness blocked the phrases that would have sprung to his lips. Josefa was meeting her trial without a murmur—magnificently fulfilling, in the direst circumstances, her vocation of motherhood. She obviously expected him, for his part, to fulfill his vocation of a religious. If she could, without any reservation whatsoever, entrust the welfare of her little ones and herself to the mercy of Heaven, could he, her dedicated son, do less?

So Miguel, too, battled with his natural affections through the final dry-eyed moments which testified to the profundity of the pain they shared. Would he ever again be blessed in being able to look upon this dear, already-aging face? When would he see any of them again—or even return to his homeland? For that matter, where was he going? Would he be required to pass his life and, perhaps, to die in some distant exile? Then, as all these questions boiled dangerously close to the surface from the depths of his turbulent heart, an instant of clarity pierced his agitation to restore, miraculously, his inner calm. Memory flashed before the eyes of his soul that great and moving scene of more than a year past when he had promised himself *forever* at the foot of the altar as a soldier of Christ—a soldier who obediently, unquestioningly, goes where he is sent and loyally fights to his last breath for his commander. Where in all this war-torn world of 1914 was there another such Commander as his?

The Pros were standing on the station platform together, waiting for the departure of the untidy train which was to carry the young Jesuits far into *"el norte."* As Miguel Agustín felt the grateful relief of certainty surge through him, he smiled confidently into Josefa's worn but unfaltering eyes. He knew, from the texture of the smile with which she met his own, that she was understanding exactly what had taken place in his heart. This exchange was like a pact between them and transcended all their previous shared emotions. For the first time in Miguel's nearly twenty-four years mother and son would now part—and against the most tragic background—without a tear. As might have been expected, this moment was to prove the final triumph of their great love. For as the groaning wheels beneath the battered, mud-plastered old coaches rolled them out of the station and Miguel's big white handkerchief fluttered a brave *adiós* to the little knot of Pros upon the platform, he was looking upon the face of "his dearest Doña Pepecita" for the last time, as it receded to a white pin point amid the thickening smoke.

It was a dolorous journey. The train itself was a disaster— filthy and devoid of the most rudimentary convenience. This much they had anticipated, as well as the innumerable protracted delays and breakdowns between their periods of crawling progress into the vast scenic monotony of the desert which must have been desolate enough before the cataclysm. More painful to contemplate was the utter devastation unrolling before their car windows. Trains which had been attacked, derailed, and then irresponsibly tumbled among the giant cacti were already red with rust, ruined beyond reclaim. The blackened remains of the burned stations along the line rose starkly against the serenity of México's incomparably blue sky. Shattered bridges cried reproachfully of long labor under a burning desert sun to effect the nation's comparative modernization—all lost before the whirlwind. The full length of the route was spotted by ghost towns which, before having been battered and blown apart, must have been so very picturesque. The farther they rode into the north, the more frightful became the scenes that filled their eyes.

It depressed Miguel extremely. Could all this have been necessary to the cause of "constitutional normalcy"—or anything else? How had a land so docile between the hard hands of old Don Porfirio during a third of a century, and then so cheerful and grateful in welcoming the independence and "freedom" promised it by the ill-fated Madero, merited any such castigation as this? In what way could all *this* be related to social justice, a cause to which no Mexican youth was more devoted than Miguel Pro? The lad who had been revolted by the ordered ruthlessness of the *Rurales* against the rioting miners of Concepción del Oro had seen nothing to equal the disordered ruthlessness here revealed to the seminarian—this nation-defacing signature of the self-styled "saviors of the people." As their train creaked wearily along, he saw this signature stamped across five hundred miles of his beloved country, in but one direction from the Great Spoils—México City.

But at last this part was over and they found themselves face to face with the international boundary where it cuts between the two Laredos—of Tamaulipas, and of Texas. Everything was still sufficiently confusing. It was sad, very sad, to be driven from their homeland under the ridicule and vituperation of its border officials, their compatriots, over a difference of opinion on the definition of the word "patriotism." It was also a bit terrifying, this abrupt, final step into a brusquely competent foreign atmosphere whose inhabitants exhibited—though perhaps unintentionally— a strangely cold attitude of aloofness and superiority to the pain which had engulfed the land lying but a small river's breadth from their own doorsteps. No, none of this was immediately reassuring, though when they had mastered the English "idiom," perhaps everything would appear much easier.

At San Antonio, however, they were given a notably kind and understanding welcome by the hospitable Oblates whose house was opened to them with the utmost good will. Here they relaxed in an atmosphere of peace which refreshed their sagging spirits. After a few days of this came the still more consoling (since more familiar) refuge provided by their brothers in religion at El Paso, where they were able to speak their native language with many of the members. But this, too, was only a brief break in their hegira. Their orders were to continue on westward almost at once, inasmuch as their destination was the

Jesuit province of California where they would be stationed in the small town of Los Gatos.

According to the account of one of the seminarians who accompanied Miguel's party: "The Mexican Jesuits exiled from their country in 1914 owe an immense debt of gratitude to the Padres of the Province of California. The doors of their house were always open to all their brothers who, driven out by the revolutionary ferocity, made their way into the neighboring Republic; but the delicacy of their generous charity was especially [exhibited] toward the younger men.

"They had immediately offered the Mexican exiles the villa pertaining to the novitiate where, freed of all their anxieties, they could independently and conveniently [re-establish] the pacific mode of life [which had been] now interrupted for many months. But this house, being unconditioned for winter, and there being no time to make the indispensable improvements, it was more prudent for the newcomers to live in the novitiate [proper].

"The novices occupied two small wooden houses situated some meters' distance from the main edifice, while the juniors were housed in a special apartment. One of the difficulties [attending] a sudden and numerous addition to [any] community is the crowding; and, in this case, it was a double community [in the sense that] each group had to follow its particular distribution [of occupations]; but the tact, the unfailing charity, and benevolence of Father José Piet, the current Rector of the house, obviated the [effects of] the inconvenience." [2]

Such was the highly appreciated hospitality which was offered to Miguel and his Mexican brothers from the day of their arrival at Los Gatos, October 9. "The impression we received, following the bitterness of such a long and painful trip, could not have been more agreeable. The first object we saw, where it stands dominating the highway that winds among the pleasant chalets,

[2] Quoted by Portas, pp. 36–37, who credits "Padre J. M." whose relation the author follows throughout the chapter on the exodus. Avoidance of the use of the full name was obviously to prevent political reprisals against the original reporter. (F. R.)

was the statue of the Sacred Heart in the attitude of the Loving Father waiting to receive His sons." [3]

This welcome vision must have comforted the spirit of Miguel Pro, who had left his beloved family, amid the desolating poverty and danger of their recent circumstances, under an identical Symbol of the Eternal Love. How this reminder of all to which his life was irrevocably dedicated and bound must have fired his heart to new hope and fresh determination!

". . . and then [we saw] the ample edifice surrounded by gardens whose extensive, vine-covered brick walls rose above an open esplanade upon the hillside; and finally, turning to view the road over which the approach had been made, the wide and lovely Santa Clara Valley with its picturesque villages and towns, its almond, apple, and plum orchards and vineyards, bounded on the right by the dark green line of the distant mountains and the abrupt canyon which forms the course of the Los Gatos River.

"But more than by the natural charm of this region, was [Miguel] gratefully surprised by the wonderful affability and the demonstrations of affection with which [we] were received by the superiors and the forty junior students, [our] future companions; and he, on his side, captured the sympathy of [them] all from the first moment, by his characteristic frankness and joviality." [4]

The winning personality and happy, responsive nature of Miguel Agustín were to prove the very best passport to esteem and confidence in any company in all the lands he would traverse. And soon, besides the new friendships which he immediately won among the California brothers, he was also enjoying a reunion with his former comrades, some of whom had arrived at Los Gatos before him, and others who kept appearing as the days went by.

Each fresh group brought its own news, its individual reports of the adventures which had dramatized its pilgrimage toward the tranquillity of this high-perched house overlooking the Santa

[3] *Ibid.*, p. 37.
[4] *Ibid.*, pp. 37–8.

Clara Valley. Miguel soon heard about the excitement attending the journey of the second division from Guadalajara. The flight of these brothers, commenced the day after the departure of his party, seemed to have been the most disagreeable. At ten o'clock on the first evening out, when they had pulled into the Yurécuaro station (so close to their beloved El Llano), their train had been boarded by the revolutionary chief Valladares who, with a large military escort, invaded the coach occupied by the students. From the moment of this bully's appearance, the entire conversation of the military took the form of the most insulting ridicule of the persecuted clergy, and particularly of the indignant seminarians' esteemed superiors at El Llano. It was as much as they could manage, just to hold their tongues.

This natural resentment was soon transformed, however, into acute terror. At Irapuato their blood congealed to see introduced into this same coach under a heavy guard Padres Maina, Leturiondo, and Moral, the only Jesuits who had remained behind at the novitiate after the dispersion. As the students knew, the priests had very soon been seized and, despite Father Moral's serious illness, the revolutionists had routed him out of bed to carry him off with the others to Zamora. From there, the trio had been transferred to Morelia where, after some time in prison, they had been condemned to death on the pretext that they had preached and "composed verses" against the Revolution. This savage sentence had been later commuted to exile for life upon the intervention of some "very powerful influences."

Notwithstanding this fortunate alleviation, the seminarians watched with heart-constricting dread their respected Minister and teachers enter the car dominated by the hate and blasphemy of Valladares. Fear for the padres held them in a vise until the moment they saw the good men safely over the border.

With the arrival at Los Gatos of the last groups of dispersed Mexicans, the re-establishment of their regular community life commenced with the annual eight days of Spiritual Exercises. Then they resumed their studies; but now, "besides the ordinary problems, there was the special difficulty of their complete lack of books [in Spanish]." Padre Mier y Teran had to teach his classes in the library by an *ad lib* method of questions and answers far from satisfactory either to professor or students. To add to the inefficiency of this system, the seminarians were forced by the unaccustomed cold to huddle about a small oil stove, so defective that it kept them fighting to overcome the effects of the rancid fumes and the smoke it produced in much greater abundance than warmth. The physical discomfort attending the classes and the disconcerting lack of textbooks precluded a satisfactory progress which, for Miguel, was a trial aggravated by the lugubrious reports on the latest developments in México and on his family's unimproved situation. All this combined to accentuate whatever it was that afflicted his stomach which, by now, held him clutched in constant pain. At this time, also, he was threatened with the loss of hearing in his right ear, result of the puncture of that eardrum by a sliver of straw.

Withal, he maintained his easy and jovial exterior. In referring to his ills in the letters he wrote with faithful regularity to his young brothers he made light of them, strove to interpret them as merely embarrassing jokes which, having overtaken the prize jokester himself, were that much funnier. Meanwhile, he went on cultivating friendships among the California Jesuits, many of whom would contrive to keep in touch with him until shortly before his death. None of them could ever forget the enlivening tales and vivid descriptions of México which sprang from this gayest of hearts in "a charmingly confused mixture of English, Latin, and Spanish words."

But the California interlude was destined for an early conclusion. During 1914 Miguel Agustín found himself commencing a five-year period of consecutive study in a city which he could only reach by crossing a vast continent and a vaster sea. This, his next home in exile, was that ancient jewel among Spain's legendary glories—Granada.

XIII

BETWEEN TWO GRANADAS

TO THE youth who had longed so fervently for "bigger things," more stimulating and beautiful places, from the midst of the crudity of the Mineral, Granada must have been sheer delight. Her streets, buildings, and battlements carried loveliness in their lines; upon them were graven the vestiges of the resplendent history which, for centuries, had evoked some of the world's richest music, poetry, and painting.

For a sensitive young fellow whose most natural instinct was to translate his impressions into verse and song, could there be a more inspiring spot in which to pursue knowledge? Miguel was convinced there was not. If in the life he now took up in the land of his ancestors he sometimes knew anguish, that was owing to the tragic cause of his exile from his own, dearest daughterland of this same Spain; and to the knowledge of what his loved ones were suffering there. Were things but normal in México, if he could only believe that life was improving for Josefa and the children, know that his father was safely beside them once more, Granada would be unmitigated joy.

But even in the lack of such reassurance, he fell to work eagerly and gratefully to make up the time lost to study. He still had the humanities—commenced at El Llano and continued, only more or less satisfactorily, at Los Gatos—to complete. And he was already well into his twenty-fifth year.

The acquisition of learning was still difficult for him, but he was heroically transcending his limitations as a scholar by spiritual mastery. No documents or letters remain from this period to help us trace the methods he employed in his discipline, but his brother seminarians have duly attested his consistent advance toward spiritual perfection—most notably observed in his almost joyful acceptance of sorrow. One of his classmates, Father Rafael Ríos, affirms: "We all knew when he had received bad news from home, because on such occasions he displayed more gaiety than usual in order to dissimulate in [the cause of] virtue, his grief." [1]

Another of his close friends during the Granada period has written: "How many times [when] we all believed his jokes to have come forth spontaneously, some sudden gesture would betray the great pain he suffered from his stomach; and meanwhile, only a very few [of us] were able to plumb the profound hurt from which his heart bled in the knowledge of the prolonged misfortune of his family, [a tragedy] partly witnessed by his own eyes and partly revealed to him, month by month, in their correspondence." [2]

The achievement of such control by one who had been born with the most impulsive of natures is, in itself, proof of his amazing progress toward sanctity while he was still, on the intellectual plane, but a half-formed Jesuit. Even this was not the sum of his attainment. The commentator continues: "I am wholly persuaded that he hid very many beautiful acts of virtue beneath the pranks which appeared to be merely impulsive. With them, he covered offenses, made a thousand favors and services, diverted his brothers [while supporting] his intense physical pain and worry over his family's afflictions. He sacrificed his own diversion during the long vacations in preparations for the festivities with which we might be amused, [facts which] perhaps not everyone fully appreciated since [all he did] was considered natural." [3]

[1] Quoted by Portas, p. 42.
[2] *Ibid.*
[3] *Ibid.*, p. 43.

Of the great humility he was perfecting at this time we read further: "Censurings and cautionings were never lacking for him. They were occasioned by the small exterior faults occurring in a temperament such as his; but I am convinced that, on one hand, his superiors held him in high esteem and, on the other, that he used these reprehensions to bring himself to a self-depreciation that I have observed in very few; not becoming dispirited, but rather acquiring the habit of regarding 'his *Padre Dios*' as his only Witness and Judge of his actions. Actually, Hermano Pro was very little bothered by the opinion of men, and [it was] this spiritual attainment [which] marvelously aided his fearless and flexible spirit to go gracefully through the most grievous perils. . . . The humiliations he occasionally experienced, as when he was notified that he had failed to pass the second-year philosophy examination, were carried bravely and without any lessening of his cheerfulness, *verbigracia*. He always demonstrated himself superior to this wretched [hurt] to his own keen sense of punctiliousness." [4]

It is hardly surprising that such a felicitous victory over self had soon made the young Mexican one of the most popular members of Granada's Jesuit community. His companions of this period wax enthusiastic in speaking of the unerasable memories he everywhere left behind. And to the present day they cherish as relics anything he happened to give or send them. His old friends from seminary days carefully preserved every note of congratulation or greeting which he wrote them on the occasions of their saints' days, or in honor of their first Masses; his caricatures and sketches to remind them of incidents they had, as students, experienced together; his playful epigrams and the verses which, "though they fell from his pen casually and in haste, were always beautiful."

"But there were more intimate souvenirs [than these], not preserved on paper, but engraved upon [our] hearts. . . . And I am certain that, if there be any who may recall some prank to have escaped Padre Pro which may have seemed a trifle 'heavy,'

[4] *Ibid.*, pp. 43–44.

they also recall, not one, but various, finenesses of charity, perhaps wrapped up in new pranks, but undertaken [by him] to the
end of repairing [the earlier] fault." [5]

As we have seen, he had progressed beyond the humanities
and into philosophy and the sciences. Meanwhile, he had become
one of the seminary's most meticulous and successful catechists.
In several towns of the beautiful Vega Granadina, Fargue el
Alto, Lanjarón, Huétor Santillán, and Albolote, he instituted or
took charge of courses in catechism. One of his most frequently
mentioned successes in this labor, which he loved, was achieved
among the gypsies living in Albaicín.

His was an indefatigable zeal for the good of souls; and he
had a gift for attracting the people, adults as well as children, to
his classes. His great humor drew the love of the simple folk, almost on sight. Old and young followed him about the village
streets, gathered around him to listen to his instructions for hours
on end, according to his friend, Father Marcelino Moreno,[6] who
was frequently his companion on these excursions which they
called "our apostolic rehearsals." Miguel's irrepressible jokes,
which never failed to evoke hilarity, and the dramatizations, by
which he graphically illustrated his teachings, formed a large
part of his attraction for these people. But mainly it was his
friendliness and unaffected interest in their welfare which drew
them to him.

At Lanjarón, whose inhabitants were already referring to him
as "Padre Miguel," his visits invariably provoked keen excitement. As soon as his presence in the little town became known,
the whole populace would lock up their houses and set out to
swell the throng that never diminished until it was time for him
to make his departure.

His growing success never affected his humility. At the seminary he was always the first to offer his services, even for the
most menial tasks, for the benefit of his fellow students. On his
own initiative, he would cheerfully substitute for a missing

[5] *Ibid.*, p. 44.
[6] *Ibid.*, pp. 45–46.

Oval: The best known picture of Padre Miguel Pro Juárez, S.J.
Upper left: Padre Pro at his studies in Belgium. *Middle left:* Miguel Pro as a boy and his sisters, Concepción and María de Luz, playing for their parents and the younger children. *Lower right:* Miguel Pro as a youth with his family.

Upper left: The house in Guadalupe, Zacatecas, where Miguel Pro was born, January 13, 1891. *Center left:* Miguel Pro "made up" for a masquerade. *Center right:* Padre Pro and Jesuit companions in the mountains of Nicaragua. *Lower center:* Padre Pro's brothers, Roberto and Humberto.

Upper left: Picture of Padre Pro made the night before his execution. *Middle left:* Luis Segura Vilchis going to his execution. *Lower right:* Padre Pro disguised as a laborer in México City, 1926–27. *Lower center:* Padre Pro a few moments before his execution.

Top: General Staff of Calles' government watching the execution of Padre Pro. *Oval:* Padre Pro receiving the executioners' bullets. *Lower left:* Humberto Pro awaiting execution. Padre Pro's body on ground. *Lower right:* Padre Pro's workingmen before the Jesuits' crypt in México City.

servant to wait on tables in the commissary, or to perform any other necessary chores.

"His talent was eminently practical," wrote Father Pulido,[7] and this was considered full compensation for his lack of brilliance in metaphysics. However, although he did have one failure in philosophy (doggedly conquered later), he was to prove an excellent student of theology, and canon law always fascinated him. Undoubtedly, his strongest subject was sociology "in both the theory and practice of which he made great advance in a remarkably short time."

But for all his increasing scope and activity, he remained basically the Miguel Agustín who had ever been keen for play or ready to construct the harmless plot which might achieve the end of diverting his comrades. He could not bear sadness in others. One day when he judged that the downcast spirits of some of his friends from México might be lifted by a *día de campo* (a picnic in the country), he made all the preparations for such an outing before approaching the rector for the necessary permission. With everything ready, he sought out the superior.

"Padre," he said with his most ingratiating smile, "wouldn't you like to make us, the Mexican brothers, the great favor of joining us on a picnic?"

"I would be very pleased to do so," replied the busy rector, "but it happens that I have so much to do that it is quite impossible."

"What a pity! We would so very much enjoy the company of Your Reverence!"

"That is all very nice, but have you already secured permission for this *día de campo?*"

"No, Padre, because we thought that, as you would be going with us, that would be all the permission we required."

"Well, but I can't go!"

"Bueno," responded Miguel disarmingly, "perhaps in that case we shall be able to go alone."

As he began to comprehend this little stratagem, the rector

[7] *Ibid.,* p. 50.

was betrayed into a smile, after which it would have been rather awkward to refuse the permission. Whereupon, "the Mexican brothers" enjoyed a wonderfully relaxing day in the country.

When the Mexican Jesuits were first forced into exile, they opened a Colegio in another, and very distant, Granada— Granada de Nicaragua. In 1920, as soon as Miguel Agustín had completed his philosophy, his Spanish superiors sent him back across the sea to become an instructor in this school before continuing his own studies. This transfer was attended by both consolations and disadvantages. Miguel was happy to be serving again under his countrymen; to feel the good earth of America beneath his feet once more. But it was tantalizing to see himself so near his family yet as unable as ever to visit them or even to re-enter his native country. Then, too, while this Granada enjoys an exquisite situation upon the shores of the vast Lake of Nicaragua, it cannot compare in stateliness or gracious mellowness with that historic city for which it was named. The new move deprived Miguel of many things he had learned to cherish during his five years in Spain. He missed his Spanish friends— particularly his dear villagers and the gypsies whose devotion and open admiration had given him the confidence to believe that his natural gifts might be utilized for great good in his vocation.

In Nicaragua an appallingly hot and humid climate must be supported, together with multitudes of dangerous insects and reptiles. The avoidance of these last was no easy matter in an as yet only half-completed building such as the Colegio. It was by no means extraordinary to encounter, gliding along the bare earthen floors of some of the rooms or through the still unclosed apertures in certain of the walls, the poisonous snakes which infested the tangle of tropical undergrowth pressing in on them from all sides. Occasionally the reptiles even invaded the dormitory beds.

As for the young *internos* to whom Miguel was assigned as teacher, they were still unaccustomed to a life of discipline since this was the first year the school had accepted boarders. Many of them were inclined to challenge authority at every step. Quite apart from the problems posed by the perverseness of the lads, there were other difficulties. Father Portas tells us: "Padre Pro suffered . . . from other causes, one of which arose from [the fact that] his characteristic manner of covering his illness with a constant show of gaiety was misunderstood by some; [8] although I knew that what appeared to these [persons] as sheer extravagance was his effort to dissimulate his pains, in combination with his natural high-hearted courage and jocosity.[9] And the same biographer states elsewhere: "There [in Nicaragua] he who writes this had the consolation of knowing [Miguel Pro] personally, of being his confessor and spiritual director and of establishing [at that period] a friendship with him which was not to terminate until the triumph of [his] martyrdom." [10]

Father Pulido, who was a classmate of Miguel Agustín and with him in Nicaragua, describes his friend's activities at this time: "The first year, teaching the little fellows their letters was merely diversion for him; and hardly more labor to look after the *semi-internos* and day scholars. In addition [to these duties], he held an hour's class each evening for the Colegio's servants, who loved him dearly. He also assisted in catechising the townsfolk; and as he had such a gift for [handling] people and mingled fearlessly with everyone, his [classes in] catechism achieved most beneficial results and were very well attended." [11]

During his second year in Nicaragua Miguel was made supervisor of the boarding upperclassmen, which turned out to be quite another matter. This charge required him to be on the alert day and night against irregularities in behavior, infractions of rules, the thousand-and-one unexpected and exasperating situations which only the tragi-comic period of adolescence seems to develop.

He slept—or better, was supposed to sleep—in an alcove con-

---

[8] Priests and seminarians, presumably. (F. R.)
[9] Portas, p. 52.
[10] *Ibid.*, p. 51.
[11] Quoted by Portas, p. 52.

necting with the main dormitory, which also had to accommodate
a certain number of the younger boys. But what with one thing
and another, he was up and down throughout the course of almost every night. There were seasons during which the scorpions
dropped from the ceiling onto the beds—like rain. There was
the real rain that, descending in cloudburst proportions and
hardly impeded by a defective roof, would rapidly soak any
number of beds if he failed to leap from his own to help move
those threatened. No orderly arrangement of the dormitory could
possibly keep all of them clear of the leaks. There were the
fantastic electrical storms which frightened the little fellows out
of their wits as the shafts of lightning bolted earthward about
the great lake; as the immense cacophony of the thunder cracked,
rolled, and reverberated across its waters. On such nights as these
Miguel did not even attempt to retire, but sacrificed his needed
rest to comfort and reassure the nervous children.

Daytimes, he taught a primary class which, according to the
later affirmations of the lucky youngsters who had comprised it,
provided their happiest school-day memories. They particularly
recalled the occasions when, during the oppressive heat of the
vacations, the gay Hermano Pro was always on hand to organize
games for their entertainment, or to dispel discomfort and
boredom by singing for them, to the accompaniment of a cheerfully twanging guitar, the rollicking popular melodies of his
lost but unforgettable México. Their *profesor* was still the
dominant ringleader and organizer he had ever been. But by
now experience—so much of it the pain and sorrow he meticulously concealed—had tempered his naturally aggressive character with a new docility, an ever-more sensitive conscience, and
an almost incredible fund of charity.

When the letter ordering his return to Spain to undertake his
theology course arrived, Hermano Pro had just rounded out two
years in Nicaragua. He was thirty-one years of age.

XIV

A JESUIT GOES INTO THE MINES

MIGUEL set sail from Corinth on the Pacific Coast bound for Le Havre in July, 1922. Disembarking at that port, he traveled overland across France and on to the Spanish town of Sarría near Barcelona, where he would continue the arduous study demanded by all who hope for ordination as priests of the Society of Jesus. In Sarría he applied himself earnestly to moral and canon law, which seemed to him the subjects most immediately vital to the salvation of souls.

His two years at Sarría increased his stomach affliction. But the heavier his pain, the more sensitive he became to the sufferings of others; the more careful not to oppress his companions with a revelation of his own misery. His *Padre Dios* had sent him a private cross—and he would keep it such. No one would be asked to aid him in bearing it.

He found other means of self-discipline, too. A brother acquaintance who in 1924 attended the Exercises with him at the Casa de Manresa [1] said: "I shall never forget this [occasion]. Padre Pro knew how to hide his spirit of mortification in a joy which overflowed [upon all] about him. But during the retreat our rooms adjoined his, and every night we heard him disciplining himself with extraordinary vigor." [2]

[1] Where St. Ignatius composed the Spiritual Exercises.
[2] Quoted by Portas, p. 56.

By now his spirit, gifts, and inclinations seem to have been well understood by his superiors, and this same summer he was sent to the School of Theology conducted by the Fathers of the Province of Champagne at Enghien, Belgium. The reason for this transfer was stated in a letter written by Padre Crivelli, at that time the Provincial of the Mexican Jesuits. "I recall that once while making a visit to Orizaba [3] where I perceived the much that should be done with the countless factory workers at that place, I found myself immediately thinking of Padre Pro for this labor. I sent him to Enghien; and he had been destined for Orizaba." [4] The Mexican Jesuits all knew Miguel's background and that his affection for his miners and his sympathy with their problems had never lessened. They had also seen his success with those who gained their livings by manual labor. He possessed the common touch with which, it was to be hoped, he would prove an especially valuable apostle to the industrial workers.

In Belgium, where Catholic labor was excellently organized, there were many highly competent men with long experience in dealing with the working classes. These experts, the proximity of the Louvain University, and the Belgian Jesuits' close association with the intensely active Popular Action in their country, would provide Miguel Agustín with fine opportunities to gain knowledge of the practical sociology that interested him so deeply.

At Enghien the new arrival found himself attached to a community comprising a hundred men from thirteen nations. In these circumstances it had seemed convenient to adopt Latin as the common tongue. Even so, the wide disparity in accents—French, Spanish, English, German, and so on—caused considerable confusion. In consequence of this language problem, the ordinary conversation of the house "was not, at the beginning,

[3] In México's state of Veracruz—a textile manufacturing center whose workers were rather prominently identified with the Revolution; and which is today a strongly syndicalized city reputed to include a substantial quota of Communists.
[4] Quoted by Portas, p. 56.

markedly animated," notes Father Portas. This situation somewhat impeded the cultivation of new friendships. Sometimes it
seemed to Miguel Pro that hardly any of the busy theologians
even knew his name. Nevertheless, whenever one of them had
occasion to rap on his door to deliver a message from the superiors or to ask his aid in anything, the caller was sure to receive
a warm welcome, to see the smile that invariably lighted up
the face of this Mexican brother, and to hear the cordial response, "What a pleasure, *Padre mío,* what a real pleasure!"

Thus in this big house, too, he soon became known for his
great good nature and merry disposition. For some time no one
was cognizant of his rapidly worsening infirmity, though he was
in a state of unceasing torture which now caused him to suffer
severe insomnia and frequently made it impossible for him to
take any food whatsoever for days at a time. But his unrelenting
pain could not keep him from participating in the games he
was invited to join. He formed the custom of playing ball during
recreation with the American padres studying in the house. This
contest he labeled "the battle of Calles against Coolidge."

For now it was Plutarco Elías Calles, self-styled "First Chief
of the Revolution," who reigned supreme in México. Carranza,
Villa, and other formidable persecutors of the clergy and the
faithful were dead—killed by the same brand of violence they
had unleashed upon their country. But not Álvaro Obregón,
who had passed the power he had snatched from Carranza on to
Calles, for safekeeping. For the average Mexican, as for the
Church, this succession had changed nothing—or certainly not
for the better. In fact, this dangerous duo—Obregón and Calles
—in its greater strength as the double symbol of revolution ac-
complished and consolidated, was carrying a conquered, rather
than "liberated," people further than ever away from its human
rights: to profess and practice its chosen Faith; to control the
education of its children. To a greater degree than ever justice
was mocked by privilege in every tribunal of the most cynical
rule the nation had yet known.

Miguel had not lost hope that he might live to see an end of this tyranny; that he might one day return to minister to his own. But any such possibility had certainly not been hinted by events. México continued helpless beneath the adamant anti-Catholic fanaticism of these super-chieftains who, while noisily extinguishing "the power" of the Church in the land they controlled and intended to continue to control between them, were failing to evidence adhesion to the vaunted "humanitarian concepts" of the Revolution. It was true enough that the rich had been impoverished. But, meanwhile, the poor were poorer and more miserable than ever.

Thus there was irony in that quip dropped on a Belgian ball field by the exiled theological student from México: *"Calles contra Coolidge."* As unnotable for piety as their country was reputed to be, Miguel knew that these carefree, ballplaying American padres would soon go home to their comfortable parishes and long-dreamed-of labor for the Faith in all peace and security. Would such good fortune—it seemed like paradise!—*never* bless the Mexicans? Was he himself never to be granted the privilege of laboring for and amid his own people?

All his efforts were now wholly consecrated to his preparation for "the apostolate to the workers." As he read and reread the encyclicals of Leo XIII which expounded the Christian means of achieving justice between classes of men, he was shaken by the enormity of his gratitude. This much-belabored problem, social justice, was not, then, the great mystery it had appeared to be! The Church had always held the formula defined by the great Pope with such clarity in *Rerum Novarum.* And there were, besides, the inspiring encyclicals of Pius X on labor. The true principles of this primary problem had been clearly articulated by these pontiffs long before the revolutionists launched their savage persecutions upon all of México's classes in the name of, and as so brazenly manifested, *merely* in the name of, social justice. The original abuses of selfish Christians had supplied selfish pagans, ignorant and hypocritical men, with an excuse to fall voraciously upon the whole nation. It was clear to Miguel that the sum of his own ministry, and likely his life as well, must be offered in recompense for the blindness of Christians who had remained indifferent to the sufferings of their own employees until both classes were forced to reap the whirlwind of compounded crime.

At least now, poring over his theology, Miguel Pro knew exactly what he was after. It was that body of doctrinal Truth which would give force to his future sermons and other efforts to proclaim God's will. His mercy on individual lives and His justice hereafter demanded the reciprocation of men's mercy and justice toward one another in this imperfect world. Miguel also possessed himself of the wisdom, the full mind of the Church, upon the central question of individual salvation through faith, moral living, and piety. But he would not detain himself in time-consuming ponderings upon the speculative fine points of this fascinating subject. He was already thirty-four years old. Perhaps he sensed that such privileges were only for those granted longer ministries on earth than he was to be permitted.

But now, just when he had fully grasped the spirit which lay behind his vocation, he was assailed by a new agony. This was the sickening fear that he would not, after all, be conceded ordination. As the time for this incredible blessing drew near, he was stricken by the prospect of seeing his long battle for learning, his dreams of serving his fellowman, come to nought.

Although this desolating inner crisis was never revealed to his Enghien associates, he wrote a poignant letter to Father Portas baring his misery and consternation before the thought of his impending failure. Reminding his confessor and confidante of the Nicaraguan days of his many faults and lacks exposed during his work in Granada, he pleaded to be told whether Father Portas believed it was *reasonable* for him to hope for the great grace of the priesthood.

Father Portas recounts the joyful sequel, "the triumphal hymn" that arrived a few days later. "I must send this letter," wrote Miguel, "to give you a little piece of news: they have conceded me the Mass; I shall say my first on August 31!" And the future Padre Pro reverted here to his playful style which had been suppressed in his previous letter. "And this was but natural, according to the indications of your expert spiritual authority (received after I had deposited in your royal bosom the griefs for which there wasn't sufficient room in my own, exposing not only the wound in my pure and angelical spirit, but even the cosine and the back-room, the tangent and the counter-tangent of my simple, devout, mystic, cold, and edifying heart); it is natural, I say, that the Mass should come as it has to make my beatific spirit happy, to rejoice, rejuvenate, and animate [me] . . . in its three or four natural or supernatural powers.

"Be happy with me and aid me with your sacrifices and prayers to give thanks to God for this new favor and to procure from Him my better preparation to receive such a great Sacrament.

"You will doubtless wish to send me a gift for my Mass, isn't that so? *Pues,* just see what a spiritual son Heaven has given you . . . and clearly! I shall not oppose [the gift], for why should I oppose it? Don't think such a thing. So send whatever you wish (even if it be a letter) as long as it isn't a scorpion, a papaya, a vigorón [5] or a banana.

"If you were to see me now (*quod spirituale*) you wouldn't know me; I have turned myself into a mystic, not easily put out of the twentieth mansion, and—I say it with a blush: I've even written to the nuns, my sisters!

"Bless your spiritual cub who doesn't forget you in *Corde Jesu.*" [6]

A postal card to his good friend Father Pulido, dated July 7, 1925, read: "The 19th I shall receive the sub-deaconate, the 25th, the deaconate; and on the 30th of the month, I enter the priesthood." [7]

Along with twenty others—eighteen French, one Brazilian, one North American—Miguel Agustín Pro was ordained a Jesuit

[5] A Central American dish made of yucca and crackling.
[6] Portas, pp. 60–61.
[7] *Ibid.,* p. 61.

priest by Monseigneur Lecomte on August 31, 1925.[8] It was real sadness for him that, almost alone among this company of new priests, he was denied the joy of bestowing his first blessings upon his beloved family. At the time, this deprivation induced a profound pain in his heart, but it was not enduring. Soon he was able to say to one of his newly ordained classmates, "At last we are priests; and that is enough."

During the vacations that followed, Padre Pro's deficient command of the French language denied him full participation in the joys of his companions who immediately commenced their ministries. Before he could preach in this area there would have to be still more study. He was, however, able to celebrate Mass at the parish church, at the Convent of the Sisters of Charity, and in various other churches. And now, too, he obtained permission to visit the famous soft coal mines at Charleroi in order to put himself in contact with the Belgian miners and familiarize himself with their working conditions and problems. In this way he hoped to prepare himself better for his future effective apostolate to the workers.

He accompanied the miners down into the deepest, darkest galleries at Charleroi where he observed at firsthand the exact circumstances of the labor by which they lived, an experience which brought back sharp memories of the lad who once went below with "his *barreteros*" at Concepción del Oro. "He paid these visits," says one of his biographers, "with the seriousness [attaching to] a pilgrimage, listening intently to the complaints [in order to] penetrate the sense of the words in which [the workers] presented their troubles and fatigues." [9] He also made such excursions of investigation to factories and foundries.

His friends in the Catholic Worker Youth had organized a Social Study Week to be held at Fayt-Lez-Manage during September, from which great results were anticipated. Padre Pro attended this meeting with tremendous enthusiasm. He wanted

[8] Instead of August 30, as he believed when writing Father Pulido.
[9] Quoted by Portas, p. 67.

to understand exactly how this potent organization operated, what means it employed to revivify and extend the Faith among labor and the underprivileged. He held long conversations with the young worker delegates who had gathered at Fayt-Lez-Manage from every quarter of Belgium. From the directors he sought advice upon how he might one day implant a like project in his unfortunate México. Her lack of such a Christian movement, he felt sure, had abandoned her to the bombastic Russian demagogues who were moving into the forefront of Calles' régime to slant its policies.

The ardent interest of this new priest from distant México was widely noted at the convocation. His unshakable devotion to the cause of justice to labor now and, as rapidly as possible, the workers' full conversion to the Faith, sparked several edifying discussions. And before many months had passed his admirers were confirmed in their estimate of his sincerity and value by his success in winning the respect and affection of the Belgian workers, an achievement which soon became a legend. It was said that the Mexican padre had a positive magic for Belgium's miners, a fact that was still hailed by the official organ of the Catholic Worker Youth years after his departure from Europe, years, even, after his death.[10]

One day Father Miguel found himself in a third-class railway carriage reserved for workers, along with ten miners who were making an excursion from Charleroi. He had been the last passenger to enter the compartment and had not failed to notice the frigidity of the men upon seeing their intimacy invaded by an unknown priest. To his affable salutation there had been one or two ungracious grunts. Most of the men maintained a stony silence, staring rudely at the bronzed face and eyes as black as their own coal.

Miguel Pro had never been a silent type and it served his purpose now to break down the hostility he saw reflected in these rough countenances. Producing the best French at his command,

[10] Of special interest is the article published in the issue of November, 1932.

he commenced to put innocuous questions to the fellow seated nearest him. "What is the name of this station?" "Is it a large town?"

These amiable sallies were met by a cool and quite irrelevant announcement: *"Tiens, Monsieur l'Abbé:* we are all socialists."

"Ah, magnificent!" responded the Father imperturbably, "I, too, am a socialist."

This declaration riveted the attention of every man in the compartment. The one who had spoken only to warn or offend him made no attempt to cover his astonishment.

"Monsieur l'Abbé a socialist!"

"Yes, gentlemen, I'm a socialist, but not exactly one such as you who don't know what socialism really is. Tell me, now, is there one of you who can explain just what it is to be a socialist?"

After a moment's uncertain hesitancy one of the miners ventured, "It is to take from the rich all their money."

Father Pro scratched his head reflectively and then suggested, "Well, about that there is this: when we have all that money in our hands what arrangements are we supposed to make to protect it from *thieves?*"

This response drew some smiles but it would not do to let this joker think he had won the day. So the last speaker added what he hoped would be a real threat.

"There are also among us some Communists."

"Communists, too, eh?" observed Father Pro with a wide smile. "Good! I am also a Communist. Look, it's already one o'clock and some of you are eating. Well, fine, I'm hungry, too. Wouldn't you like to divide your lunch with me?"

The laugh was now general, and the man who had let himself into this trap was obviously disconcerted. He shrugged the topic aside. "Weren't you afraid to come in here into our compartment?"

Father Pro appeared not to have heard correctly. "Afraid? Why? I'm always well armed."

"Perhaps you'd best show us your pistol, *Monsieur l'Abbé,* the socialist!" demanded the miner on a note of real menace now.

The priest immediately began to rummage in his pockets until a smile of relief showed that he had located his "arms." There was a certain tension in the air. "Here is my weapon. With it along, I have no fear of anyone." And Padre Miguel displayed his crucifix for the consideration of ten faces on which arrogance was replaced by sheepishness. From there on to their destination the miners permitted this remarkable cleric to hold the floor—which he did with a talk on the effective operation of his "weapon"—much more efficient than a pistol. While we cannot know how deeply his words may have penetrated the hearts of these miners of Charleroi, there were several who removed their hats as their new acquaintance continued to hold the crucifix before their eyes.

At Chatelineu the miners left the train, but not until one of them had pushed a small package into the hands of Padre Pro. All alone in the carriage, he opened this to find it filled with chocolate pastry! [11]

This little anecdote was one of his favorite reminiscences in later years. "Bravo for my Communists," he used to say, his eyes full of tender mirth, "who diverted me so greatly, who fed me and, as you see, certainly didn't kill me."

[11] This much-cited anecdote and dialogue is found in *Entre Obreros* by Adriano Xavier, pp. 27–30; also in Portas, pp. 67–69.

XV

PAIN

FATHER PRO could no longer conceal his illness. The marks of its ravaging progress suddenly startled everyone about him. His disposition, bland and jovial, was not affected, but pain and undernourishment had altered his physical appearance distressingly.

Besides his regular activities as a newly ordained priest of the Society and his special efforts in behalf of the workers, he had entered his fourth year of theology. He felt there was no time for physicians, for the elaborate treatments they would doubtless find it necessary to prescribe. But his superiors deemed otherwise. So in November he undertook a weary routine of doctors' consulting rooms, diets, medication. Finally, he entered the sanitariums which claimed more than six months of his time—right at the beginning of his ministry! The attending specialists confirmed the worst fears of the superiors—his life depended on surgical intervention.

Enghien's spiritual director, Father Bouvy, persuaded the patient to submit to the operation, arguing that such a trial now might cure or at least preserve him for years of fruitful apostolic labors. To this solicitude Padre Miguel replied, "I have no fear of physical suffering," by which he meant that he was prepared to accept the will of Heaven for him whether it imposed surgery or a continuance of the pain he had now endured for years—on to the end. Not greatly encouraged by his counselor's optimistic prognostications, he agreed to the operation. Whereupon he was immediately sent to the Saint-Rémi Clinic in Brussels.

It was at Saint-Rémi that he received the word of Josefa Juárez' death. This was a blow to obliterate any merely physical agony! Throughout his thirty-five years of life in this world his mother had been closer to his heart than any other human being. Distance, long separation, nothing had changed his devotion to her. Each day he had lived with his concern for her. For although a religious is wholly consecrated to the love and service of God, this accession of Divine love but deepens his tenderness in all his human affections.

"I can't be certain whether my first reaction to the news was one of serenity or stupefaction," he told Padre Enrique Basabe, a Jesuit friend who paid him a visit of condolence at the hospital. "It seemed that I simply had no tears. But later, at nightfall when I was alone, I clasped my crucifix and the weeping commenced." [1]

Father Basabe closed the letter in which he described this scene for Father Portas: "He showed me a photograph of his mother surrounded by all her family and told me how greatly consoling it was to him that she had made a holy death; about his sweet presentiment that she was already in Heaven. It was one of those afternoons very difficult to forget."

Padre Miguel also mentioned to several of his brother religious his conviction that Josefa had died in sanctity. "My mother is in Heaven. This morning I wished to say Mass for the peace of her soul, but [found] I *could not* pray for her; from this I'm certain she is already in Heaven." [2]

As he was being prepared for his second complicated stomach operation, the surgeons informed him that on this occasion they could not risk an anesthetic. He exhibited no consternation, merely replying that, in such case, he would like to be given his Code of Canon Law. To offset this new inconvenience he would

[1] Quoted from a letter from Father Basabe by Portas, pp. 71–72.
[2] *Ibid.*

occupy his mind with study. They gave him the volume; and while the amazed doctors were cutting and stitching his tortured body, Padre Pro quietly read the Code, giving no evidence of the excruciating pain that attended the process.

One would so greatly wish to be able to say that such fortitude and superhuman patience were rewarded by a final end of illness. These first two operations, however, left him not only dangerously weak but suffering the severest pain he had yet endured. Everything he ate provoked an agony in his stomach that could only be likened to a vast blazing fire, not to be quenched until it had consumed him. This, too, he bore with serenity and cheerfulness. The nursing Sisters who attended him had never seen anything to compare with the patience of this young Mexican padre; and the friends who came to hearten, entertain, and console him with their attentions remained to be heartened, entertained, and consoled by his blithe greetings, jokes, and amusing stories. He laughed at everything, but first of all, at himself and his misfortunes. Other than humorously, he refused to speak of his pitiable condition. How was this possible? The only hint of the source of his courage appears in his remark to Father Couvreur: "I pray almost all day and during most of the nights. After this, I find myself refreshed." [3]

The third operation did somewhat alleviate the pain. But his state of debilitation was now so alarming that his concerned superiors determined to send him to the Riviera. If anything could help rebuild his shattered constitution, it should be the fresh, healing air of the better climate, in combination with the good food and tender care of the Franciscan Sisters who conducted a *pension* for sick priests at Hyères.

But Padre Pro did not look upon himself as a really sick priest. From the moment of his arrival at the famous health resort he insisted upon being permitted to say the first Mass each day in order that the other Fathers might rest a bit longer in the mornings. "Do let me say it," he countered all objections. "As I can't sleep anyway, arising early is no great sacrifice for me."

[3] Quoted *ibid.*, p. 77.

Then, at the termination of his own Mass, he would take no more time than was required by his quick, light breakfast before returning to the chapel to assist the Masses of the others. When the Mother Sacristan insisted he was undertaking too much, he replied, "I only wish I were able to serve all the Masses that are celebrated." Nor did he neglect any other duties of his ministry. He attended the dying, administering the Last Sacraments; he attended the living, hearing confessions, giving instructions and First Communions.

The Sisters had in their employ a strangely aloof young gardener named Amadeo. It was known that this youth had never made his First Communion; that, despite the tactful suggestions of the nuns, he firmly, though respectfully, refused to do so. This attitude of a lad who was an honest and dependable sort perplexed and worried the good women. As soon as Father Miguel heard of this problem, he made an occasion to open a conversation with Amadeo during which he mentioned that he had come all the way from America to prepare for a life mission to the laboring classes. The ideas of this friendly, foreign invalid appealed to the gardener, who readily accepted an invitation to visit Padre Pro in his room.

The following evening when Amadeo presented himself, he found a table well supplied with fruit, pastry, and a large box of chocolates. A delightful repast was followed by more interesting conversation before Father Miguel put his quiet question: "And do you attend Sunday Mass, Amadeo?" There was a moment of profound silence. The kindly manner of his host was irresistible, however, and Amadeo soon confided his story. It seemed that, when a youngster, he had been expelled from a minor seminary for a misdemeanor he had not committed. His natural indignation at this injustice had determined him to keep clear of priests for the rest of his life. The warm understanding with which this one received his confidence won the affection of the embittered youth in a single evening. Following a few weeks of instruction, Amadeo received his First Communion from the hands of his new friend. . . .

These unceasing exertions did not speed Padre Miguel's recovery, and with the passing weeks his superiors saw no improvement in his health. In June it was reluctantly suggested that it might be better for him to return to México. It was possible that the more favorable climate and the familiar scenes of his homeland might work the necessary miracle. If not, he would have the consolation of dying among his loved ones.

Upon hearing that he was to be sent home, Miguel instantly interpreted the news as proof that his condition was considered hopeless. "Why wasn't I told before?" he exclaimed. "I would have offered my life long ago. God has no need of me to work His good for México!"

This reaction proved that he was more competent to estimate the situation prevailing in his country than were his superiors. He was aware that his life would be more endangered in México by political conditions than by his poor health. To the Belgian Jesuits it was still incredible that the mere reappearance of an ailing young cleric, sent home to die of his physical afflictions, was tantamount to condemnation to an aggressive persecution.

But he explained none of this as he made preparations for his departure from Europe. He asked only that before embarking he might visit Our Lady of Lourdes. This permission was granted, and we have his own description of the pilgrimage in a letter written to Padre Magín Negra from Paris:

"My beloved Father in Christ:

"Now I can say with Simeon: *Nunc dimittis* . . . ; I can now leave for the other world, and not that which our ancestors called the Indies, but the true other world which is Heaven.

"What mischief have I, weak and good for nothing as I am, done now? I don't deny it. What imprudence to spend two nights on the train without sleeping or eating? I don't deny this either. But what I shall never be able to deny also is that yesterday was one of the happiest days of my life.

"I left Paris at seven o'clock Wednesday evening, arrived at Lourdes at eight forty-five the next morning and, from the first,

had the aid of *Nuestra Señora* because, on the road, I met the
Bishop's secretary who, when I had presented the paper, gave
me permission to celebrate [Mass] in the Basilica. When? At the
end of the last requested Mass at the main altar. I commenced
my Mass at nine and it took more than the usual time since in
the remembrances I had many families of México, Sarría,
Enghien, Brussels to pray for . . . and you know that your
family and mine have, thank God, many members.

"From the church I went to the grotto—or to a little piece of
Heaven—where I saw a Virgin who flooded my soul with an
immense happiness, an intimate consolation, and a divine sense
of well-being, so vitally felt that . . . But there aren't words
to express it. The poor, unhappy Pro saw nothing, heard
nothing, took notice of none of the pilgrims there—no, that isn't
altogether true. Once, raising his eyes to his *Madrecita,* he saw
a sick woman lying on her little cart at the Virgin's feet, praying
the rosary with her arms extended to form the Cross . . . and
this was not a loss, for the faith and confidence that he saw in
this sick woman revitalized his own and he commenced an intimate conversation with our most holy Mother in which she,
more than he, produced and released in my soul things I have
never felt before.

"How long did I kneel there, I who cannot continue [in this
position] for more than five minutes? I don't know, [but] at
twelve, I went to eat. I wrote four postal cards and at twelve-
twenty I was back at the grotto. Don't ask me what I did or
said; I know nothing [about it] excepting that yesterday I
wasn't miserable as I customarily am.

"At three o'clock a priest came up to me and said: 'If you go
on like this, you will become ill. I would advise you to go outside to the pool where there is shade.' Why did he tell me this
or what face or posture did I have? This, too, I do not know. I
only know that I was at the feet of my Mother and that I felt
very deeply within myself her blessed presence and action. At
the pool I saw hundreds of poor little sick ones in search of
health. A Capuchin preached between the decades of the rosary;

and I did as all the others—sang, prayed, kissed the earth, made a cross, and invoked the Virgin. At four-fifty I was in the train.

"And . . . I was at Lourdes? *Pues.* . . . How was it I didn't go to the Calvary? Why didn't I see the river? How is it I don't know the shape of the Basilica, nor what things are there or not there? And nevertheless I was there. Because for me, going to Lourdes was to find my Heavenly Mother, to speak to her, to pray to her; and I found her, spoke to her, prayed to her.

"At eight-thirty I arrived in Paris and, at nine, said Mass in the house.

"I could sleep today no more than an hour; Sunday I leave at eight-thirty in the morning and shall arrive Saint-Nazaire at five in the afternoon. The sailing is at midnight. My voyage will not be as hard as I had anticipated, for the Virgin has told me so. *Ay, Padre!* It is very trying to my miserable nature to return to México without health, without having finished my studies, to find my poor country undone by its rulers, and without the pleasure of being able to go see my saintly mother who gave me being and for whom I weep even in the midst of my resignation and acceptance. But my trip to Lourdes has given me new vigor and encouragement, this trip to Lourdes which is owing to the love and delicacy of you and your family." [4]

The face and voice of Miguel Pro could hide his innermost feelings more easily than his always expressive pen.

From Saint-Nazaire he embarked for México on the *Cuba*, June 24, 1926.

[4] Padre Magín Negra had sent Father Miguel the "fifteen *pesitos*" with which to make the pilgrimage to Lourdes. Letter quoted by Portas, pp. 81–84.

XVI

HOMECOMING TO TERROR

WHAT did this ailing, inexperienced priest expect to meet when he arrived at Veracruz and attempted to re-enter his country? He knew well that Calles' rabidly anti-Catholic government was constantly apprehending and casting out the religious and clergy, condemning them to wander about the earth in quest of whatever receptions they might be extended, whatever services they might be permitted to perform in strange lands for strange peoples. Were the port authorities likely to allow an *incoming* Jesuit to escape their vigilance? Having made the crossing with a shipload of Mexicans for whom, being the only priest aboard, he matter-of-factly fulfilled all the offices required by his ministry, he could hardly feel assurance that he might not be exposed by one of his fellow passengers. Or, dating from his pilgrimage to Lourdes, did he simply know that he would pass the immigration officers unchallenged? He did not say so.

"It was by an extraordinary concession of God that I was admitted into my country; for with the government ejecting the priests and brothers I don't understand how I was permitted to pass. But they didn't even open my bags in customs. We left the port at six in the evening and at seven the following morning I was at Lerdo.[1] At ten I saw the *Jefe*, and at eleven I was a work-

---

[1] Headquarters of the Society's Mexican Provincial alluded to by Padre Pro here as "the *Jefe.*"

ing priest in Enrico Martínez [2] under this order: 'As soon as you are rested from your journey, you will make another to the Colegio in Chihuahua.' " [3]

When Padre Miguel was delivered into the hands of the Brussels surgeons, he had barely begun his last year of theology (which St. Ignatius called "the third year of probation"). Under normal conditions, the completion of this work would have been a requirement for the teaching and other offices included in the full Jesuit ministry. But the abnormal conditions in México had reached a point where all the known priests could function only in the most precarious circumstances; and things were growing more terrible by the day. There was a multitude of occasions when an unknown newcomer would be of the utmost value to the faithful of México City. For the present, therefore, the young invalid who had been returned for the improvement of his health, or to die in the consolation of familiar surroundings, was now ordered to pursue privately his preparation for his final examination, and meanwhile to devote himself to the greatest amount of ministerial labor he could perform in this hostile ambient.

The first development after his arrival in the capital (July 8, 1926) was the official order, issued July 31, suppressing all public worship. And now, too, any priest encountered by the police at any time was a legitimate victim.

Had Father Miguel with his penchant for slang been familiar with the current North American vernacular, he might have exclaimed, "This is where I came in!" Instead, he described the confusion in which he immediately found himself: "This is where my labors commenced. My confessional was a jubilee. Having just left the clinic's smooth pillows, my annoying constitution was unaccustomed to the hard bench of the confessional that I warmed from five until eleven in the mornings and from three-thirty in the afternoons until eight o'clock. Twice I fainted and had to be carried out. And simultaneously there were all the talks—to enfervorize—to admonish. . . .

[2] México City's Jesuit Church of Guadalupe in Enrico Martínez Street.
[3] Quoted by Portas, p. 87.

"With the closing of the churches, I had thought I might relax, rest from the strain of these last days in which all the world wanted to confess. And truly it had been a fantastic strain, which kept us at it from very early morning until eleven or twelve at night. But the anxiety of the faithful to continue receiving the Sacraments gave no time for rest. Talks, conferences, baptisms, marriages consumed every moment of the few priests who, thanks to being less known, were able to work with relative security, for that which would have taken an hour in church could hardly be achieved outside in an entire day. I was named chief of the consultants and this, yes, did turn me whiteheaded, for the consultants were the most select of the capital's youth, persons of talent and training who assaulted me with questions in philosophy, ethics, sociology, literature and, above all, on politics and civics. I had to give them conferences and to the public as well, passing from the carpeted salon to the warehouse shrine; from an audience perfumed and educated to the open-hearted and vulgar fraternity of labor.

"And this isn't the whole story. As most of us are unable to minister on account of being known and hunted, here I am substituting [for many], running from Herod to Pilate, day and night. The departure of [Padre] Otón increased my work greatly, for to my own parish I had to add the one he left. . . . How did I stand it? How *do* I stand it?—I, the weak, the delicate, the interesting guest of two European clinics who passed the day stretched out upon a divan drinking broths . . . all of which proves with a most evident evidence that without the fullness of the Divine Element which uses me merely as an instrument, I'd have made a mess of everything. Not in the minutest [thing] can my vanity flatter itself even a little, for I know that, of themselves, my person and results are worthless. *Unde, non ego, sed gratia Dei mecum.*[4]

"I have what I call eucharistic stations where, fooling the vigilance of the police, I go each day to give Communion, some days to one place, others to another, with an average of three

---

[4] "Not I, but the grace of God in me."

hundred Communions daily. The first First Friday I had six hundred and fifty Communions; the second, eight hundred, and the third, nine hundred and ten.[5] This is a terrific labor, but we go ahead. A terrific labor, I repeat, of confession, and with affected *beatas*,[6] with scrupulous men (which is worse), with worldly youth, stubborn servants, and mischievous children; but all, all worthy, not only of the work of a little sin-sifter such as I, but also of the apostolic and loving zeal of thousands and thousands of missionaries (before me), the result of which is what moves our unfortunate compatriots to repair the offenses committed against the divine Heart of Christ by our infamous government and evil rulers. And oh if I had time to tell of the examples of virtue which I have seen! They leave me so *small,* these people, rich and poor. My confessional is for me an exercise in modesty, just to see how far am I from imitating [some of] those who come to me for direction. Aid me with your prayers that, as we Frenchies say [this effect], may not rub off, may be fruitful for my soul, [so that] it will not resemble the statue of Padre Rodríguez which points out the road while it, itself, is left standing still.

"All this is being written moments before entering the Exercises, which is to say, the first moment of rest since my arrival in México. Exercises! Another *toro* and *olé!* because not only am I to take part in them, but give them to a brother Coadjutor, and this without the Third of Probation. The first retreat I have given. How will it come out? However it may be, I pity the poor brother in his spiritual part because his human part is sure to be 'stood up.' I'll put him to sleep for eight days!

"The [counter-] Revolution is a fact; the reprisals all over México will be terrible. First to feel them will be those who have mixed their hands in the religious question, and I—I have mixed them in up to the elbows. I hope I shall have the luck to be among the first, or among the last, but to be one of the num-

---

[5] These First Fridays have been identified by Portas as those of August, September, and October, 1926.

[6] Overly pious women.

ber; if so, prepare your petitions for Heaven. But honey wasn't made, etc. . . ." [7]

The postscript of this letter which was signed, *"El Barretero,"* explained the need for anonymity: "The censorship of the mails is terrible. For this reason, I don't write my name." [8] But his friends easily recognized the correspondent who had ever been the miners' champion. On other occasions he closed his descriptions of the confusion and danger in which he was finally serving his own people with "Miguel Enghien."

The counter-Revolution of which he spoke was the great new organization of laymen determined to free themselves and the Faith from the savage persecution of Calles' regime. Thousands were planning—and arming—for revolt. There had already been outbursts of violence, but so far little had been achieved save an increase in the government-imposed terror that had, for years now, made life hideous for the majority of the Mexican people. Generally speaking, the clergy had obeyed the orders of the hierarchy and taken no part in this movement; but, of course, the nation's fanatically anti-clerical dictators accused the priests of being the "prime motivators of disorder."

Father Miguel's letter sketching the situation in the fall of 1926 contains the first indication that he harbored a desire for martyrdom. It would also seem to indicate that he had a strong presentiment of its approach.

[7] Old Spanish saying: "Honey wasn't made for the snout of a jackass."
[8] Letter to a brother Jesuit. Quoted by Portas, pp. 88–92.

XVII

BICYCLE MINISTRY

THE Pros, Don Miguel, the younger brothers, and Ana María, had moved to the capital and Padre Miguel was now living with them. Of his joy at this reunion we read nothing in the correspondence which has been preserved. In fact we have no letters written by the desperately busy young priest between October of 1926[1] and February of 1927 because, although he had mailed three to his Father Provincial during this period, none had reached its destination. From the February letter, however, it is clear that he had been carrying on, ever more energetically, the labors outlined in October.

His *conferencistas*—the "consultants" previously alluded to— had become a band of one hundred and fifty zealous youths who continuously circulated about the city giving conferences to as large groups of the faithful as could be convened with comparative safety, and Christian instruction to as many as they were able to reach of those who, during the Revolutionary years, had been deprived of such teaching. At first the results of this drive were excellent; but as the consultants came to be known, the police lost no time in falling upon one after another. They were carried off to prison, exile, or worse. Periodically someone would be executed by the firing squads charged with keeping matters

---

[1] That quoted in the foregoing chapter.

in hand for the most brutal dictatorship México had yet known.

Padre Pro was spending more and more time preaching to office and factory workers, bus drivers, and the population of the very poorest quarters (*mis descamisados*), who stood in dire need of consolation and counsel as they pursued their miserable lives and labors in the midst of persecution and tyranny. To fulfill his strenuous schedule he must incessantly cross and recross the big, sprawling city so fearsomely patrolled by Calles' gestapo. To preserve his life while doing so, he had to call upon every resource of his talents for impersonation. Dressed in a flashy but shabby sweater, rumpled trousers or overalls, and a rakishly tilted cap, with a cigarette dangling impudently from the corner of his mouth, he might have been any fresh young man of the city's lower middle class as he whizzed and whistled his way up streets and down alleys astride a bicycle belonging to one of his brothers. Wheeling carelessly past a *cuico* [2] (cop), he would nonchalantly throw the law a casual jest or salute calculated to be "unpriestly." And somewhere along the line he grew a rather disorderly mustache.

Humberto and Roberto, both active members of the Religious Defense League, had already fallen under police suspicion. On December 4 the resistance had released six hundred *globos* (balloons) in a display which caused intense excitement when it was seen that they were disgorging a rain of brightly colored leaflets upon the city. There was a lively competition to capture the papers with their religious propaganda. This exploit aroused the towering rage of Plutarco Calles. He demanded the apprehension, at all costs, of every participant in the making and distribution of the leaflets, which had made him ridiculous right in his own citadel. Running down the instigators of the balloons became the prime business of a police corps now said to number ten thousand agents. One of the first houses raided was the Pros'.

"My blood brothers are involved to the ears in all the doings of the League and, as the supposed promoters of the famous *globos,* they attracted the glances of our government friends,"

[2] Also "squealer," "tattletale," "half-breed."

wrote Father Miguel in his February letter to the Provincial.[3] "Bandala[4] searched the house. He found nothing; but left an order that any man entering between twelve and one was to be carried off to jail. I was the only one to arrive (the house is my refuge); and thus, the only one to visit Santiago Tlaltelolco.[5]

"What an experience! Seven of us younger men were taken to prison on this matter of the balloons between double lines of soldiers at seven in the evening. There, the lieutenant who read us the order of arrest told us laughingly, 'Tomorrow we'll have Mass.'

" 'Bad,' I told myself. 'They've already recognized me!'

" 'Mass?' we all asked, terrified.

" '*Sí,*' replied the lieutenant, 'as one of you is a priest.'

" 'Bad, *very* bad!' I repeated to myself as we all looked one another over from head to foot wondering who might be the unfortunate priest among us.

" 'He's a Miguel Agustín,' said the lieutenant.

" 'Stop!' I cried loudly. 'This Miguel Agustín is I, but I'm going to say Mass tomorrow just like I'm going to sleep on a mattress tonight. And this *presbítero* before the name? That's only my family name, Pro, which someone has confused with *Pbro,* the abbreviation for *presbítero!*'

"That night . . . whee! We spent it under the open sky in the patio. The arrest order read: 'Do everything [possible] to annoy the apprehended' and *Vaya!* this was certainly carried out! An extensive bed of cement, which is to say the whole patio, was placed at our disposal, together with some enormous pillows, otherwise serving as walls; [but] there were no sheets save those the night chill was able to provide. We seven prisoners huddled together closely, for the cold was even more intense than usual; and, quite regardless of the guards, began to pray the rosary and to sing softly whatever occurred to us. I, who in the Granada Observatory once spent the dead hours measuring the distances

---

[3] Living in exile at El Paso, Texas.
[4] One of the police chiefs.
[5] The military prison.

of the stars, infuriated because they moved so slowly, was, on this night, given an opportunity to repeat the experience. . . .' The next morning they came to waken us with pails of water but, as we hadn't slept, needless to say, the first splash had us running about the patio to the laughs and whistles of the soldier convicts.

"Our common purse contained the reasonable sum of three pesos, ten centavos, which sufficed to pay for a whole *olla* (stewpot) of unsweetened orange-leaf tea which didn't taste like nectar and, being encrusted with frozen particles, left us as cold as icebergs.

"I took my departure from the prison at noon. My more privileged companions didn't get out until the next day. However, I had to appear twice more at the Gobernación to declare. To declare what? I didn't and don't know. It was a farce during which in all certainty and conscience I pulled our worthy rulers' legs, using a humorous tone to tell the truth without compromising anyone. And yet, thinking it over, I'm amazed I wasn't shot for one strong statement. When Bandala asked me if I were willing to pay a substantial fine, inasmuch as Calles was furious about the balloons, I replied: 'No, Señor—for two reasons. In the first place, I haven't a cent; and secondly, even if I did, I wouldn't care to suffer lifelong remorse in the knowledge of having supported our present government with a half centavo from my pocket for even the ten millionth part of a second.' "

We, too, may well wonder how Padre Pro passed through this dangerous experience to resume his former liberty of the México City streets. Was his insult softened in the sight of the dreaded Bandala by some deft touch of the humor Miguel Pro commanded so readily; or was he released on this occasion simply because his work for his country was not yet finished?

There were to be repercussions, however, and these impeded his labors for several months. The same letter continues: "After this burlesque, the scope of my ministry was reduced. Withal, I was able to prepare the Christmas feast in some six asylums and at the Good Shepherd, with the talks, benedictions and general

Communion on December 25; and with suppers, *piñatas*,[6] and toys.

"This was my final public exploit because on the twenty-ninth some of the reserves arrived with an order of arrest for me and my family. Vainly did I make myself very small before them; vainly implore them with tender phrases; just as vainly invoked influential [persons] and recommendations. The hard heart could only be softened with fifty pesos, which I gave. But my father, sister, two brothers, and I had to flee with whatever we could carry along with us to seek refuge among friends and relatives where we have been ever since. [Although] there have been a thousand versions, the prevailing one is that I was the author of the leaflets and my brothers responsible for the *globos,* which is false on both counts.

"A recluse confined to a narrow room with no other horizon than a neighboring corral, prohibited to show myself, I am studying. In order not to be indolent I am also, *sotto voce,* building my granary, filling empty houses with cereals and eatables of all sorts for the families of the young men who are so bravely defending our liberties. I have various people, more or less organized, who act for me in all this. With them for a front, I do the planning from here. So far, I've managed to provide two months' provision for eighteen families. What a pity that I can't get out because I'm almost sure I could do the same for others who are in critical circumstances.

"I am preparing for my examination, after a fashion. After a fashion? Yes, since I have no books excepting the Bible, an Enchiridión, and a volume of Pesch, the first edition. Two or three other books which I might be able to use are in my house which is watched. Don Carlos [7] hasn't been able to get me even a poor Tanquerey. The text is Hurter, and the treatises I must present are *De Gratia* and *De Fide.*

"In my earlier letters I asked you for a Hurter but, as [the letters] weren't received, I have waited for this in vain. If you can

[6] Suspended jar filled with candies, which children break with a pole.
[7] Carlos Mayer, S.J., acting local Provincial.

send me the book, I shall appreciate it infinitely because June is drawing near and for lack of material 'ex quâ' I am unable to finish my study for the examination."

This restriction to a cramped room after the great consolation he had known in his short but prodigious ministry was a heavy cross to Father Miguel. He would be much happier taking all the really desperate risks that lay in the streets for him now that he would be readily identified. However, it was his superiors' command that he remain in hiding. Nevertheless, he believed he might reasonably present his point of view on the obligations of the priesthood under persecution, even though it might not wholly correspond with their ideas for him.

"Obedience is superior to sacrifices, which is why I haven't budged from where I am. However, permit me to say one thing without pretending to criticize or complain. [True], the situation here is very delicate; there is danger for all and I know that God helps those who help themselves. Nevertheless, the people are in dire need of spiritual assistance. Every day I hear of persons who have died without the Sacraments. There are no priests to meet the situation because, owing either to obedience or fear, they are in hiding. To contribute my little grain of sand would be to expose myself as I was doing before, but with discretion and moderation, it doesn't seem to me too daring. . . . I judge that, between temerity and fear, there is a middle course, as there is, also, between an extreme of prudence and rashness. I have indicated this to Don Carlos, but he fears for my life. My life? But what is that? Would it not be to gain it if I were to give it for my brothers? Certainly I shouldn't give it foolishly, but are they sons of Loyola who run away at the first shot? I do not generalize, for there are many individuals who will serve greatly in a future day and it is best that these be preserved with care. But such types as—I? This is not humility, Padre, nor from a wish to be considered valiant. It is merely my conviction before God of my uselessness and of the small value of my capabilities; and [I feel] it would be very animating to an infinite number, priests or not priests, for us not to abandon our poor brothers who *today* need the aid of the Faith so badly. The most they can do is to kill me and that only on the day and in the hour which God has appointed. Furthermore, the situation seems to be prolonging itself and there are few, very few, pastors guarding God's flock. . . . I know that I better serve the Church hiding here in a poor room than I might in the middle of the plaza of my own will; but it is not disobedience to ask my Superior's permission to do something which I can perform without much danger, and this, in spite of the order of my immediate superior. You be the judge, Padre; and you already know that in everything I shall respect your commands and those of Don Carlos."

This appeal sprang from his deepest desire and it demonstrates the abnegation of a soul which had already attained a stature rarely seen in men, even in those who are priests of the Church. He was not a theorist who merely perceived the truth that in giving his life he would, indeed, be gaining it. He was a man of action who was generously offering his life during a nightmare epoch which was his "today," in order that he might do today what would be most beneficial to his human brothers in Christ. The magnanimity of this proffer was not lessened by the possibility that his health might, in any case, cause his early demise. For he was nearly cured. A postscript appended to this same letter affirms: "My health is like bronze. I haven't had a single day in bed. Only very rarely does my stomach remind me that it was operated upon. And these occasions are, in my opinion, merely its final protests after almost eight years of daily pain." [8]

It was with every reason to believe that he was making a full recovery and might lead a normal, pain-free life that Padre Miguel wrote his Provincial acknowledging the superiority of obedience to sacrifice, but still, pleading for the opportunity to make his own sacrifice—inside obedience.

[8] Extracts in this chapter are all from the letter of February 19, 1927, quoted by Portas, pp. 94–99.

XVIII

"FROM THE POCKET
OF GOD, MY FATHER"

TO HIS great joy his plea was granted. The Father Provincial was profoundly moved, not only by the abnegation and holy charity so serenely expressed by this brother, but by the valiance that proved him a true son of their great soldier Founder. Such richness of soul might not be rebuffed—particularly inasmuch as it was so patently prepared to accept rebuff, if such were its duty under obedience.

"Like the May rains came the permission to leave, with the needful precaution, this narrow retreat in which the illustrious Calles of the Plutarchs has had me confined," he wrote on April 21, 1927, to Father Henry Valley, the Provincial's secretary.

"I was really smothered in that enclosure of scarcely five square meters which was almost airless owing to the windows having been bricked up. The only outlook was upon the corral of an adjacent house where an old burro grazed peacefully. Moment by moment there fell on my ears the moans of those who surrounded me, the lamentations occasioned by the imprisonment of Fulano, the exile of Zutano, or the assassination of Mengano.[1] And there I was, caged, powerless even to study since I had no books; and burning with anxiety to throw myself into the thick of the fray for the encouragement of the countless champions of our Faith. . . .

[1] Names equivalent to "Tom, Dick, and Harry."

"With the arrival of the letter, I quit this isolation and began giving retreats left and right, an heroic ministry which somewhat frightened me as I'd had no practice in it. By way of rehearsal, I commenced with six-and-a-half dozen old *beatas* whose moans and groans, sighs and sobs showed me that if I'd managed to strike the key to their sentiments, I'd also touched that of my own mirth; for such was the laughter which bubbled in my body at the sight of all this bawling and these compunctious faces, that I cut it short and abandoned the feminine gender for the masculine. For the too masculine, as it turned out. These were some hundred and fifty district chauffeurs of the type that affects Texan hats, dangling forelocks, and which spits through the teeth; but people of *pro*,[2] even though exteriorly rude and filthy. In speaking to these, I proved to my amazement that I hadn't lost the old flow of coarse and resounding words. (I had thought that down the years I'd forgotten this vocabulary which makes a trifle of the sixteen since I left the mines); but, *córcholis!* it seemed I might have acquired it but yesterday. I refrain from describing the solemnity of this conference [held] in the big corral of some very ordinary folk, about which, in my mechanic's costume and with cap pulled down to the eyebrows, I shoved my sympathetic listeners. Blessings on the chauffeurs of all the world!

"Following this, I rose a bit to [the level of] a group of women teachers and government employees. There were close to eighty of these forward and decided young females who feared not even the morning star. Perhaps, perhaps, I obtained more fruit with them than with my chauffeurs. . . . But just see how we are quite unable to entertain vainglory, since it is only and exclusively the grace of God which operates in such matters. All the force of my arguments to achieve anything would, as I have seen, result uselessly but for the fact that His grace touches souls through the simple phrases I improvise on the spur of the moment. Blessed be *mi Padre Dios* Who is the very best! . . ."

---

[2] A pun. *"Pro"* means "worth"—thus they were both "people of worth" and "Miguel Pro's people."

Working again to restore the vast vineyard which had been
Christian México, Miguel Pro was very happy. His joy flooded
all the lines dashed off to his brothers in religion during the brief
moments available between the Exercises, confessions, Communions, baptisms, marriages, and rites for the dying which filled
his days and, frequently, his nights. Even his recitals of the risks
and perils that beset his activities abound in high spirits.

"One droll incident which might have ended tragically occurred on the first night of the Exercises for the government
workers. [At nine-thirty when I left the meeting], I saw two
characters waiting for me at the street corner.

" 'My son,' I said to myself, 'say good-by to your skin!' But
based on the maxim that he who takes the first step takes two,
I walked directly up to them and asked for a match to light my
cigarette.

" 'You can get one in that store,' they responded.

"I made a great show of following this suggestion, but they
trailed me in. Could it be coincidence? [In the street again], I
turned one corner and then another—and so did they. 'My
grandmother—on a bicycle!' I told myself, 'this is really *it!*'

"I took a cab—and they did, too. By good luck the chauffeur
was a Catholic and, seeing my fix, placed himself under my
orders: 'Now look, son. At the corner where I tell you, slow
down. I'll jump out and you just go on ahead.'

"I stuck my cap in my pocket, shed my jacket so my white
shirt would be what showed and—leapt. I got to my feet immediately and leaned against a tree where they would have to
see me. A second later these fellows passed so close to me that
they almost scraped me with the fenders of their car. They saw
me all right, but never dreamed it was I. I turned around but
not with the desired bravado because I was just beginning to feel
the blow this leap had given me. 'All right, son, now we are
ready for the next time,' was my final ejaculation as I started
limping home through the streets.

"No one knows where I live. There are four different spots
where I keep appointments and receive letters, messages, and

donations for my poor families which now number twenty-three. I touch those things of which we read in the lives of the saints (take note that I shan't be one of them!) for, without knowing how, when, nor who has sent them, I receive now fifty kilos of sugar, now, boxes of cookies, now, coffee, chocolate, rice—and even wine. And the Providence of God is so paternal that even while I'm scratching my head, trying to think whom I may sponge on next, I find the larder already filled. I know hardly anyone, and still it has been scarcely any trouble for me to obtain loans of vacant houses for as long as six to eight months; in one of which we actually have a telephone. The best of all this is that my *holy figure* doesn't appear at the front, for I merely pull the strings and other generous souls do it all.

"And my own impudence has attained such proportions that once when we were sent a hundred kilos of beans which turned out to be spoiled and so, good for nothing, I went to the very person who had made the contribution to beg for a few *frijoles* inasmuch as some we had just received were unusable! And sure enough, by petitioning the Father, I achieved my results in chick peas! . . .

"When shall we have even a half-hour to relate the thousands and thousands of incidents of a life so agitated as that which we support? I sigh, yes, for the quietude of our houses, for the order that reigns in everything, for the facility with which we do our ordinary work. But here, in the midst of the vortex, I am amazed by the special aid of God, the very special graces He grants us in such perils, the Presence now more intimately felt when discouragement comes to make our souls smaller. I understand very well—and three times over—the cry of Saint Paul in which he asked God to take him from this earth. But at the same time I feel the truth of the divine reply: *'Sufficit tibi gratia mea, quia in infirmitate perficitur.'* " [3]

Notwithstanding the achievements of Father Miguel and his faithful aides (which they themselves viewed as miracles of

[3] St. Paul to the Corinthians II, Chapter 12, v. 9: ". . . My grace is sufficient for thee: for power is made perfect in infirmity."

God), there was certainly no perceptible general improvement in the Mexican picture as spring drew on toward summer.

"Things go very badly here. No brightening of the horizon can be observed and, lacking a direct intervention from God Our Lord, human means are not going to remedy the situation. Blessed be He Who arranges all and Who gives us the grace to live this life which is not a life," he wrote to the Father Provincial on May 15. "The scarcity of priests is extreme; the people die without the Sacraments, since the few of us who are left do not suffice. Those who are left? If only all of these would work a little so that things wouldn't continue quite so badly; but each is the owner of his fear. I employ the caution you have recommended and nothing has happened to me; just scares which, more or less, don't pass beyond that and which serve me by causing me to depend still more, both in the spiritual and the material, upon the loving Providence of our *Padre Dios;* and which, after the threat of the moment has passed, make me laugh at the comic aspects of our dissembling.

"I haven't a centavo, nor do I believe myself able to find one, since now nobody cares to give anything and, nevertheless, I maintain (pardon me the occupation) thirty-nine families, supplying their food, shelter, and some, a very little, clothing. Each day I feel the direct action of God upon us, for it is only through Him that these poor ones exist. This auxiliary work is my favorite. What? Who gives me the rice, beans, sugar, corn, etc.? I don't know. Or rather, yes, I do know: *Mi Padre Dios*—because in an infinite number of cases and without my having asked anyone for anything and right when all had run out, I have received gifts of supplies without knowing who made them.

"In regard to the ministries, I mostly hear confessions and attend the dying and for [only this last] I wish I were a hundred [men] so that I might be everywhere at once. The perils in which we live are terrible if seen with the eyes of the body and not with those of the spirit. Now, indeed, can I appreciate the community life, the holy life of the community. Withal, my soul puts its trust in the [priestly] estate for, on my own, I would already have failed in all. *'Nos vos me elegistis, sed Ego elegi vos'*—and God knows what a piece I was. . . ."

On May 25 for Father Henry Valley he detailed more fully the inconveniences and threatening circumstances of his daily life: "Right now I should be giving ecclesiastical sepulture to a pair of *tacos* of avocado and a half-dozen *zopes* [4] of *frijoles* as it is two o'clock in the afternoon—but the exhaustion from a heavy morning of confessions has ruined my appetite and I prefer writing this as my recess before facing the session of afternoon confessions which won't terminate before ten or eleven tonight.

"Things here go ahead full sail, since the Christians are now being expedited to Heaven without any difficulty whatsoever. The privileged souls who fall into the dungeons of the police are now quite assured they won't return to repeat their indiscretions, and the persuasion in my house that this will be my fate is so strong that all my tender relatives, instead of simply bidding me *adiós* when I go out in the street, make an Act of Contrition. Now we know that, when Fulano fails to return by eleven o'clock at night, he is one more target for the treacherous bullets of the 'dignitaries.' We held a family reunion to take leave of one another until the Valley of Josafet. We made no will because they have taken from us the two straw sleeping mats and the one cooking pan we had, but instead of tears, the hearty laughter sprang forth inasmuch as it is a bargain to go to the Celestial Court in such a noble cause. What wouldn't I give for Your Mercy to be able to pass a day with us! We live three to a room in a reconstructed house where it is impossible to receive visitors as it contains nothing but the essentials to existence.

"We are seven and there are five chairs, four plates, four knives, eight beds, three mattresses, and a broom—all loaned, which means given, because it is almost certain that neither we nor our inheritors will return anything.

"In the three [police] raids we've suffered, they left us not even a cuspidor, but as none of this is needful in getting to Heaven, we give it a very low rating. Books? *Újule!* and here

[4] A corn-meal coating for *frijoles*.

I have to sing the public recantation. I don't know into the hands of what technician your Pesch has fallen—but anyway, I formally promise to return it to you in Heaven where the technicians count for nothing.

"In the ministries we carry on like slaves. Jesus help me! If there isn't time to breathe even, and I am mixed to the eyebrows in this business of feeding those with nothing—and they are many, those with nothing—I assure you that I spin like a top from here to there, and with such luck (exclusive privilege of petty thieves) that it doesn't even faze me to receive such messages as: 'The X. Family reports that they are twelve members and their pantry is empty; their clothing is falling off of them in pieces, three are [ill] in bed—and there isn't even water.' As a rule, my purse is as dry as Calles' soul, but it isn't worth while worrying since the Procurator of Heaven is as generous as [the little dialogue] I shall relate here indicates.

" '*Señor Barretero,* here are a hundred little pesos they gave me for you. Take charge of them for right now I have no use for them'—and, of course, I must send a note to a place two blocks away immediately: 'Of these hundred pesos, give forty to Fulano, forty to Zutano—twenty to Mengano.' I see His hand so palpably in everything that almost, almost I fear they won't kill me in these adventures, which will be a fiasco for me who sighs to go to Heaven and start throwing out arpeggios on the guitar with my guardian angel.

"They give me valuable objects to raffle off and thus we are able to obtain forty pesos for an item worth ten. Once I was going along with the purse of a *señora* which was quite cute (the purse, not the *señora*) presented to me but five minutes before, when I met a much-painted lady, *ut in pluribus.*

" 'What have you there?'

" 'A lady's pocketbook worth twenty-five pesos that, seeing it is for you, I'll sell for fifty pesos which I beg you to send to such-and-such a family.' With such indirections we break down the resistance of all."

In view of an unbroken continuity of incidents of this order we are inclined to agree with the affirmation made many times throughout Padre Miguel's communications to his friends that he saw all his needs supplied from "the pocket of God, my Father."

"Lately I have had no brushes with the police, but the most recent was with one of the reserves who assured me by the fifteen Peers of France that I was going to jail and to whom I almost swore by the beard of Mohammed that I wasn't. He was so annoying that I came near to wanting to take a punch at him, but I managed to say: 'Look, you vulgarian, if you cart me off to prison, I shan't be able to confess your *mamacita*.'

"'You must pardon me, little Father, but you know how times are now. So go away, go away at once!'

"'I go? He who will go is you—and not to the police station, but simply to tell your *mamá* that I shall hear her confession tonight and carry Communion to her tomorrow morning to learn whether in that way I can't achieve your own confession, you good-for-nothing, shameless demon.'

"'Ah, what a little three-stone padre!'[5]

"'Well, one would be enough to break your head.'

"The next day my *big* friend attended the Communion of his mother—and I believe that soon I shall carry it to him.

"And now, I must cut this short. Three are waiting to be confessed. What this act has cost me in these days! *Mi Padre Dios* has sent me a torture in the teeth and molars and sometimes the pain is so intense that I would like to take the confessional gate and bounce it off the head of the unhappy penitent. This is how I pay to God the interest on the much He gives me for such a great family."

We cannot doubt that his superiors and friends in exile marveled at the heroism revealed so ingenuously in his casual and largely humorous reports. They were kept fully informed, from many sources, upon the creeping horror that might yet so easily

[5] An idiom signifying "jokester" or "kidder"

end in a spiritual black-out for México—of which "predilect daughter" His Holiness Pope Pius XI had already stated: "Yours is a great country because it has demonstrated its faith, faith such as has never been manifested until now." [6]

To the May letter the Father Provincial replied, congratulating Padre Pro upon his unfaltering apostleship. Then he brought up again the old problem of the final theology examination which still lay ahead for the student who had returned to México presumably to die of a stomach ailment and whose presence was now preventing the starvation of numerous Christian Mexicans. What was the exact situation with regard to Father Miguel's study program? How many months now had he been preparing for the examination? Would it be necessary to seek a dispensation in the matter of the date for taking it?

We may imagine something of the weariness in which the desperately-driven Father Miguel, who was struggling so valiantly to compensate for the scarcity of the clergy as well as the fear which curtailed the activities of those who did remain, patiently sat down to respond to these anxious inquiries upon his purely intellectual progress.

"You ask me how much time I have studied [this course]. I worked two-and-a-half months in Enghien before entering the clinic; here, since January, I have studied all I could from Tanquerey.[7] I say 'all I could' because, owing to the exceptional circumstances of the jails, enclosures, flights, etc., I haven't been permitted all the peace which might be desired.

"I anxiously await your word on the date of the examination since Don Carlos has said nothing concrete about this to me. Does it seem to you that I shall have to take it at the end of this year—or at the opening of next?

"You say it is necessary to have all the data to 'legalize a dispensation of the course.' On this point permit me to remind you

---

[6] To a group of Mexicans in audience during this same year, 1927 (José A. Romero, S.J., *La Virgen de Guadalupe,* p. 82).

[7] This letter, written June 11, 1927, would seem to indicate that no one had *yet* sent him the required and missing Hurter!

of what I told you when I had the opportunity to see you. In Sarría and again at Enghien, not once but many times, this final examination was dispensed in favor of my companions when, for special reasons, it was impossible to take it and when the third years of philosophy and theology had been completed. Moreover, the dispensation was proposed to me, myself, but I would not accept it until I might confer with you—and then, as this was just when the order to depart arrived, all was left in *status quo.* An [alternate] proposal was that I prepare in eight days' time five or ten theses for presentation before my departure inasmuch as I didn't care to accept the dispensation lacking your consent. This seemed to me puerile and I didn't do it. None of this means that I am now asking the dispensation, for I wish to do only what you order me.

"In a previous letter you indicated that I am [scheduled] to leave this country in June or July. Don Carlos has never made mention of such a thing to me. Would it be undue curiosity to ask about this matter? You well know that I have no particular inclinations and that even though, for me, it would be a trial to lose here the opportunity to gain Heaven, to take the Universal Examination and to acquire the perpetual chaplaincy of the Islas Marías,[8] nevertheless I prefer (above all) to obey since in this way I shall accomplish more for the same [interests] for which I wish to labor.

"So now, without for any reason meaning all this to influence your judgment, and always under your direction in obedience, I shall say what Sr. Crivelli said in Rome: 'Permit me to remain in my place until the persecution passes.' Fear, which is what impedes the doing here of much in favor of the flock, is not one of my dominant defects. Will this [fact] perhaps be my ruin? What will it do or undo for my person? This is for God to say. How I wish I were worthy to suffer persecution for the Name of

[8] Padre Pro obviously means "the Islands of María" to refer to Heaven though this is also the name of the islands holding México's most formidable federal penitentiary, and a pun was evidently intended.

Jesus, the more so as I am one of those who carry the glorious distinction of belonging to the Light Cavalry! But—as in the 'Our Father'—thy will be done." [9]

The spirit of Miguel Pro indubitably longed for martyrdom, even while he knew himself duty-bound to extend every effort to preserve his life for its utility to others. His whole soul coveted the assurance of Heaven that any day the one little slip, the carelessness of an instant, might so easily achieve. He had no illusions about his intellectual capacities; no brilliant future as a shining light of the Society to look forward to. His one great chance for maximum service was *now!* He probably recognized, too, that his beloved country's salvation might be secured through some rash excess destined to surge from Calles' anti-Catholic frenzy which, running away with the last vestige of the tyrant's political acumen, would make martyrs of prominent and popular figures—figures such as Padre Pro. If in dying for Christ he might be the means of saving his country . . . ? But it was this glorious privilege that he must resist with all his might. Even more vital than his incessant labor for his people was holy obedience—his vow. Beyond his sacrifices, works of charity, and unfaltering fortitude, this subjection to obedience was the true badge of his priesthood.

[9] All letters quoted in this chapter are taken from Portas who quotes them between pp. 99–114.

XIX

AMERICAN NERO

LET us briefly examine the record of Plutarco Elías Calles, this master of México who, in retrospect, seems to resemble a bad myth. It tells us that, although officially represented as having been born into a middle-class, politically-minded family in Guaymas, Sonora, on Christmas Day (!), 1877, Calles' Mexican birth has always been doubted in the land where he is still alluded to as *"el Turco*—the Turk."[1] In any event, it was in Guaymas that he commenced his career as a public school teacher, an employment from which he was dismissed when, during his term as treasurer of the Teachers' Association (1900), the organization's funds mysteriously disappeared. This inauspicious beginning, rather than having a subduing effect on the otherwise unpunished young man, seems to have been adopted as a pattern for future operations. When, through the efforts of an influential relative, Calles was soon appointed to the post of municipal treasurer of Guaymas, the ex-professor barely escaped arrest after his second ejection from public service—for embezzlement.

Unabashed, he next accepted employment as a bartender at the local Hotel México, from which humble berth he made a

---

[1] Although usually called a Turk or an Arab, Dragón writes: "He was born in the United States of a Semite and a Mexican woman and adopted by her relatives who resided in Sonora." *Vida Íntima del Padre Pro*, p. 305.

meteoric ascent to the status of proprietor of the same establishment—which promptly burned down. In this case the charge was
arson, but once again there appear to have been no inconvenient
repercussions save for the refusal of the insurance companies to
make full payment on the policies covering the hotel.

His immediately following positions (as manager of an uncle's ranch and of a flour mill) coincided significantly with the
successive bankruptcies of these enterprises. Thus México's future dictator had figured in no less than five scandals involving
monetary irregularities during his first few years as a "public
servant" and businessman.

But before 1912 Calles had practically abandoned commerce
for that easier route to wealth and power—politics. By tying on
to Madero's Revolution, he captured an appointment to the post
of chief of police in squalid little Agua Prieto, located on the
Sonora–Arizona border. There, as a side line, he opened a general
store, saloon, and gambling house which was soon picking up its
full share of American tourist dollars. It was incontestable that
a certain amount of capital would come in handily in making
the ambitious transition he envisioned.

The blood-chilling cruelty which he exhibited very early seems
to have been quite as much an infirmity as it was a weapon for
advancement. With no other excuse than "loyalty" to Madero
(a man who easily overlooked personal insults), Plutarco condemned a harmless peasant who had made the mistake of shout-
ing "Down with Madero!" to hanging by *barbed wire* from a
railway bridge! And in 1918, just six years after *"el Turco's"*
own life had been spared through the intervention of Dr. Manuel Huerta (before whom, ashen-faced and trembling, he had
gone on his knees pleading mercy), Calles ordered the hanging
of his benefactor. To achieve this classic ingratitude, Dr. Huerta
had been kidnaped from asylum on American soil and carried
back to México by Calles' agents.

He made his first bid for military distinction by joining
Obregón in the field during 1913; and soon won a colonelcy
from which, with little difficulty, he rose to the command of the

Sonora troops. Although his early war exploits were unnotable, he clung to the Revolution—the shortest route to fame and fortune—and became, in 1915, Carranza's provisional governor of Sonora. Following an adventure in Indian fighting through the Yaqui country (1917), he returned to Hermosillo, now as "Constitutional" Governor of the same state. From there, he moved up, in 1919, to Carranza's cabinet as Secretary of Industry, Commerce and Labor. But with far more ambitious ends in view, he resigned this charge, alleging as his reason: "All the errors and all the acts of the most corrupt administration yet recorded in the annals of Mexican Government." [2] In this accusation he may well have been right, but what is surer is that, with Plutarco Calles on the scene, Carranza's "corrupt administration" would not long be able to maintain any such record.

Throwing his full support behind the presidential candidacy of General Obregón at this time (1920), Calles brought about the formidable collaboration that was to make short work of Carranza, whose assassination rivaled the murder of Francisco Madero for barefaced perfidy. This crime cleared the way for Obregón's seizure of the executive prerogatives of the nation, and the launching forthwith of México's historic epoch of Rule by Cynicism. For Obregón had displayed just enough activity in the expropriation of the large landholdings (battle cry of the rebellion) to pay lip service to the revolutionary aims [3] and, naturally, to show the proper consideration for the enrichment of his constituents. Meanwhile, he made a more thoroughgoing job of placating North American Big Business, thereby securing the support needful to the consolidation and stabilization of his regime.

Nevertheless, in view of the passion with which the old military men had adopted the slogan deriving from the 1917 Constitution: *"Effective Suffrage and No Re-election,"* Obregón dared not risk trying to succeed himself in the presidency. This is where Calles (now Left Wing leader and Secretary of *Gober-*

[2] Quoted by Magner, *Men of Mexico,* p. 524.
[3] After ten years of Revolution, a full third of México's agricultural workers were still bound to the haciendas in semi-serfdom. (F. R.)

nación) came in. These two "old soldiers," both tough and ruthless politicians, were still in accord on most matters. Thanks to
the arms supplied them on credit by Washington in appreciation
for the first Mexican guarantees to American capital since "the
good old days of Don Porfirio," they could easily manage to put
down all challenges to their might.

Thus, the rebellion of Adolfo de la Huerta (1923) was swiftly
smashed, its leading figures jailed, exiled, or executed, according
to the whims of the strong-arm team. The intrepid General
Ángel Flores defied this warning to become an opposition candidate with the realistic pronouncement: ". . . What has happened is simply that the rich man has been impoverished while
the pauper is not better off than before. Rural property has been
destroyed, farmers have no resources nor credit and are unable
to mortgage or sell their properties because no funds are available for upkeep and development owing to the fear of impending confiscation . . ." [4] Flores met a swift end by poisoning.

The misfortunes of De la Huerta and Flores served to convince
the nation and so, in 1924, Plutarco Calles from Guaymas and
Agua Prieta, as a matter of course, "inherited" the presidency
from his crony, Álvaro Obregón, on the flagrant platform:
"dictatorship of the proletariat; suppression of private property;
total submission of the family to the state; the uprooting of religion."

Calles' term as President, the first stage of a rule that he
would manage to extend over a full decade as "First Chief of the
Revolution," was unalleviated terror. Thousands upon thousands
with the means to do so fled their beloved homeland. The opposition which remained—and could be identified—was meted
out the most outrageous violence. The robbery, torture, and
slaughter which had marked the early days of Calles' personal
history were made operative on a nationwide scale until there
was no safety for any independent thinker in México. We already know how all this had affected the nation's pursuit of its
spiritual life, and the functioning of the Church.

[4] Quoted by Magner, p. 527.

Under the original plan, Calles was to return the executive power to Obregón in 1928,[5] a magnanimous gesture which, it was supposed, would be reciprocated by the latter in 1934. Once more opposition candidates denounced this high-handed procedure of government by closed combine, but they, too, were dispatched by Callista bullets.[6] Meanwhile, México's real heroes, her apostles and self-sacrificing, suffering patriots, could be left to the brutal attentions of the loutish police spies and their humid, rat-infested dungeons beneath the Inspección de Policía.

[5] To which end the 1917 Constitution had been amended to legalize re-election after an intervening term which had been increased to six years.

[6] There were 300 political assassinations during the first week of October, 1927. Among this number was General Francisco Serrano, one of the opposition candidates; and before the end of the month General Arnulfo Gómez, another candidate, was shot.

XX

THE BOMB

THESE were the circumstances, the figures, and the deeds whose ominous shadows fell across each hour of Miguel Pro's ministry to his fatherland. The lanes and alleys through which, by day and by night, he furtively bore the gifts to console the spirits and preserve the lives of his suffering compatriots were filled with these lurking shadows, the threats to his own life and liberty which, "when the danger of the moment had passed," he could humorously relate while being grateful for their profit to his soul.

As the days marched forward toward the opening week of October, 1927, he was moving faster, working harder, than ever. In August: ". . . the day has only twenty-four hours. . . . A shining court of chauffeurs is my crowning glory; how good it is among these strong-spoken, utterly fearless ones who are, nevertheless, most docile when they see themselves treated with consideration! I wouldn't trade them for all your haughty matrons and sissy *caballeros*. The ministries are most varied and beautiful: marriages of [former] Lutherans and heretics; [preparation of] the dying of all ages and religions; conferences à la Nicodemus' with armed guards on the door to protect those who enter; First Holy Communions to touch [the heart]; Masses in the catacombs, at which the celebrant is left very small before the faith of his listeners; confessions by day and by night—to wear out the old man and make him detest sin [if only] for what it costs him.

"If there were a community life [here], the load would be lightened 90 per cent but, running to and fro, sweating and riding busses guiltless of springs, covertly alerted to spy out those who are spying [on us], and with the Sword of Damocles threatening us with the police dungeons at every turn—this is how we go on, who would almost prefer *being* in jail, just to obtain a little rest. Really, one might rather be dead than forced to support such barbarity: poor people!—the poor little people —postponing the good of their souls for the body's convenience!" [1]

An added concern was now piled upon the compounded burden he already bore. This was the thesis which he wrote, not once but, after seeking the criticism of the scholarly Father Alfredo Méndez Medina, a second time. On September 16 he sat down for the worrisome, much-discussed final theology examination. Padres Méndez Medina, Luis Benítez, and Joaquín Cordero, the trio of erudite Jesuits who were his examiners, were unanimous in their report: *"Attigit mediocritatem."* "From which it is to be seen," wrote Father Portas, "that although it couldn't have been a brilliant execution, it was sufficiently good to be passable." [2] After sixteen years of striving, laboring, and suffering on two continents and in five countries, Miguel Agustín Pro had at last qualified for full membership in that select body of men which he was to cover with undying glory. What vistas did this success open before him?

Five days later, as he was preparing to say Mass in a house occupied by a community of nuns, he supplicated them all to pray that God might grant him the privilege of offering himself as Plutarco Calles' victim in the cause of the Faith and to the benefit of the priests of their country. His Mass on this morning was offered for the same intention. One of the Sisters present upon

[1] Quoted by Portas, p. 115.
[2] *Ibid.*, p. 109.

this occasion wrote later: "All during that Mass I was most deeply affected. It was celebrated very slowly and I wept the whole time. At its termination [Padre Miguel] told one of the nuns [who still lives and can testify to this]: 'I don't know if it could be purely imaginary or if it really happened, but I feel sure Our Lord accepted the plan of this offering. . . .' " [3]

Of his indubitable desire to be sacrificed in behalf of his brothers in religion and for the relief of the miseries of his countrymen, México's Jesuit Provincial, Father Carlos Mayer, affirmed: "Padre Pro repeatedly demonstrated his longing for martyrdom in the cause of the defense of the Church; and, especially during the last months, he frequently asked [our] prayers to that end. . . . [Although] he subjected himself to the precautions required of him, because he was very obedient, he pled to be given ever more liberty to extend his works of zeal. The perils to which he necessarily exposed himself [in his labors] certainly justified fear. But owing to his unwavering desire for sacrifice, he was never afraid while doing all that was possible for God." [4]

And now October was half gone, that indescribable October whose first week had run with the gore of the three hundred citizens. Their slaughter had been *"el Turco's"* grand gesture of "loyalty" to Álvaro Obregón—or, more realistically, to the fat future of Plutarco Elías Calles. To Father Miguel the horror of this week was of a single piece with the rest; his duties, strains, and heartaches a depressing tapestry woven on an evil loom— the tyranny of Godless men. His labors, his movements across the terror-haunted city, were all motivated by one consideration: what did his *Padre Dios* ask of him this hour, this moment? How much of all that cried so loudly to be done could he personally accomplish for his "poor little people"—*today?*

Sometime on October 17 he found the moments to dash off a note to Father Henry Valley whom he addressed nowadays as "My Very Appreciable Cousin, D. Enrique," while signing himself simply "Enghien" ". . . We are now supplying ninety-six

---

[3] Quoted *ibid.*, p. 126.
[4] Quoted *ibid.*, p. 127 (from Province Archives, November 28, 1927).

families with everything from A to Z—though we have no
definite income upon which to depend. All the better! Vainglory
can't even raise its head amongst us because we must always be
acknowledging, in all its loving splendor, the direct action of
God. And how certain it is that He Who feeds the little birds of
the field isn't going to leave the sons He created and redeemed
with His Precious blood to die of hunger. My personnel has
reduced itself to half-a-dozen pious women and the same number of unemployed, pious men. . . .

"This week's highlight, and this in my personal life, was the
gift of a six-months'-old baby boy whose infamous parents
abandoned him. There wasn't room for him in any nursery, and
so nothing to do but carry the little jewel home with me. My
papá, sister, and two brothers received the babe with open arms
and he has become the diversion of our family life. This is the
sixth I've been given, but the others were easily placed. His name
is José de Jesús and he is a *Tapatío* [5] and altogether such a good
piece that he smiles all day and cries little. My friends disapprove
this adoption, but doesn't it seem just that we care for the *niño*
God gives us when He has protected everyone of our house
through these days of mourning and misery?" [6]

Ten days after this writing Father Miguel was conducting
exercises for all classes of the society of Toluca, capital city of
the State of México, which lies some forty miles southwest
of, and at a still higher elevation than, the Valley of México.
From there, apparently in high spirits, he mailed a postal card
to Father Henry, the wording of which may strike us as less
enigmatic than might have been desirable. "Dear Cousin: Am
on an excursion to this city of butter and *chorizo* where I shall
remain until November first. I came to sell my *medias* [7] on the
modern coupon plan under which I give talks to demonstrate
their utility. Am at it all day long: at 5:30 A.M. I talk to servant
girls; at 8, to children; at 10, to young ladies; at 3, to menserv-

---

[5] A native of the state of Jalisco.
[6] Quoted by Portas, *ibid.,* pp. 117–20.
[7] A pun. *"Medias"* means "hosiery," and in mathematics, also "propor-
tionate means."

ants; at 5, to ladies; at 6, to my friends in the trade;[8] at 8, to men. Have to strike while the iron is hot to win the advantage. Public has responded well and I hope to earn enough to meet my debts. Only wish my employers would let me make a tour of the Republic."[9]

This was the sort of jest that had always delighted the heart of Miguel Pro—and there was very little fun left save in pulling the legs of the humorless henchmen of tyranny. Perhaps the thinness of the disguise he threw over his meaning in this instance demonstrated his small respect for the perspicacity of his would-be persecutors. This unclosed report on his mission to Toluca was followed, on October 30, by a serious letter to the same good friend which is of interest because it is believed to be the last he ever wrote. We place here only the closing lines.

". . . I've just forgotten all about the medical prescriptions that have burdened me for the three years since I had to have the first operation and during which time a greasy alimentation has been mortal sin. I've been eating [Toluca's] famous *chorizos*[10] and *pambozos*[10] which, up to now, haven't protested in my stomach. This certifies that I'm now bombproof and that these excursions which (I am told) 'contribute prestige to the constituent mentality of the nation' could be more widely extended without fear of anyone or anything. What will Don Carlos think of this [plan]? What will you people? Ah, little Cousin Enrique, interpose your influence that my rope may be loosened so that I may go to all these people of God! Just see that it's the 'constituent mentality of the nation' with which we are dealing.

"*Adiós.* Remember me to all, never forget me and, any time you lack someone for whom to say an *Ave María,* know that I shall accept it with the greatest pleasure. Enghien."[11]

With the opening of November he was back in México City; and on Sunday the thirteenth so was Álvaro Obregón. Following

[8] Other priests.
[9] Quoted, *ibid.,* pp. 120–1.
[10] *Chorizo,* a highly-spiced, greasy Mexican sausage is a filling for *pambozos,* heavily-crusted rolls, almost hollow.
[11] Quoted, *ibid.,* p. 123.

the campaign tour (more a convivial than a political gesture), this lusty, urbane, one-armed *ex-ranchero* from Sonora had been automatically "re-elected." Now nothing but the calendar stood between him and his resumption of power over the land of "Effective Suffrage and No Re-election."

On this beautiful Sunday, shortly after noon, the General, flanked by his bodyguard companions, Juan H. Jaime and Ignacio Otero, descended from the train into the enthusiastic embraces of a reception committee composed of faithful adherents; and then swung smartly through the smoke and grime of the battered old station into the thin, clear air of the hemisphere's loveliest and most ancient capital. As he was deferentially handed into his Cadillac to be whisked up the sun-gilded, green-canopied Paseo de la Reforma, he must have been savoring a satisfaction greater than he had ever experienced, a triumph never to have been granted to México's other revolutionary chieftains. For, after a full term in the presidency and another full term during which the office had been held down by a contemporary "strong man," he had "come back" to take possession once more.

It was still *his*—the nation first won for him by the hard-bitten desert troops which had swarmed south across its jagged terrain in the victorious push of 1914. His great "Army of the North" had indeed made him master in this broad land. But it was he who had created that formidable force and led it to glory as it was his shrewdness which had built upon the initial advantage to catapult himself into the presidency. And hadn't he chosen Plutarco? Even years ago everyone had hated the fellow. But it had been given to Álvaro Obregón to spy out the germ of genius lurking, one might almost say, festering, in this unprepossessing man of malice and menace. Despite Calles' mediocre military talents and demeaning private record for cheap peculation and brutality, he had possessed—or been obsessed by?—a truly inspired quality that had proven very useful in the pinches. Plutarco not only enjoyed his atrocities, he never bothered about the amenities that a ruler who covets popularity, too, must try to keep in mind. For *"el Turco,"* power was enough; power and riches together the whole point of existence.

For himself, Obregón wanted a little more than this, for instance, that edge of esteem on which to base a feeling of superiority to his widely-detested partner. It helped to lull the unease occasionally experienced in contemplating the pathological fiendishness of Plutarco's behavior in some very picayune matters, the inconceivable lengths to which he would go, so pigheadedly, to impose his will. México's *next* President had no fear of his old protégé, and it was probably sheer foolishness, this sometime resentment that the *Viejo* [12] had gradually become so indispensable. After all, Calles had done a superb job on that amendment which had made his former chief's new grab so exceedingly simple. There wasn't any sensible doubt that they could stick by their original deal to play the nation back and forth between them. But it was a pity that, as the years slipped along, they who had always complemented one another so surprisingly as a political team seemed to be pulling further and further apart on certain basic concepts. For Calles went right on talking like a fire-eating radical; while Obregón, himself, was growing ever sicker of this socialistic ballyhoo. It had served its purpose, hadn't it? The Revolution had been won—long ago. The trouble with Calles was that he couldn't leave well enough alone! The downtrodden masses meant no more to him than to anyone else—or why so many savage persecutions against all the peasant held most dear? Well, no matter, one had to have Calles and he had done well in summarily dispatching their recent opposition,[13] in smothering the various *Cristero* [14] outbreaks. One hadn't fought a tough campaign and lost an arm in the process to be expected to endure molestations of organized opposition, that was sure.

---

[12] "The Old Man," another of Calles' nicknames.

[13] Generals Serrano and Gómez, both assassinated in October, had announced their intentions of running against Obregón.

[14] A lay movement determined to regain religious liberty, by insurrection, if necessary. The battle cry, *"Viva Cristo Rey!*—Long Live Christ the King!" is still México's most popular slogan.

Nevertheless, this business of turning fire hoses into churches on doddering old ladies who only asked to be allowed to say their rosaries in their priestless temples seemed unnecessarily antagonizing to a lot of citizens besides the old women. And why employ such extremes of brutality with these tiresome priests and nuns as to convert them into martyrs? That could be dangerous policy. Once safely re-established in the Palacio, however, a less impassioned chief executive would experiment with discreet modifications in the methods to be applied in this fight to eradicate the ingrained Faith of a remarkably stubborn nation. If a slightly softer attitude would ease the undercurrent of sullenness, which only a fool could completely overlook in any tour about the country, wasn't that the indicated course? It would also increase the personal prestige of Álvaro Obregón.

Some such reflections as these were occupying part of his mind while he listened to the jovial flattery of his satellites and ran an indulgent eye over the festive scenes typical of all Mexican Sundays which enlivened the parkways and the bridle path of the Paseo. Thus distracted, he failed to notice the shabby Essex which doggedly tailed the Cadillac from the station right into Avenida Jalisco where the General's party was driven through the heavy steel gates into the Obregón premises. Nor did he or his guests observe the same small car as it thereafter studiously circled the block.

At three o'clock the cheerful politicos, after dining very well, pulled away from the Avenida Jalisco residence in two automobiles: Obregón and his friends, Tomás Bay and Arturo Orcí, in the Cadillac driven by the General's chauffeur, Catarino Villalpando; the ex-soldier bodyguards, Jaime and Otero, with their friend, Ramiro Ramíres, immediately behind in a machine chauffeured by Rodolfo de la Torre. As ordered, Villalpando headed for Chapultepec Park where the General wished to pass the hour which must elapse before the bullfights. To "make the *paseo*" in México City is to join the traditional Sunday motorcade in a slow drive back and forth through the boulevards of Chapultepec, two, frequently three, lines deep in either direction. This leisurely progress permits one to take the air amid incomparable natural beauty and—vastly more stimulating—both to see and be seen by those few thousands of inhabitants of the capital who may be said "to count" in a metropolis which then already numbered more than a million inhabitants. The hour was now so advanced that the procession-paced, formal *paseo* had thinned out for the afternoon dinner, but a cruise through the Bosque de Chapultepec would be most agreeable for a weary traveler.

Just inside the majestic park the Cadillac swung about the "Fountain of the Frogs" and, bearing to the left, entered the Avenida Principal, heading for the bridge which spans the canoe-dotted lake, closely followed by the second car. Behind them both rolled the still-unnoticed little Essex. The only reason why Juan Jaime eventually found himself taking note of this modest vehicle was that it suddenly pulled out of line to pass, first, the car in which he was riding with Otero and Ramíres, and then, at a considerably accelerated speed, that of the General. Not far beyond it made a horseshoe turn and doubled back down the avenue for another passing from the opposite direction. This dodging in and out attracted his attention, although it did not cause the guard any conscious foreboding. In his subsequent sworn statement concerning this day's events, he said that "without knowing why" he had just happened to make a mental note of the Essex' license number: 10,101.[15]

Now, as the Essex met the Cadillac, he became aware of one of its occupants' tossing an object full upon the Obregón car. Simultaneously, the air was split by a deafening explosion and filled with a burst of smoke which became denser following a second detonation. Through this choking fog a rattling of pistol shots was emitted by the Essex, before it commenced its flight from the scene. To ascertain the result of the attack upon the life of General Obregón, the guards ordered De la Torre to pull alongside the Cadillac before taking out in pursuit. Had their

[15] *Acta en la Inspección de Policía* of November 19, 1927, photostatic copy in *Novedades,* México City, November 13, 1952, part of documentation submitted to Rome in the cause of Padro Pro.

Jefe been killed? Or seriously injured? He had been seated on the left—the more exposed side of the tonneau.

Amazingly, he was not seriously hurt. The blood they saw on his face and hand was merely from minor wounds inflicted by powder and a splinter of glass. To their agitated inquiries Obregón snapped, "I'm all right. Follow them!"

Pistols in hand, both Jaime and Otero were already riding the the running boards of their machine and, as their driver wheeled about and opened the pursuit back toward the park entrance, they commenced firing upon the disappearing Essex. The chase flashed out of the Bosque and on down the Reforma as far as the Independence Column where it veered right into Florencia Street. Meanwhile, two of the Cadillac's tires having been demolished by the explosion, Villalpando moved it only as far as "the Lions," [16] at which point the General, Bay, and Orcí caught a cab back to Jalisco Street.

Much farther downtown, amid a perilous cross-fire (or so was Jaime to testify, insisting that the bombers' car had returned their shots), the pursuit continued until, at the juncture of Liverpool and Insurgentes, the Essex collided with a Ford. Three, perhaps four, occupants of the assault car were sprinting down Insurgentes. One of them, being frightfully wounded in the head, was easily overtaken by Otero. A second, unhurt, was captured by Jaime close to the busy intersection of Insurgentes and the Calzada de Chapultepec. One of the regular police on this corner, alerted by the shots, laid hands upon a third individual, Francisco Olivera (who seems to have been an innocent bystander with the singularly bad luck to have sought refuge from the ricocheting bullets behind a streetcar right alongside an unnoticed bomb on the pavement). [17]

According to the closing lines of Juan Jaime's signed declaration: ". . . the detention of these individuals having been attained, the declarant and the policeman returned to the assail-

[16] Chapultepec's main entrance is flanked by ponderous sculptured lions on huge pedestals.

[17] Facts sworn to by Olivera, *ibid*. Reproduced in *Novedades*, November 13, 1952.

ants' car and upon examining same, discovered numerous blood-stains on the interior and, in the rear of the automobile, a pistol with one vacant and one loaded chamber: they immediately placed the detained at the disposition of this Inspección de Policía: the undersigned is fully certain that Antonino Tirado [Jaime's uninjured captive] and the wounded Nahum Lamberto Ruíz are two of the assailants: he is unable to affirm whether Francisco Olivera was or was not at the scene of the assault." [18]

However, as would be assumed by anyone familiar with the *pistolero* psychology, this was not all that had taken place. Jaime omitted to say that the injured prisoner, Ruíz, was first dragged to the house in Jalisco for "interrogation" and the in-structions of the *Jefe*. But this fact was mentioned by Tomás Bay [19] and by Otero,[20] both of whom testified that the half-dead Ruíz asserted to Obregón: *"Mi General,* I didn't shoot." After this, Otero stated: "General Obregón ordered that this individual be brought to this police station, which I did."

Inasmuch as it appeared that Ruíz' head wound had claimed an eye, that he might expire momentarily, and was, meanwhile, bleeding profusely over the disgusted General's carpets, he was dispatched as rapidly as possible. The President-elect had no more time to waste in such a stupid business. He had an engage-ment. Only slightly disfigured by his iodine-splashed scratches, he set out at once with Bay and Orcí for the Plaza de los Toros where, by great luck, they succeeded in arriving in time for the first bullfight of the afternoon.

[18] Jaime statement, *ibid., Novedades* reproduction, November 13, 1952.
[19] Bay statement, *ibid., Novedades* reproduction, November 15, 1952.
[20] Otero statement, *ibid., Novedades* reproduction, November 17, 1952.

XXI

THE PRETEXT

PADRE MIGUEL had been driving himself hard all week. Knotty problems posed by a hundred destitute families, decisions and plans requiring his judgment and advice, had been held in abeyance pending his return from Toluca. This pile up of work had to be tackled immediately because so many of the issues were emergency matters.

Humberto and Roberto, at twenty-four and twenty-two years, were splendid aides for the routine detail, but their time was largely allocated to the printing and distribution of propaganda for the civil branch of the Religious Defense League. (Edmundo appears not to have been involved in the League's activities, but it seems certain he shared his family's hardships and interests.) To Ana María fell the task of making a home of their ramshackle Pánuco Street rooms for her aging father, brothers, and one or more extra adults. (Padre Pro mentioned seven in their almost unfurnished quarters.) The "adopted" infant, for whom there was no other refuge in all the city, must have been an added care for Ana María.

Their program was necessarily extremely flexible. As they lived wholly to serve the persecuted and the poor who came seeking their beloved Padre Pro in all their spiritual and material crises, the family must be available at all hours; likewise constantly alert against a sudden descent of the police in raids such as had driven them from their previous shelter (in September) and despoiled them of their household goods. Although no scrap of incriminating evidence had been uncovered on their premises, the government spies were still not entirely convinced that some of the Pros had not been at the bottom of the balloon affair. There was, too, that old rumor that one of them was a priest. Neither charge had been proved and, furthermore, we know that Father Miguel had categorically denied their implication in the matter of the balloons but, even so, by reason of their labors for religion they were all technical outlaws. In Calles' México, it was sedition to print so much as a prayer or an article of Church doctrine.

Before the heroic example of their eldest brother and emulating his audacity, the young Pros pitted their dedicated and hazardous efforts against the tyranny which had enslaved Christian México. Theirs, therefore, was a life of unremitting tension. There were, however, many merry moments in Pánuco Street, and none more enlivening than those brightened by Miguel's humorous re-creations of his hairbreadth escapes in the crazy adventures he constantly entered upon for the good of "his people." (In these days, under a hundred disguises and dissimulations, he continuously outwitted the guards to carry Holy Communion right into the cells of the political prisoners and to patients in the public hospital wards, an exploit at which, almost incredibly, he was never detected.)

On Sunday the 13th all four Pro brothers dined at home, and then played ball until past four o'clock when they broke up their game in order to keep the appointments to which they were individually committed. By seven young Roberto was back again—with the startling news of the afternoon's excitement in the Bosque de Chapultepec, a report which Padre Miguel, who returned before nine, had also heard at the Valezzi home. But it was the arrival of Humberto a few moments later, his face drawn and gray, that brought the shock which was to destroy forever their hard but happy life together in Pánuco Street.

Humberto had a copy of the *Universal Grafico's* extra. Beneath the headlines proclaiming the attack on Obregón by dynamiters so ineffective that they almost had to be amateurs was a fearsome disclosure. The assault had been made from an old Essex bearing the license number 10,101. For—and this, at last, was indeed disaster—until the previous Wednesday that Essex had been Humberto's property! It was licensed under the pseudonym, "Daniel García," which, however, carried a photograph of Roberto.

The Essex had formerly been employed to distribute the propaganda, but as the League had recently replaced it with a Studebaker, Humberto had, during the past week, sold it for three hundred pesos to one José González, a stranger whose address was unknown. In any case, it would seem that González had turned the car over to a third person. At least Humberto had seen Luis Segura Vilchis driving it subsequent to the sale to González. Could Segura, whom he had known casually for a year or so as an amiable young engineer who held a responsible position with the Light and Power Company, be mixed up in a plot to do away with Álvaro Obregón? It was hard to credit, although there had been indications that he was involved with the armed defense branch of the League (whose activities were sharply divided into two totally separate categories). While thousands of peaceful Mexicans—the Pros among these—were dedicated to the civil works of the movement, this did not mean that they were in any way implicated in its parallel plan of resistance by violence. Thus, that a car so easily traceable to them should have been used in an attempted assassination was a great injustice.

And that was not all. As the worried family pored over the news report someone recalled that a chauffeur associated with Luis Segura had recently rented a room and garage from a *pensión* which Humberto had obtained for two resourceless sisters named Hernández through the generosity of the Señora Montes de Oca. Had the Essex been located there? If so, would the Señoritas Hernández be likely to mention the name of Pro to the police? A number of coincidences might lead the investigators of the attack to their own door. And certainly this time they could not hope to conceal the fact that they were, at the least, important cogs in the organized opposition to a religion-hating regime.

But there was no time to waste in conjectures. They must flee this humble dwelling place before Calles' police spies swarmed down upon them. The faces of Father Miguel, Humberto, and Roberto were already entirely too familiar for them to risk dallying here—or being sighted anywhere. For the present they would have to go into strict hiding. Then, perhaps, they could try to make their way north to escape across the line into the United States. For old Don Miguel, Ana María, and Edmundo there would hardly be much danger if they remained quietly with friends under assumed names until the commotion blew over.

What did Padre Pro think of all this? Did he really believe he might manage a successful second flight from his homeland, especially now that he was so well known? At thirty-six years of age, did he *wish* to face starting all over, an exile once more from the land to which his heart wholly belonged? In view of his sincere desire to sacrifice himself for the liberation of the Faith in México, it seems most unlikely. But as he was morally bound to do all in his power to protect his young brothers and to preserve his own life as long as possible, he quickly set up the plan. And thus, before the arrival of the police for a fourth raid on their pathetic little house, the birds had all flown.

Nahum Ruíz, the injured prisoner, had been removed to the Juárez Hospital where, having lost the sight of the remaining eye [1] and fallen into a state of coma, no hope was held for his recovery. On November 15 *Excelsior* declared: "As Ruíz is dying and unable to pronounce a single syllable, he has said nothing . . ." [to throw light upon the plot against Obregón's life].

[1] This fact is disputed by one of the biographers, but was claimed by both the press and the police at the time.

And Tirado, the other man who was captured by the General's guards, had simply refused to talk. According to *Excelsior,* November 17: "Juan Tirado continues to maintain silence or, better said, persists in affirming that he knows nothing about the attack. The *Inspección de Policía* is convinced that he is one of the dynamiters; but although the Chief of the Security Commission [Mazcorro], as well as other agents, has used all his skill[2] interrogating him in an effort to lead him into contradictions and thereby obtain a confession, the prisoner still maintains his original declaration . . ." [of innocence].

Meanwhile, the third detained individual, Olivera, having verified his movements up to the luckless moment when he had ducked behind the streetcar to avoid the bullets whizzing through Avenida Insurgentes, had been released. The authorities were inclined to the opinion that there had been four men in the Essex. The exoneration of Olivera, therefore, left two still to be apprehended. Of course the hunt was on for "Daniel García," but so far this "person" had not been located.

Could not General Obregón or his friends throw any light whatsoever on the identity of their assailants, or at least describe their appearance? When, on the nineteenth—nearly a week after the bombing and following a number of arrests—they finally presented themselves at the police station, Obregón, almost indifferently, made a cool, objective statement in which he said: ". . . that he hadn't seen and so wouldn't be able to identify the fugitives . . ." [dynamiters].[3] Orcí testified: ". . . that during the assault he had observed that one of the Essex' occupants had a swarthy complexion [in México!] and thus, he might be able to recognize him . . ." if seen again.[4] Bay stated: ". . . that, not having had time to see them, he couldn't expect to identify the assailants."[5] No accusations of any nature against any individuals appear in the testimony of Obregón or his two

---

[2] Tirado was repeatedly tortured by the police, according to Antonio Dragón, S.J., *Vida Íntima del Padre Pro,* p. 321.

[3] *Acta de Inspección,* photostat reproduction in *Novedades,* November 13, 1952.

[4] *Ibid.,* November 14, 1952.

[5] *Ibid.,* November 15, 1952.

friends; and the aides, Jaime and Otero, had nothing to offer beyond their personal conviction that their captives, Ruíz and Tirado, were unquestionably two of the would-be assassins.

On Monday the fourteenth the detectives Valentín Quintana and Álvaro Basaíl were assigned to head the bombing investigation. The former immediately fell to work on the Ruíz angle. He located the dying man's wife, Luz del Carmen González de Ruíz. The woman accompanied him to the Juárez Hospital where, according to Quintana,[6] she willingly represented to her husband (who, if the *Excelsior* report was accurate, was not only totally blind but "unable to utter a single syllable") that the detective was either Ruíz' own brother or brother-in-law.[7] When she began to quiz the injured man about the attack, he responded (still following Quintana) with reproof of her inquisitiveness, despite which, Quintana passed the night at the agonizing man's bedside. On Tuesday morning he emerged from the hospital with several pages of notes purporting to consist of information supplied by Ruíz after his acceptance of the detective's—and his wife's!—misrepresentation.

It is obvious that there was something wrong about this story. Even granted that the newsmen erred and that this dying man with a bullet hole through his head (drilled with sufficient force to blow out an eyeball) was really capable of speech and to chide his spouse on her curiosity, would he have chanced committing himself to a "relative" he could not see? If equal to a detailed recital, would he have been incompetent to detect the difference between his brother's voice and that of a stranger? (If we are to grant three such unlikely premises, or even any two of them, we must then accept the inference that Nahum Ruíz judged his wife's discretion to be inferior to that of the individual to whom he believed himself speaking.)

But to get on with Quintana's declaration: It affirms that,

[6] *Ibid.,* November 28, 1952.
[7] In the *Acta,* Quintana merely stated that Ruíz' wife referred to him as "a relative," but from his comments to the press, *El Universal* quoted "brother"; *Excelsior,* "brother-in-law" (both reports appeared November 22, 1927).

during his all-night vigil over Ruíz, the latter frankly revealed his involvement in a plot to overthrow the government; named his immediate *Jefe* as a "Luis" who could be located either at an address in La Villa de Guadalupe or at the Light Company office; and, somewhere amid a jumbled but incredibly extensive exposure of the plans, names, and addresses of his companions in the conspiracy, adverted: "Humberto Pro is at 24A Alzate Street where the bombs are made, which has a broken windowpane." How exceedingly strange that only his *Jefe* was unsupplied with a family name among so many fully cited, while still two addresses (and correct addresses) were given for Luis! And if Ruíz was delirious, would an exposition so definite and detailed—aside from the only partial identification of his director—have been possible?

Were not such scraps of information as pointed the finger at a husband's closest associate what an overly inquisitive wife would have managed to piece together from her own observation? As for the much fuller identifications of persons only distantly known to Ruíz, Quintana was more than equal to elaborating these from details already known to the police. Moreover, four incident-packed days which produced an abundance of new information were to elapse before the detective described his night in the hospital room for the official record. Finally, never would there be the slightest shred of testimony to substantiate his assertion that Nahum Lamberto Ruíz uttered, or had been capable of uttering, a word.

Assuredly, the unrelated and incorrect comment touching Humberto Pro was not made by the dying man. But before November 19 Inspector Quintana had his own reasons for inserting that into his transcribed notes. Humberto was not at the Alzate address (which the investigator *had* obtained from someone, probably the Señora de Ruíz).[8] When he and his assistants sped out to this site, it was found that there was no such number.

---

[8] An editor's footnote to Dragón's work (p. 322) suggests that Ruíz' wife was played for a fool by the police who led her to believe she was aiding her husband by co-operating.

However, there was another clue on the "house where the bombs are made." It had a broken windowpane. And so did the one numbered 44A on the same street!

Alzate 44A was occupied by two young women named Hernández who appeared willing enough to permit the policemen to inspect the premises. They explained that they did not have access to one of the rooms nor to the garage. These were kept under lock and key and visited only occasionally by another tenant, sometimes accompanied by a friend or two. Of course no more than this was needed to start the police bashing in the door of the locked room, where they certainly did uncover a stock of ingredients necessary to the manufacture of bombs—tubes, wicks, and explosive chemicals.

The sisters were hurried off to the police station to be grilled by Quintana's "skilled" chief, Mazcorro. It soon became fairly obvious that they had been ignorant of the room's contents. Perhaps they knew nothing else of interest to the police, though there were one or two details which, terrorized before the threat of prison, they soon divulged. They had been established in the Alzate house, they said, by a certain Señora Josefina Montes de Oca whose generosity had been extended through her friendship for their helpful acquaintance, Humberto Pro. Excepting that they had been charged to guard the house and show every consideration for the privacy of the other roomer—apparently the collector of whatever had been found in his quarters—they knew nothing whatsoever. Altogether, it was a triumphant afternoon for Valentín Quintana for, although the name of Pro had not yet been linked with "Daniel García," there surely were several police-blotter allusions to a family of that name. To run into it again, and in connection with an ammunition cache, was a most significant coincidence. So in this revelation by the Hernández we unquestionably find the basis for Quintana's later testimony in the police department *Acta* that he had been "tipped off" on Humberto by Ruíz. Atttributing his private suspicions to a "confession" by a central figure in the case would render them infinitely more convincing.

The next step on the Pro angle was to locate the Señora Montes de Oca which, from the information supplied by the Hernández, was a simple procedure. Quintana, now accompanied by Basaíl,[9] burst in on this lady of many good works on November 17 to find her hastily packing for a journey. A young woman with a baby on one arm who claimed to be the wife of a traveling salesman was assisting. The visitor seemed of small interest. In a rapid ransacking of the house a number of suspicious-looking papers came to light. One of these consisted of a single line that appeared to have been scribbled in haste: "Don't go to Pánuco. Miguel." Wasn't one of those confoundedly elusive Pros called Miguel, the one they'd had in on the balloon deal? In any case, this Montes de Oca woman owed them a number of explanations. And they fell to work to obtain them.

She was a widow, she said, with a son, José Bolado Montes de Oca, adding that he was not in México City at the moment—a statement that was soon discredited when Basaíl answered the señora's telephone to hear a youthful voice inquiring for his mother. This "break" caused Quintana and Basaíl to pack the distracted woman off to the police station; and also led them to the son who was at the home of his grandparents in Chiapas Street. According to Quintana's formal declaration, already suspect in many of its details, the boy readily explained that his mother had sent him to stay with his grandparents, but for what reason he couldn't imagine; that the young woman they had seen with her was Ana María Pro and, of course, a sister of the famous Pro brothers; that the latter were at this moment in hiding at Londres 22, a boardinghouse. While it is true that this information was supplied by young Bolado, the editor of Father Dragón's book[10] states that he did so after having been subjected to a brutal beating and from a desire to protect his mother who (threatened Quintana and Basaíl) would surely be condemned to prison if he failed to tell them all they wished to know.

[9] Reputedly by far the more unscrupulous of the two.
[10] *Vida Íntima del Padre Pro,* footnote, p. 326.

The inspectors should have been most grateful to this lad for thus simplifying their labors. Now, in their considered opinion, they possessed enough information to clear up the bombing "incident." They had already apprehended Ruíz' *Jefe,* right where someone had assured Quintana he might be found: at the Light and Power Company. Seated behind his desk in that most respectable establishment, he had turned out to be a handsome, clear-eyed fellow of twenty-four years named Luis Segura Vilchis. Surprisingly, he had made no protests of innocence nor any objection whatsoever to being arrested and hauled off to prison. In fact, he had courteously and calmly averred that he would accompany them "with all pleasure."

Everything was well in hand and the sleuths could afford to congratulate themselves. Their demonstration of "brilliant deduction" and "redoubtability" could hardly fail to be rewarded by very acceptable promotions for Inspectors Quintana and Basaíl. Even so, they must not relax until they finally had those Pros all safe and sound in the police station's waiting dungeons. In closing the net upon this trio of "desperadoes" it might look very well to utilize an impressive company of soldiery.

Miguel Pro was a man who had long since abandoned fear, as other men are said to abandon hope. For at least a year he had prayed that he might be accepted as a sacrifice for the Faith in his country. If he were to be apprehended now, his prayer almost certainly would be granted: not because he was guilty of complicity in the bombing, or believed to be, but simply by reason of his calling.

Plutarco Calles, so resolutely and yet so precariously established in the Palacio, was afflicted by a hatred of the Christian religion—not just of the priests of the Church, as has sometimes been argued—that was a deadly malady. Had he not stated openly: "I have a personal hatred for Christ"; and: "Three times I've met Christ in my road and three times I've struck Him down"? [11] This deranged rancor, as Padre Pro well knew, was

[11] *Ibid.,* p. 352.

symptomatic of the indwelling misery of the man. It was nothing so simple as atheism. The detached atheist can coolly, unemotionally, persuade himself that religion should be suppressed as a harmful or retarding influence in the life of a nation. But for Calles there was no such easy route. He could not deny the existence of a Christ he had "met"—and "struck down." And that he did, indeed, bear within him a corroding, personal hatred of Christ was because he was terrified of the very idea of Christ.

El Turco was not only capable of, but bound to, murder any priest of Christ's Church who dropped into his hands in any such propitious circumstances as this situation offered. He was also capable of murdering the blameless brothers of that priest. It was this knowledge that caused Padre Miguel to spend Monday and Tuesday, November 14 and 15, seeking out a safe place for Humberto, Roberto, and himself to hide until they could manage to leave México.

By Tuesday afternoon everything had been arranged. A lady who conducted a *pensión* at Londres 22 would receive them. She had asked no details, but understood she was offering her hospitality to a priest being pursued by the police. This circumstance alone was a sufficient recommendation in those days to the sympathy of just and courageous Mexicans. In order that she might be able to identify her guest the instant he appeared at her gate, this lady, María Valdés, tore in half a leaflet of the *Apostleship of Prayer* and gave one of the pieces to the intermediary who had solicited her generosity.

This countersign was handed back to her at seven o'clock the same evening by a mild-faced young man who asked gently: "You aren't afraid of compromising yourself by receiving a priest into your house?"

The Señora Valdés' answer was to throw the door wide in welcome to Padre Pro and his companions. Although she never asked their names, she was soon able to distinguish them as "Miguel," "Humberto," and "Roberto." At first she didn't take them to be blood brothers. *"Mis hermanos"* had suggested that they might all be priests—brothers in religion. For this reason she inquired if they might not prefer separate rooms.

"No," replied the eldest gaily, "the bed will accommodate my brothers very well, and I am enchanted by this divan."

He immediately produced his chalice and ornaments. A small commode was soon transformed into an altar where for two mornings an unworried fugitive was to celebrate Mass in a most privileged house. María Valdés was touched to see the brothers praying together frequently; as also the kindly efforts of the priest to distract and amuse his juniors. But she did not look with favor upon the penitents who began to present themselves at her door, wishing to make their confessions to her new lodger. "This displeased me because it seemed a very dangerous procedure for a priest who was being sought by the police; and I told him so. But he replied that his visitors had taken all the needful precautions and that, for himself, he feared nothing." [12] The señora said no more, although her fears had not been illogical. Two of the penitents attended by Padre Pro that first day were Josefina Montes de Oca and her son, José! Wednesday, however, passed tranquilly enough.

It was during Mass on Thursday morning (November 17) that the Señora Valdés had a rare experience: "At the moment of the Elevation, I saw [Padre Miguel] seemingly transformed into a white silhouette and plainly raised above the level of the floor. I became aware of great happiness. Later, my servants told me spontaneously that they had observed the same phenomenon; and, simultaneously, had experienced an exceptional consolation." [13]

In the evening, after blessing the marriage of a young couple, Padre Pro had a few words with the Señora Valdés: "My brothers will leave for the United States tomorrow; and on the nineteenth I shall be going along to resume my business of souls." At this moment, however, his fate was already settled, which is

[12] Quoted by Dragón, *ibid.,* p. 324.
[13] Quoted, *ibid.,* p. 325.

to say that the prayer Miguel Pro had put in writing on the previous Sunday, that fatal thirteenth day of November, 1927, had been answered.

"I.H.S.," he wrote, addressing Our Lady, "Let me spend my life at your side, my Mother, the companion of your bitter solitude and your profound pain. Let my soul feel your eyes' sad weeping and the abandonment of your heart.

"I do not wish in the road of my life to savor the happinesses of Bethlehem, adoring the Child Jesus in your virginal arms. I do not wish to enjoy the amiable presence of Jesus Christ in the humble little house of Nazareth. I do not care to accompany you on your glorious Assumption to the angels' choir.

"For my life, I covet the jeers and mockery of Calvary; the slow agony of your Son, the depreciation, the ignominy, the infamy of His Cross. I wish to stand at your side, Most Sorrowful Virgin, strengthening my spirit with your tears, consummating my sacrifice with your martyrdom, sustaining my heart with your solitude, loving my God and your God with the immolation of my being."

Oh, yes, his prayer would be conceded—in its totality!

With the first dark on Thursday, the police had commenced to surround Londres 22; were probably in their stations, many of them, before the departure of the young newlyweds. For some inexplicable reason no move upon the house was made during a long evening. At 1 A.M. the last members of the unsuspecting household retired. (It would be interesting to ascertain why the simple arrest of three young civilians was deemed to warrant such elaborate preparation as a nine-hour vigil on a chilly November night by a large squad of soldiers.)

At 3 A.M. the barking of a dog, followed by suspicious noises from the roof, awakened María Valdés and her three servants. The kindhearted landlady described the events of this unforgettable night: "Hearing a discreet call at the door of one of the interior apartments and thinking it might be a nocturnal visitor to see the padre, I went to the window.[14] What I saw with alarm was that there were at least twenty armed soldiers in my patio. Since I knew that the police were pursuing priests who celebrated Masses in private houses, my first thought was to find a means of escape for the padre. I went to his door and knocked, but nobody heard me, so I hurried up to the roof where I found the rifles of four soldiers aimed at me point blank. There were soldiers everywhere, from which I understood that the assault had been especially well prepared. I took it for a miracle that I wasn't killed up there on the roof because, afterward, the soldiers told me their orders were to shoot on sight anyone who put in an appearance there. . . .

"When I got back downstairs, still other soldiers were demolishing one of the doors with their rifle butts; and by the time I had dressed ten or twelve, with drawn revolvers, were already inside the room occupied by the padre and his brothers." [15]

How had they managed to sleep so soundly, right through to the moment of that brusque command, "Don't move, anyone!"? Because they were God-trusting, clean-living youths, healthily exhausted by their arduous labors—all in the interests of others? And didn't the prevaricating Quintana, the cynical Basaíl know them for what they were, the valiant and dedicated flower of the nation's young manhood? If so, we may be sure that the Quintanas and the Basaíls, who lived by terror, experienced their own moments of fear. Swaggering about the capital in pursuit of priests and nuns, defenseless widows and girls, slight youths and the helpless children who could so easily be beaten into talking, they could not *always* forget the fact of their brotherhood with all these victims—in Baptism.

"Repent your sins as if in the very presence of God," were the next words María Valdés heard in that crowded sleeping room, and they were, of course, addressed to his brothers by the perfectly composed Father Miguel. And then deliberately raising

---

[14] This would be a window giving upon the patio and thus upon what she termed "an interior apartment."

[15] Quoted, *ibid.,* pp. 326–27.

his voice, he pronounced the sacramental absolution upon them. This concluded, he lowered it again, "From here on, we're offering our lives for the cause of Religion in México. Let us all three do it together that God may accept our sacrifice."

Inspector Basaíl was admonishing the Señora Valdés: "Did you know that you were harboring the dynamiters in your house?"

"What I *know*," came the flat reply, "is that I've been hiding a saint."

Father Miguel intervened, "This lady is innocent. Leave her in peace, and do with us whatever you wish." And then he turned to the Samaritan who had served him so well. "As they are going to kill me, I am leaving my sacerdotal ornaments to you."

"Oh, nothing of the sort," jeered Basaíl. *"You've* nothing to fear at the Inspección!"

Ignoring this baiting, the priest crossed over to the cabinet from which he took nothing but a small crucifix. He kissed it and slipped it into his pocket. Now he was ready, and nodded to his waiting brothers.

"Aren't you going to bring your overcoat?" asked Basaíl. "It's cold tonight."

"I gave it to the poor."

María Valdés slipped out of the room ahead of them, and before they had reached the door below she rejoined them with a serape which she pressed upon the padre. Grief-shaken, she and her maids dropped to their knees before him, whereupon he gave them his blessing. No other utterance broke the sounds of the absurdly numerous escort's shuffling feet and the sobs of the women until, just outside the street entrance, Father Miguel turned to cast one final glance back upon this, his last earthly shelter. Then, drawing a deep breath, he startled them all by calling in the loud, clear tones which must have suggested the Avenging Angel himself, *"Viva Dios, Viva la Virgen de Guadalupe!"* [16]

[16] All dialogue in this chapter follows the relation of María Valdés, as quoted by Father Dragón, *ibid.*, pp. 324–28.

XXII

"VIVA CRISTO REY!"—THE
SHOT THAT ROCKED A NATION

BASAÍL, writes Father Dragón, had a flair for "refinements of cruelty which he disguised under a cloak of condescension." From the record, it seems sure that some such unhealthy complex largely inspired his whimsicality in now detouring his star prisoner, Padre Pro, by the Montes de Oca home to permit him "to embrace his sister for the last time" en route to the police station.

Or perhaps he anticipated seeing or hearing something of further interest to the case. If so, he was disappointed. It was only the prisoner who learned anything new. His good friend Josefina Montes de Oca had been in jail since the previous evening. Deeply concerned for Ana María, who would now be alone in her suffering for them all, Father Miguel improved a moment when Basaíl was out of hearing (!) to telephone the García Belaunzarán family. To the excited lady who answered his ring, also Ana María by name, he spoke quietly, "Do me the favor to come to the Señora Montes de Oca's to be with my sister. My brothers and I are just leaving."

"Wait for me a bit. I'm coming right over to see you!"

"No, *hija*," he replied hastily, ". . . not until Heaven"—and hung up the receiver. It was exactly five o'clock; and this his last act in relative liberty.

After the preliminary questioning of the three brothers at the police station, Basaíl took them to view the battered old Essex.

"Just look at the result of your handiwork!" he exclaimed self-righteously; to which Humberto replied: "We had nothing whatever to do with this affair."

Padre Miguel merely smiled. His characteristic humor was all that was discernible in his face or manner. And he was already making friends with the guards.

Soon enough they made their acquaintance with the dark cellars beneath the police station where Humberto was thrust into a cell already occupied by Josefina Montes de Oca. The priest and Roberto were assigned to that marked: No. 1 (which their tenancy was so to distinguish that its subsequent "guests" would count it an honor to be granted confinement in these famous quarters). Actually, No. 1 was an appalling place, a damp, dark alley ($4\frac{1}{2} \times 9$ feet), entirely unventilated and permeated by a most obnoxious miasmic stench. At this season, too, the cold was disagreeable, penetrating and, in the absence of adequate clothing, dangerous.

The inhabitants of the dungeons of the police station were by no means indulged at the public expense. They were provided with neither cots nor food. They managed their sleeping however they might. Their meals must be brought in by families or friends. The Señora García prepared the Pros' food which Ana María carried to the prison. She was not permitted to see her brothers, however. Before the meals were eaten the various dishes had been reduced to unappetizing shreds, the hot liquids chilled by straining, in the routine search for concealed messages.

Otherwise, however, Father Miguel and his brothers seem to have been accorded reasonable deference. They were not beaten nor tortured, which had been the lot of the unfortunate Tirado —now so ill that Padre Pro immediately sent him María Valdés' serape. The brothers also divided their food with the other prisoners who lacked sufficient provision.

To occupy their time they prayed and sang, these young men

who had prayed and sung all their lives. Padre Miguel began with morning prayers. Then he and Roberto said their rosary. With the arrival of others to crowd their cell, this program was shared by all. After prayers came songs which filled the grim cellars with the incongruous resonance of cheer—first the religious hymns and then the countless popular ditties so long stored away in Miguel's retentive memory. All this devotion and merriment, as well as the bounding exercises in which they engaged in an effort to keep from freezing, must have mystified the guards, hardened to the sorrow and suffering which had always ruled this fetid cavern. Every so often some of these guards would conduct the Pros into the presence of the almost amusingly pompous officials, but the inquisitions came to nothing. The brothers were innocent of the slightest knowledge of the bombing; said so repeatedly; and were ordered back to the dungeons by their disgusted captors. Whereupon it would start all over—the praying, singing, the games of leapfrog. They had soon added a new activity to this routine, the decoration of the walls of No. 1 with their fondest sentiments. In huge letterings they printed triumphantly: "VIVA CRISTO REY!"—"VIVA LA VIRGEN DE GUADALUPE!" What could you do with such people —that is, short of shooting them?

It was now known, via the grapevine, that Luis Segura Vilchis, of his own volition, had calmly, dignifiedly confessed to having been author and director of the plot against Álvaro Obregón. This left only one occupant of the Essex unaccounted for. Then what was wanted of *three* Pros? For that matter, in view of the many witnesses who could swear to their whereabouts on the afternoon of the assault, on what theory were any of them held? It was decidedly a bad sign that no witnesses were being called, nor even heard when they came forward spontaneously to testify. (But it was also somewhat amusing that, although lying right on Mazcorro's desk, Roberto's photograph attached to the "Daniel García" registration had not been recognized by the man reputed to be México's shrewdest investigator.)

The *Acta*[1] was opened on November 19 with the testimony of General Obregón, Jaime, Orcí, Bay, Otero; immediately followed by that of Tirado and Luis Segura Vilchis. We already know the substance of the first five statements. Now, Tirado (in a really pitiable physical condition) talked—for the first time. He acknowledged his presence in the Essex, but denied having known anything of the plot prior to starting out with his friend Ruíz and two others (Segura and a total stranger, but the actual driver of the car) for what he believed was no more than a Sunday outing. (It is obvious that this was not the full truth, but Tirado knew that Segura had already assumed responsibility for the plot; and, of course, that Ruíz was in his death agony. He wished to save himself, if possible, and, although his efforts to this end show him to have been a weaker character than the heroic Segura, he had, until Segura's confession, withstood torture without informing on anyone.)

Luis Segura now amplified his earlier admissions, testifying: ". . . that he was twenty-four years of age, a topographical engineer, native of Piedras Negras, Coahuila . . . ; that it was he who had prepared and planned the attempted dynamiting of which General Obregón was victim on Sunday, November 13; that three other persons had been involved in the scheme, two of whom had been detained by the police and one of whom was still a fugitive; that the prisoner who calls himself Antonino or Juan Tirado, but who had been known to the declarant as José or Juan Gómez, was a party to the assault, though declarant doesn't know whether or not [Tirado] actually threw one of the bombs; that Nahum Lamberto Ruíz also participated in the attack; declarant cannot say exactly how long he has been acquainted with [Ruíz], but probably about six months; that Nahum Lamberto Ruíz had knowledge of the planned assault upon the person of General Obregón and had committed himself to participate in it the Thursday previous to the said occur-

---

[1] This consisted merely of the preliminary sworn statements for the police complaint and was not a court action.

rence; that declarant had spoken of it to Juan Gómez, or Tirado, on Sunday morning, whereupon [the latter] also agreed to take part in the attack; that it was he [Segura] who had constructed the four bombs which were [to be] employed against General Obregón's automobile, only three of which were thrown, and said bombs were constructed in the house numbered 44A in Alzate Street in this city, but that he refuses to name the person who assisted him in this labor; that he personally purchased the materials and ingredients for the fabrication of the bombs; that the formula employed for their manufacture is an origination of the declarant; that apart from the persons who participated in the attack, no one else knew of the project until the deed had become public knowledge; that the Alzate Street house had been rented by Señor Humberto Pro whom declarant requested to secure such space; that he never knew Señora Montes de Oca and nothing of Señor Humberto Pro's understanding with her on the matter of the house in question; that the Essex car which had served for the attack and which, during the immediately preceding days, was garaged at the said house, was the property of the declarant who had bought it from Señor José González; that this José González, whose address declarant does not know and whose description he refuses to give, was the person who drove the Essex at the time of the assault; that he was unaware [at the time of purchase] that the Essex had been the property of Humberto Pro, since he had paid José González for it or, better said, had commissioned González to buy it; that previous to the assault there had been no meetings [of the conspirators]; [but] that on the Thursday before the attack declarant had individually committed himself with Ruíz and with González to make it, and, on Sunday, with Tirado; that the motives for it were political; that the seven thousand Mauser cartridges found by the police at 38 Jesús María Street were declarant's property; that he refuses to say for what these cartridges were destined; that the money for their purchase had been supplied by several persons, among them Señor Jorge Téllez Pizarro Suárez; that he had shipped cartridges outside México,[2] but refuses to say to whom; that Téllez Pizarro had forwarded money from the city of Guadalajara. . . ."[3]

Segura's statement closes with an account of his movements on November 13, when he had found it impossible to stage the attack at the railway station in accordance with the original plan, owing to the crowd there; the eventual assault in Chapultepec; the pursuit of the Essex by Jaime and Otero; and his own escape. He had managed to catch a streetcar on the corner of the Calzada de Chapultepec where Ruíz and Tirado were captured and had then, like his victim, proceeded to attend the bullfights. Segura's closing lines in the *Acta* read: ". . . that the declarant assumes all the responsibility, moral and material, as author of the dynamite attack; and has nothing more to declare."[4]

From this it will be obvious to all that Luis Segura Vilchis was an intrepid and forthright young man. It also proves that he had dedicated his life to the Cristero counter-revolution, convinced that only violence would serve to eradicate the violent men who were tyrannizing over his country. He had come to México City a year earlier, already obsessed by his intention of eliminating Álvaro Obregón whom he believed bound to continue Calles' persecution of the Mexican faithful. He had failed in his mission, but held no regrets that it would cost him his life.

The melodrama's "man of mystery," so-called José González—whose address no one knew and whose description no one would give—was, unquestionably, an important Cristero chief. It is likely that he still lives. One of Padre Pro's biographers, who repeatedly refers to this figure as "El *Prófugo*—the Fugitive," comments that "as he ran from the scene of the Essex' collision, he is still running." The Pros may well have possessed certain information about the Cristero organization and activities, but their own labors were of a very different order from any procedure involving Mausers and dynamite bombs.

[2] Outside México City.
[3] *Acta de Inspección,* photostat reproduction in *Novedades,* November 18 and 19, 1952.
[4] *Ibid.*

Whether the statements of Humberto and Father Miguel, which immediately followed Segura Vilchis', were taken the same day or the next morning, we cannot say, since they are not dated. At eight o'clock on the morning of November 20 Nahum Lamberto Ruíz died in the Juárez Hospital. It is significant that this occurrence definitely preceded the testimony of Quintana and Basaíl, who were now able to attribute to a dead man whatever they wished to place in the record. Moreover, they were the sole witnesses, with the exception of Obregón himself, who had access to the statements of the others.

Humberto testified that he had received his first information of the attack from the columns of the *Universal Gráfico* during the evening of November 13; that he recognized from its description that the Essex used by the assailants had been, until recently, his property. This fact caused himself and his brothers to hide from the police. He affirmed the sale of the car to José González and mentioned that he had thereafter seen it in the possession of Segura Vilchis. It was true that he had been acquainted with the latter for more than a year, but they had never been intimate friends or closely associated, owing to the divergence of their activities. Ruíz he had known only through the coincidence of having, at one time, carried foodstuffs to a building occupied by a group of needy persons which included Ruíz. He admitted his dedication to the propaganda work of the Religious Defense League, but denied ever having participated in any acts or plans of armed resistance. In soliciting the co-operation of the Señora Montes de Oca in the matter of the Alzate house, he had intended merely to secure shelter for the Hernández sisters who were without resources. Later, he had introduced Segura to the young women in complete ignorance of the latter's reason for wishing space in the house, knowing that the Hernández were anxious to establish a *pensión*. And Humberto meticulously accounted for his movements throughout the day of the attack.[5]

Father Miguel immediately identified himself as a *sacerdote;*

[5] *Ibid., Novedades,* November 23 and 24, 1952.

and then explained a letter which had been found in the room at Londres 22, directed to "Señor Cocol"—his childhood nickname—and signed "José." The writer was José Murillo, a chauffeur, to whom the priest had advanced seventy pesos with which to leave México City. The man had been alarmed to learn that the Essex had been implicated in a bombing, because, while it was in the possession of Humberto, he had been seen driving it on many occasions. He did not wish to be unjustly involved; and Padre Pro had agreed that it would be best for him to return to his home in Guadalajara. The priest could not recall having ridden in the car ever, but if he had, it was only briefly. He knew the Señora Montes de Oca as a very charitable person who gave generously to the poor. He did not know Ruíz. He had once met Luis Segura Vilchis simply by happenstance upon the occasion of a baptism administered by himself. Padre Pro also gave the reason for their hiding at Londres 22. And that was all.[6]

(It is noteworthy that he was not even questioned about participation in, or knowledge of, the Obregón attack.)

On November 20, Josefina Montes de Oca, one of the Hernández sisters, Inspectors Quintana and Basaíl and assorted policemen testified, but added nothing new. Not the remotest accusation was made against Miguel Pro. Nothing involved any of his family save the unsupported allegations of Quintana and Basaíl that Ruíz had made reference to Humberto being at the Alzate house, and that, among others, the Pros "should be warned." Now, too, Basaíl claimed credit for being the one who had induced Ruíz to "talk"! The *Acta,* which now would seem to have been closed this same day with the signature of General Roberto Cruz (Calles' Chief of Staff) before whom it was taken, was far from complete; actually, Cruz had stipulated November 22 for its continuance.

Back to the dungeons went Tirado and Segura, their fates already sealed—and the brothers Pro. What did this mean? Was

[6] *Ibid.,* November 24, 1952.

General Cruz going to consign their case to the courts for trial? Inasmuch as they had not been released, this was the only logical conclusion.

Father Miguel and Roberto now had company in No. 1. A Chinaman and one Antonio Mutiozábal, another victim of the general religious persecution, joined them. Señor Mutiozábal was to say later of his meeting with Padre Pro: "Upon hearing my name, he came up to me and asked if I happened to be related to Dolores Mutiozábal, and when I told him she was my sister, he said he knew her, that he was Padre Miguel Agustín Pro; and he presented me to his brother, Roberto.

"I had never seen him before, but I had heard him spoken of frequently. In the two days that we were together in the prison I saw him praying for long periods and several times daily, by himself; and during the nights we all prayed the rosary together and also sang together the march of St. Ignatius. He repeatedly counseled his brother and me, telling us that we were very dear to him and that, when we should leave the prison, we must dedicate ourselves with the greatest efforts to the Catholic cause. He also inculcated the thought that we must always practice the virtues with pleasure and gaiety.

"The dungeon was narrow, dark, and unventilated. In spite of all this, Padre Pro demonstrated patience, resignation, contentment, and even joy. He told us that we should be happy to be suffering something for Jesus Christ, that if worse evils, or even the firing squad, lay ahead for us, we ought to be proud to suffer and die for Christ. I heard him express his own wish to die for Christ.

"Padre Pro appeared to me to be an exceedingly virtuous priest, a saint who made virtue agreeable. In his simplicity he was like a child, and he played with us in the manner of a schoolboy. . . .

"Once, joking, he told me that one day when we would chance to meet on the street we would give one another the *abrazo* [embrace] in liberty, and that I would then have to prepare a barbecue at my ranch to celebrate that liberty.

"The last night he slept on the bare floor because he had loaned me his little mattress."[7]

General Cruz did not like the Pro aspect of this case, and he decidedly wanted no part of pursuing it. He was convinced of Segura's truthfulness. That young fanatic, as well as his weak-kneed fellow conspirator, Tirado, would be executed without more ado. Nahum Ruíz' death had saved one round of ammunition; and the fourth assailant might well be apprehended at any time.

So why the panic about the Pros? These stubborn young psalm-singers were annoying, yes, with their scurryings about the capital in the interests of a lost cause—the Holy Roman Catholic Church—but it was absurd to try to implicate them in attempted murder. One had but to look at them. More important, there was no evidence against them. Besides this, they were three popular heroes. That much had emerged from the inundation of messages, protests, and offers of evidence in support of their alibis which were pouring into his office and getting harder to discourage by the hour. Even the browbeaten Mexican press seemed to be for the Pros. No, Roberto Cruz just did not fancy himself in the role of martyr-maker in any such touchy circumstances.

The thing for him to do was to get out from under the whole worrisome business by consigning the Pros to the courts. Such an action would, of course, be tantamount to releasing them. Judges, too, no matter how venal, had their own sensibilities to public opinion, and no amount of "persuasion" was likely to be effective in the lack of a better case against the Pros. *Caramba!* there simply wasn't any case at all! But as far as he was concerned they were welcome to their acquittal. The trouble with that lay elsewhere. Plutarco Calles had caught himself another priest, or at least a pair of thick-headed coppers had turned themselves inside out to catch one for him. It was only too well known what priest-hunting meant to the *Jefe*. What a thor-

[7] Quoted by Dragón, pp. 332-33.

oughly stupid case this had been: amateur assassins, angel-faced choir singers—and a phobia-ridden sadist demanding the kill.

Perhaps it was more prudent to confine oneself to worrying about what was going on in Obregón's head. But who ever knew *that?* He had been very attentive during the first few days of the investigation, pored over every scrap of evidence. Perhaps he had figured the bombing might have been dreamed up by some realistic political competition like, say, the Leftist Labor crowd, Calles' latest favorites. But as it became clear that this fracas had been sparked by nothing more interesting than a little group of Catholic fumblers, Obregón had permitted himself to relax. He probably felt he could afford to let nature— especially Plutarco's nature—take its course. The two-time presidential winner had always been the smarter of the pair. He, the victim, would just be big and good-natured about the whole thing, prove himself above revenge. And why not, since he knew so well that Calles' fanaticism would suffice for them both? Cruz was forced to recognize that Obregón would not bother to interfere in a situation which stood to lose him nothing personally.

Roberto Cruz' fears were realized. Calles was not to be deprived of his preferred quarry by an ordinary trial procedure. This is to say that he was himself convinced of the Pros' innocence for, had there been the slightest evidence upon which a judge might have convicted, turning them over to the courts would have been both the easier and shrewder move. His enormous power over the military could also do miracles in the judiciary; [8] but what judge could risk a finding that the public would instantly recognize as dictated murder? Meanwhile, all Inspección records and processes were secret. Thus, on November 21 an irritated Cruz telephoned his attorney, Guerra Leal, to say: "Do you know what's happened now? The President's ordered me to shoot the prisoners! I told him the *Acta* hasn't been completed, nor the process prepared . . . nothing what-

[8] There was, and is, no trial by jury in Mexican courts.

ever validated. I tell you I'm going to get out of this deal, or at least send them over to the garrison so that the executions will have to be at the Target School."

Since Cruz saw his own ruin in defying his master, he attempted to soften the news for a clamorous public by easy stages. The same day the press carried his warily vague statement: "The members of the Religious Defense League are responsible for the attack on General Obregón; especially Humberto Pro and the Señora Montes de Oca in the matter of the house where the bombs were discovered." The newsmen, mystified by so many indirections, but alerted now for practically anything, kept pestering the distracted Cruz. Finally, he agreed to grant their first —and only—interview with the prisoners, but he accompanied them down to the dungeons.

The *Excelsior's* "discreet" version of the meeting with Padre Pro (November 22nd):

" 'Are you a priest?' we asked him.

" '*Sí, Señor,* a priest and a Jesuit.'

" 'Do you care to make a statement?'

" 'There is no statement I wish to make save to say that I am grateful for the courtesy extended to me by those persons by whom I was apprehended. I am absolutely outside of this affair since I am a person of order. I am completely tranquil and await the enlightenment of justice. I deny positively having taken any part in the plot.' "

However, Comandante Masuski (in *Magazine de Policía,* July 7, 1942) gave another version of this incident. Citing the names of Leopold Toquero and Carlos Villenave as witnesses to this scene, the Comandante said that Padre Pro's opening words to the reporters were: "Señores, I swear before God that I am innocent of what they accuse me. I had no participation in any of it, and I was . . ."

At this point he was determinedly shut off by General Cruz with: "That's enough! Retire at once!"

According to the same witness, Humberto Pro also affirmed his innocence on this occasion.

An identical description of the scene and quotation of Padre Pro's only words permitted utterance before the representatives of the public were also published by Armando Araujo in *Ultimas Noticias* on August 13, 1942. Araujo cited the presence of Toquero, Villenave, José Pérez Moreno, and other newsmen of the capital. In a dictatorship, the press, too, is cautious.

That afternoon Calles and Obregón met with Cruz to make a hasty decision.

Calles to Cruz: "It's necessary to make an example of this rabble."

Cruz to Calles: "But best to give the sentence an appearance of legality."

Calles to Cruz: "I don't care for forms—I want only the deed."

Cruz to Calles: "Wouldn't it be best to assign the accused to the courts?"

Calles to Cruz: "I have given my order. Your only course is to obey. And you will make me a report *in person* when you have complied with it."

Cruz to Calles: "Then what shall we do with the *Acta de la Inspección?*"

Obregón to Cruz: "To hell with the *Acta!*"

Apparently there was nothing left for Cruz but obedience. Both powers had spoken their final words on this sorry subject.

Cruz to the reporters: "Each and every one of the prisoners has been convicted by innumerable proofs, and they have, furthermore, confessed to their complicity in the attack. All was prepared, primarily, by seven persons, Segura, Tirado, the priest Pro, his brother Humberto, Nahum Ruíz, and two others, in the house at No. 1 Madero Street in Tacuba. Humberto Pro drove the car, Segura and Ruíz each threw a bomb, and Tirado didn't manage to throw his." [9]

"Everything was proved," *but,* at seven-thirty in the evening Father Miguel was called to make another declaration. When he returned to the dungeon, he told Roberto, "Now I believe our testimony is finished. I understand that they're going to turn

[9] Above dialogue quoted by Dragón, pp. 342 and 382.

everything over to a competent tribunal to which we are to be consigned. God grant that it be so!"

At this exact moment Cruz was telling Licenciado Guerra Leal that Calles had ordered him to shoot the prisoners the following morning and *in* the police station. He had been charged to make it a "big show," to invite representations from all the government secretariats, the national and foreign press, the photographers. These "social aspects," or publicity angles, of the affair, were dispatched during the early evening hours. In the barroom, La Opera, Congressman Alfredo Romo extended invitations right and left. An attorney named Becerra, who was the editor of a legal review, invited others. The diplomatic corps was not overlooked.[10]

Nevertheless, at 10 P.M. Licenciado Guerra Leal was apprising the reporters that, inasmuch as the *Acta* was now complete, tomorrow the prisoners would be consigned to the judicial branch.[11] Why this? Was it wishful thinking—or a last-ditch try to exculpate his friend, Roberto Cruz?

As the evening wore on Father Miguel, who had been enjoying increased confidence and encouraging Roberto, was disturbed to see that the guard had been doubled. However, he made no comment. It was the hour for Roberto and himself to pray the rosary.

Shortly after midnight General Cruz appeared in the dungeons in the company of General Palomera López, several other of the military, and a battery of photographers. One by one Padre Pro, Humberto, Tirado, Vilchis, and Roberto were called from their cells to be photographed. And now, recognizing Palomera López, the priest who had prayed that he might die for Christ believed his prayer had been answered. For López was the "amoral and sanguinary" character commonly dubbed "the assassin of the Catholics."[12] When the photographers were through, General Cruz ordered that the prisoners should be allowed to speak to no one. As they could receive visitors at no

[10] *Ibid.*, p. 343.
[11] Duly reported the following day, *after* the event.
[12] Dragón, p. 343.

time, this meant they were prohibited speech among themselves, or with the guards.

But Father Miguel spoke to his youngest brother and god-child. "Now yes, the thing has become difficult. Who knows what these señores want to do? It can't be anything good! Let us ask God for the resignation to accept whatever is coming."

This was when, giving his "little mattress" to their cellmate, Mutiozábal, Miguel Agustín Pro lay down upon the bare floor of dungeon No. 1 to pass his final night on earth. . . .

He started up out of an uneasy half-sleep at six o'clock, aware of an excruciating headache. He thrust, rather than lifted, his stiffened torso above the moisture-seeped floor and, leaning against the wall, fumbled through his pockets for a *cafiaspirina.* In the gloom he could just make out the thicker spot which gradually settled into the outline of his brother's figure. Peering intently, he saw that Roberto was wide awake. He swallowed the pill which, as it scraped down his dry throat, felt grimy—like everything else, and said: "I don't know why I have a pre-sentiment that something's going to happen to us today. But don't worry. We'll ask God for His grace and He will grant it to us."

Ana María had been prevented from carrying their food to the prison that morning. When the two little maids whom she had dispatched with it returned at eight-thirty, they were con-siderably excited. There was a big commotion at the police station, they reported. The place was all overrun by a *"muche-dumbre"* of soldiers. They'd hardly been able to find anyone willing to receive the breakfast for the Señorita's *hermanitos!*

Ana María froze in her tracks, but as she recognized this au-tomatic paralysis for what it was, she set her strength against it —and the vise began to loosen. Fear was a luxury denied the Pros. Besides, there was no time for it. She must hurry. "I must hurry to them!" she breathed.

Her own words, so surprisingly unemotional and uncolorful for a *Mexicana,* by that very fact reveal the profundity of the concern which drove her through morning-fresh, new-washed streets which she did not see. "Alarmed by this information, I went immediately to [the police station]. But there was a dense crowd of people of all types; and the troops of soldiers about the door wouldn't let me enter, although I could see that the guards were passing through a large number of *militares,* who were all dressed in gala uniform, government and newspaper people and photographers. Inspectors Basaíl and Quintana arrived and I asked them what was happening, but they told me they knew nothing. 'I want to see my brothers,' I said. They promised to get me the permission; but they didn't come back."

Not an easy scene to contemplate, this: the now thoroughly aroused, anxious-eyed young woman contending with a milling, sensation-seeking mob to hold her ground near the entrance— just in case one of the detectives should have told the truth. At times the pressure of the throng would sweep her yards from that grim, yawning, but forbidden portal (especially when the soldiers flattened hard rifle lengths against it, clearing a passage from the blasting motors at curbside for those personages rating a welcome). But she would fight her way back again, step by step, straining also against that other suffocating pressure, the dread of what it all portended for her brothers.

What evil thing were they doing to her beloved brothers that they had to hide it behind lines of uniforms—to Miguel, that valiant, tender man of God, sower of the joy and gaiety with which their ever-poorer shelters always abounded? What ghastly extremity was he facing, together with their bright-eyed "little brothers" whom she alone had given a woman's loving, daily care since their loss of Josefa those few, but such long, years ago? They had been a big, vital family, carefree and comfortable. Was it now to be only Edmundo, herself and, for a little while, the prematurely bowed old father? Poor, poor man, to have lived to see all his children falling away from him one by one!

What did all these people *think* was happening? Tensely, she began to listen.

". . . I heard my brothers referred to as 'the dynamiters' who, according to some, were about to be sent to the *Islas Marías;* according to others, to the Target School.

" 'Why this last?' I asked, and someone answered:

" 'To be shot!'

"I saw the four Cruz Verde ambulances drive up. . . ."

Yes, it was a terrible scene, fraught, not only with desperation, but with the suspense that is so much more unsupportable than consummated tragedy can be. But Ana María, being a Pro, did not panic. Whatever this was—almost had to be—that she was barred from sharing with her brothers, she would stay right here, as close to the doors as the agitated throng would permit, while imploring God to hold her as bravely upright as He was, in all certainty, holding her beloved Miguel—Humberto—Roberto. . . .

It was ten o'clock on the dot when Security Chief Mazcorro presented himself in the dungeons to call loudly: "Miguel Agustín Pro!"

The sweater-clad prisoner arose and turned to contemplate the approach of "authority."

"Put on your jacket."

As his brother helped him with his jacket, the priest asked mildly, "May I know where we are going?"

No reply.

So he squeezed Roberto's hand encouragingly and, without another word, made his exit from the heavy air of No. 1, the dungeon which his presence and his sufferings had glorified forever.

Ana María saw the ponderous double doors swing shut at exactly ten o'clock. Did she see the man who was so heatedly demanding admittance—waving a thick white paper in the soldiers' faces just before the heavy bracing bars thudded into place on the inner side of the doors? Did she comprehend the clamor now being raised by those nearest the doors and the police station's iron-grated windows? If so, she understood in bitter sorrow (since this was a fruitless effort) that the man bore an *amparo*—a restraining order—against the execution of the brothers Pro Juárez; that some good soul (Licenciado Luis MacGregor) had worked a miracle in prevailing upon a daring judge (Julio López Masse) to affix his signature, on behalf of her brothers, to the most powerful instrument in Mexican jurisprudence. No one, not even Plutarco Calles, could "laugh off" the majesty and the magic of México's *amparo!*

Here it was, a force far stronger than any mere "stay of execution," a force to protect any party or parties it names, not only from death and persecution, but even from incarceration and exile, until his (or their) case is duly tried and judgment rendered. Here it was, indeed, bearing the names of the Pros and being presented in ample time to rescue them from these highly suspect proceedings. Well no, not really presented, for it could not be applied out here in the street. And there was no breaking through that line of little Indian *"sí mi jefes,"* the guards who had soon banged the doors against the bearer of this document and his annoying cries of *"amparo."* They had their orders and were taking no chances! [13]

Luis Segura Vilchis had confessed, assumed full responsibility as conceiver of the plot, fabricator of the bombs, and director of the attack upon Álvaro Obregón in which Juan Tirado had been his willing, if ineffectual, accomplice. Humberto Pro, though innocently, had been indirectly useful in helping secure the room where the bombs were made. But it was Padre Miguel, unaccused by any witness, who had not even been questioned on participation in the plot, who was to receive the firing squad's first attentions. The reason? The same that had sparked and impelled the whole crime against the Pros—Calles' implacable

---

[13] *Excelsior* (November 24, 1927) dutifully reported that the *amparo* arrived too late for application, but Gonzalo Chapela in *a.b.c.* (August 9, 1952) affirms there would have been an ample margin had not the execution been "mysteriously" advanced thirty minutes ahead of the schedule designated in the "invitations." (Note: It would be interesting to learn the eventual cost to Judge López of his heroic, but futile, gesture. Or did Calles prefer to ignore the entire affair?)

hatred of the symbol—any Roman Catholic priest. His hood-lums well knew who held center stage in this spectacle. The entrances of Segura and Tirado could be held up a few minutes. After all, there was no restraining order bearing *their* names at the door of the police station!

The prison yard was jammed. There, with his entire staff, stood General Roberto Cruz, chin jutting aggressively below the impassive face of the typical *mestizo militar*. But in his opaque dark eyes there flickered a shifting pin point of unease; and the fingers holding the cigarette in the classic pose of nonchalance were not quite achieving the triumph of holding it entirely still.

There were reporters, photographers, and more distinguished guests grouped in tight, self-conscious little knots everywhere about the courtyard before the padre's blinking, dark-conditioned eyes. Although no one had told him whither he was bound, to what he was sentenced, nor even that he *had* been sentenced,[14] he knew at once what it all meant: that the bullets of injustice and savagery compounded were, in moments now, going to blast the spirit from the body which, together, had, for thirty-six years, ten months, and ten days, been Miguel Agustín Pro Juárez.

However, his recognition of these facts had already become unimportant to him. As he walked across the compound with a measured, unfaltering tread, the eyes of his body fixed upon the ground modestly veiled the brilliance of the vision beheld by the eyes of his soul. For that brief walk toward the repulsive horror of the targets (marked off in the life-size outlines of the human form upon the shot-splattered wall) was in itself *nothing,* merely a symbol in time of his long trudge upward to the threshold of the Glory that was outside all time!

The little crucifix was clasped firmly in his right hand; in his left, the rosary which was never separated from his person. He could feel them glowing against the flesh of his palms and fingers.

A shadowy figure was drifting in to him on an oblique angle.

[14] In the lack of a formal charge, a legal trial or hearing of any nature.

The figure seemed to be a man. It spoke, and became Valentín Quintana, the Inspector, the pursuer. "Padre, I ask your pardon for my part in this."

Ironical? Not so! Rather, pathetic, with the pathos inherent in all human failures. "You have not only my pardon, but my gratitude. I give you thanks."

The shadow that, for a joyous instant, had been a man and a policeman, thinned to nothingness, too, the nothingness of the whole surroundings—and the walking was finished. Immediately before his face sprang those crude outlines shaped like men. Oh, yes, the target. But *he* was the target! So he turned about and thought of himself as lined up with them in their mutual nothingness. Together they confronted the mass of mottled dark and light which must be those knots of people he had passed and the spaces where the sun, falling warmly on the ground, separated them.

"Is there anything you wish?" It was Major Torres—just a job, a voice—and a deeply gashed scar across a broad, dark cheek.

"That I may be permitted to pray."

He was on his knees, crossing himself, deliberately, slowly (impressively—though he knew nothing of that). He folded his arms over his chest while the photographers' cameras clicked, but he knew nothing of that either. His lips moved to articulate —one time more—his offering. Would it be accepted? It was such a small thing, merely the life of one poor, imperfect, hard-driven body, that he had to give for Christ . . . for México . . . for all those pitiable, unlovable, but beloved souls clinging together out there where their ignorance, terrors, and despairs were the dark spots in the mottling.

He kissed the humble small crucifix and arose. He shook his head at the proffered blindfold. And then, as from a great distance, he smiled faintly out upon them all, the unaware beneficiaries of this moment of sacrifice—which was finished. But this astonishing serenity at least could not go entirely overlooked.

Its impact upon the fascinated audience had the effect of a blow, compelling the gasp that had lifted into the sun. In which direction were those gleaming rifles really pointed?

It was no more than an instant's impression. After all, who was this rumpled, humble figure anyway but another fugitive priest too stupid to save his skin behind the international line? That's all the big *Jefe* wanted, wasn't it?—for those foolish fellows to get out of his sight? But no, they had to make outlaws of themselves! Naturally, he did not look like an outlaw, standing there against the bullet-chipped wall, his arms now outstretched to form, with his body, the Cross. All these pious fanatics went in for dramatics of this type. So, even if it was just a grim joke to brand them as outlaws, why did they have to be so stubborn, totally refusing to keep up with the times? Why did they waste the best years of a man's life running from a lot of miserable little coppers until, at last, they had beaten a path right into the spot where this one stood, not seeming magnificent any more (in the light of reason), but just a shabby nonentity waiting to die in ignominy.

And then they heard his voice, surprisingly firm and clear (though somehow they'd never expected him to exhibit fear)— but neither was it the voice of triumph. No, there was nothing aggressive in it, just confidence, certainty and, somehow, affection. It uttered only five syllables, but *ay!* they were México's five best-known. Only the manner of delivery was a little different. It would have been less shocking if he had shouted them out—the time-honored, familiar war cry! But he did not. His was just a quiet affirmation.

"*Viva Cristo Rey,*" he assured them kindly.

A sharp explosion launched the small white smoke puffs they had come here to watch rise between themselves and a still form on the ground. And there it was, not crumpled up by the fusillade, but retaining the rigid form of the Cross quite unaffected by the fall. Understandably, this was a thing to start a trembling in the uniform bending above it to deliver the *coup de grâce*.

Someone broke the hush with an hysterical giggle and said,

"It's ten thirty-eight," but scarcely anyone heard him. Their Mexican ears were straining to catch the echo of an old beauty, an old magic known in the blood. Who can learn to ignore the pull of four centuries of priceless glory as long as there remain men like this one to reaffirm it in only five short syllables? But this man was dead! They had been brought here to watch him die. Why? By what right had such a man been *murdered?*

XXIII

A MARTYR'S BLESSING
ON THE THIRTY MILLION

ANA MARÍA heard the explosion. Sharp and decisive, it slashed the stricture of suspense. The suspense had been an unbearable compression, but the severing left her reeling dizzily. Had she been leaning upon this fetter? Before the rocking had stilled, the guns cracked again, spitting instant, ignominious death. At which targets? Segura? At the youth whose unflinching eyes and truthful tongue had claimed, rather than acknowledged, his culpability? . . . At the tormented Tirado—whose equivocation had been so human? Surely. . . . She became aware of the restless, almost impatient, stirring about her, and then of its cause. The minutes that were flashing a kaleidoscope of painful memories before her dread seemed long to the crowd. What had happened? Could it be *possible?*

A *third* volley! This, then, was *it.* Now she was condemned to listen twice again. Now dear, *dear* God, there must be five. Why? *Why?* What had they done besides their duty to Your honor? What had they done save spread consolation among Your poor? Nothing but joyously risk their young lives in Your Name!

Four! Well, they had lost their generous, their magnificent gamble, her three wonderful brothers. And perhaps that was all they had asked. What had *she* asked? What had she expected?

Why was she waiting here half-drowned in this curious, crass multitude? But of course! To hear the fifth volley from those accursed guns. . . .

There was no fifth volley. At first she could not believe it. The third report had assured there must be five. She simply had not heard the last one! An uneasy motion swelled through the crowd and broke in a thrashing wave which nearly threw her to the ground.

"The ambulances," shouted a sergeant kind of voice. "Clear the way there for the ambulances!"

There *must* have been five!

"Hmm. Only four," she heard above the buzzing. "They're leaving the young one for *Las Islas*."

Were they? "Oh, *please*," she prayed, choking. But even so— Miguelito—Humberto . . .

One day she would be able to tell it: "I was right beside the entry. A *diputado*[1] saw me there, lost among all those men. He invited me into his car and we followed the ambulances to the Hospital Juárez. After considerable difficulty they let us in . . . and I saw them, Miguel and Humberto, on the slabs, their bodies still warm. . . . I returned to the police station, where a great disharmony reigned. I found Licenciado Guerra Leal who gave me a written order for the possession of the bodies. . . . Then I went back to the hospital."[2]

She had so longed to stand beside them, be of some use to her brothers in their extremity. Now she was beside them; now there were things to do for them. Edmundo joined her in the hospital morgue where Don Miguel soon found them. The majestic old man had first had the dreadful word from the extras being screamed through the streets, had hastened to the police station where sympathetic clerks directed him to the hospital. Over her weeping Ana María heard a steady old voice demanding: "Where are my sons? I wish to see them!"

He crossed directly to the bodies and bent to kiss the forehead

[1] Deputy, congressman.
[2] Quoted by Dragón, p. 347.

of each. Then, with a worn but snowy handkerchief he wiped their faces clean in an old familiar gesture. This time, when the handkerchief went back into his pocket, it was stained with the blood of martyrs. As he stepped back, his daughter threw herself into his arms, sobbing wildly. In the consolation of his protective embrace she was a child again—a tragedy-exhausted child. Tenderly he drew her aside.

"*Hija mía,* this is no cause for tears!"

Back to the Pánuco house, a safe house now, they carried their beloved, their heroic dead, to find the premises already filled with friends, with the grieving devout, with the countless beneficiaries of the loving sacrifices made for them by the brave young men now snatched from them forever. Already there was no room left in which to receive the swelling numbers surging down upon this humble dwelling. The visitors formed a multitude waiting in the street, and then the adjacent streets, for their opportunities to enter here and pray. The rich came; and the poor. Members of the diplomatic corps mingled with Padre Miguel's heartbroken paupers. The flowers which had commenced to arrive in an avalanche before three o'clock made massive bankings in every existing corner. There was no place left! But they kept coming. . . . The Pánuco house was proving great enough for all the flowers in México and for all the world that afternoon of November 23 in the year of grace, 1927.

Finally: "At ten o'clock when I went to fasten the door to my house," said Don Miguel, "I found five or six of the government police standing there. It was an unpleasant surprise, for I supposed they had come with some new order from their *jefes* for our molestation. But far from that, they humbly begged to be permitted to visit the bodies, and I acceded. Before the coffins they all fell upon their knees and prayed respectfully. When they arose, one of them said to me, 'If there is anything we can do for you, please count on us.' " [3]

General Cruz had promised that sometime during the night Roberto would be conducted to the house to visit his brothers'

[3] *Ibid.,* p. 360.

remains. In order that the grief-stricken youth might receive Communion, a certain priest now secretly bore a consecrated Host into Pánuco Street. But the promise was broken and Roberto was deprived of this double consolation. Nevertheless, the Blessed Sacrament was placed on Padre Pro's coffin, quite openly, there to repose all through the night, as if upon an altar. This reproduced, as noted by all his biographers, "the earliest of Christian scenes: the faithful praying in the catacombs before the sepulchers upon which the Victim of Calvary was offered."

At eleven Father Soto preached a holy hour. Then Father Méndez Medina, supervisor of Miguel's last studies, heard the confessions of fifty mourners. The Rosary was recited until four o'clock the following morning, the time for Padres Méndez Medina and Soto to start the celebration of their successive Masses.

At six the door had to be opened again to a throng of Padre Miguel's beloved workingmen which clamored to enter and honor, before reporting for work, "the laborers' priest" and his brave brother. When the workers had to leave, there was no break in the solid procession of visitors. From every walk of life they came by the thousands. It was imperative to organize a special brigade to handle the crowd and reroute the district traffic. The adjacent streets were choked and impassable long before three o'clock, the hour for the recital of the Office for the Dead. All across the city the hunted, the proscribed Mexican priests were praying the Office in concert.

In Pánuco Street "this didn't seem to be [a manifestation of] mourning, but of jubilation. Sorrow ran silently in the tears, yes, but more than that were they [the tears] of tenderness and devotion.

"All the world had brought crucifixes, rosaries, and other pious symbols, determined to touch them to the bodies of 'the martyrs.' . . . Many, many there were who, upon contemplating the dead faces, crossed themselves as though before a blessed image. Among these was the heroic father of the two confessors of Christ who, in inexpressible Christian valor, knelt between the two cadavers to offer these pure victims to God. To those who [appeared to him] too afflicted by this room's tremendous scene, he said consolingly: 'The padre was an apostle; my Humberto, an angel all his life . . . they died for God and are already enjoying Him in Heaven.' " [4]

The Office had been completed and it was time to proceed to the interment in the Dolores Cemetery. Padre Pro's remains would be sealed in the Jesuits' crypt; Humberto's in a tomb nearby. The problem was how, in such utter confusion, a cortege might be formed. It was quite useless to ask the dispersion of the crowd, and for blocks about the house there seemed not to be space for another human foot. México City had never seen so enormous a turnout for a funeral. But "when it was announced that the coffins were coming out, a spontaneous cry: 'Make way for the martyrs!' was followed by a sudden deep quiet," and, phenomenally, a clear space opened before the door. For a breathless moment the silence held. And then—as the priest's coffin was glimpsed in the portal—an instantaneous, unanimous, thunderous shout went up to reverberate through the thoroughfares and across the roofs of an ancient Christian stronghold: "VIVA CRISTO REY!"

Did they hear this—down there at the Inspección, those little bullies under the uniforms of tyranny?

Did they hear it *again*—those compromised and quibbling "guests" of yesterday's "execution party" whom it had shattered when it had been a compassionate murmur of pardon?

Did he hear it—that two-time President-"elect," Álvaro Obregón? And if so, could he help but understand this cry to their Mexican heavens for what it was: the cancellation of the "luck" which had held for him through so many less meaningful explosions? Did he not feel its doom to any renewal of his power—or even the tomb's chill breath upon his own neck?

Up there behind those stout walls at Chapultepec Castle and

---

[4] From a relation prepared for the Society's Father General by Padre Méndez Medina, S.J., eight days after the Pros' funeral, inedited until December 1, 1952, when it was published in *Lectura*, México, D.F.

those chinkless walls of his egomania—didn't *he* hear it, the defaulting schoolteacher, barman, border-town copper-turned-competitor of the Deity? Did Plutarco Elías Calles hear this historic shout? If not, he would!

"Who could have believed that this was a funeral?" exclaimed Padre Méndez Medina. "It was a combat of flowers, a triumph, an apotheosis, a beatification *sui generis* by popular acclamation. It was the voice of the people which in this case, yes, reproduced the Voice of God, responding to the calumny of tyranny: 'You say that he was a dynamiter, and I tell you that he is God's chosen, favored already with extraordinary signs of power.' Because truly it was humanly inexplicable, this overflowing enthusiasm and holy intrepidity which animated so many thousands of persons drawn from the humblest to the highest classes of Mexican society when, by reason of the reigning terror, nothing but panic and desolation might have been expected at the interment of these, the executed.

"And whereas, on other occasions, the thundering Jupiter's whole apparatus of force had crashed down to impede the most insignificant manifestations of piety, now, in this veridical, most solemn act of public worship, evidenced in prayer, resonant song, in all the ceremonial pomp (a display rendered more aggravating in that it was to the glorification of those who had been branded abominable opposers of the offended tyranny), not a voice was raised in mention of the *'Ley Calles!'* [5]

"With the utmost labor, in view of the impetuosity with which the multitude launched itself in huge human waves simply to touch the hearses, the funeral procession (or triumphal march) was eventually properly organized and started on its way toward the Colina de Dolores. . . . Four interminable lines of automobiles in two double files served to protect the center of the procession which was composed of the thousands who walked, four abreast. Along the entire route the Holy Rosary was prayed with delirious fervor, religious songs being interspersed between the Mysteries. At sight of the hearses the population congregated

[5] The famous and infamous Calles anti-religious law.

at the intersections of the streets crossing the Reforma would drop to its knees and make the sign of the Cross. The trolley-cars and other vehicles circulating the Bosque de Chapultepec emptied themselves of their passengers who joined us to swell the vast concourse. As we approached Dolores, we saw another multitude, perhaps greater than ours, spread out across the extent of the plain. It was awaiting us with palms and floral offerings, and now moved down to meet us at the main highway. This, yes, was the peak of fervor, the inexplicable fervor—mixture of triumph and mourning—which constituted the appropriate note of this sepulture. And now the intonation of the hymns and songs to Cristo Rey flowed from the mesa of Dolores out over the whole Valley, an immense cataract of voices which, in its course, swept round and about the neighboring Alcázar de Chapultepec where President Calles sat nursing his secret rancors. The olympian lord was overcome by consternation, indubitably, to hear this public manifestation of the faith and piety he had so vainly desired to exterminate.

"Upon the descent of the padre's body into the crypt of the Society, a profound silence again overwhelmed the throng's enthusiasm; but hardly had we emerged from the vault when the animation, renewed and augmented, overflowed in applauses to the unauthorized cry: '*Viva the first Jesuit Martyr of Cristo Rey!*' And then, amid the songs and obbligatos of *vivas,* the crowd turned to Humberto's grave. A new interval of silence while the sepulcher was blessed, the cadaver lowered . . . the noble old father of the fervent Catholic youth cut down in the flower of life took the spade and dropped the first earth (thus converted into a sacred relic by contact with these remains), after which he advanced toward us upon steps firm and strong, saying, 'We have finished. *Te Deum laudamus.*' . . ." [6]

This was not the pain of mourning before a desolating loss to the tomb. It was glory and jubilant thanksgiving. This was the portent of great blessings ahead—for México—and for the Church of Christ!

[6] Méndez Medina in *Lectura.*

How was it that, alone among his brothers, Roberto was spared? He had shared Humberto's labors in the cause of religion. The Essex' registration bore his likeness under a pseudonym. He had been captured under identical circumstances.

It is said—and written—in México that Roberto's escape came about in the following manner: [7] The Argentine Minister to México, Don Emilio Labougle, stood high in the esteem of Obregón and Calles despite the fact that he was a fervent Catholic. He had frequently attended Masses celebrated by Padre Pro in the home of his friend, Roberto Núñez; and he knew of Don Roberto's deep regard for this zealous and sympathetic young Father. When the Pros fell into the hands of the police, the Minister, urged by Núñez, made personal representations in their favor to the President. Calles gave Labougle his "word of honor" that the Pro brothers were destined for nothing worse than exile. And this, on November 21, the day that his order to General Cruz was: "Shoot the rabble!"

During the evening of November 22 the invitations to the execution were circulated, and by morning the news was sweeping the city. Miguel Pro was shot about ten-thirty, and five minutes later Luis Segura. But before Humberto and Tirado had been dispatched, nearly an hour elapsed. Núñez' first notice of the disaster was received at ten-thirty when a hasty telephone call to Labougle sent the Minister speeding to see Calles and protest this evidence of bad faith. The ruthless man who "didn't want forms, only the deed," pleaded political expediency. He couldn't afford an open break with Obregón, he said, and it was the future President who had demanded the Pros' execution. Nevertheless, in respect for the Argentine Minister, Calles would see what he could do. It was possible that the shooting wasn't finished! In unaccustomed magnanimity, Calles telephoned Cruz, who is supposed to have reported, "In this moment we're getting ready to kill Roberto Pro." Calles' instructions: "Well, let that one off. We'll exile him."

This version is accepted by many informed persons and may

[7] Martínez del Campo, editor for Dragón, p. 359, footnote.

well be true. It is argued that Humberto, equally innocent, had to die in order to set up an excuse for the extermination of a priest. Since the Mexican did not live who could be persuaded that a priest drove the assault car, it must be made to appear that the police believed Humberto was the chauffeur, inspired and abetted by his brother, the priest. If two, instead of one, of the Essex' passengers had escaped capture, the whole diplomatic corps could not have prevailed to save Roberto—who, after a month's detention in the police station, was shipped off to the United States under orders never again to set foot in his native land. . . .

So even before the fusillade had terminated, Calles had tossed the blame to Obregón who, understandably, wanted no part of it. Forthwith, he sent Orcí to make a clamorous protest of the Pros' execution to General Cruz. Obregón, it seemed, "had never been convinced of the brothers' guilt" just as he, Orcí, had never believed them guilty. Cruz, not illogically, replied that, such being the case, Obregón should have saved them since no one but himself enjoyed sufficient influence with Calles to have effected such a feat.

The bare facts were that there was simply no one left in this shameless regime with the ordinary decency to bother with the prevention of this double murder.[8] Thus Calles' order, given without the least flicker of premonition that it was to prove the most appalling blunder of his career, invoked the crime that marked the turning point in México's long struggle for freedom —the immense blessing which Miguel Pro had prayed God he might purchase for his beloved compatriots by the sacrifice of his own life. For this time the senseless hate that shot innocent men at will had been turned on precisely the right victim to end the patience of a greatly abused nation.

Segura's bombs had not harmed Álvaro Obregón, but he would be assassinated just the same—and prior to his resumption

---

[8] If we consider Cruz' tentative gesture to have been sparked merely by his fear of public opinion, a sheerly political sensitivity which was so amazingly lacking in his chiefs.

of the executive powers he coveted so strongly. Whereupon Calles, warned at last, not daring to succeed himself openly, had to "make do" with a few disintegrating seasons of behind-the-scenes maneuvering through puppet presidents. Soon even these, his creatures, turned on him and, far less cruel than he, shunted him off into exile, an impotent, hate- and disease-raddled old man [9] still dreaming his fantastic dreams over a copy of *Mein Kampf*. By this time México's religious persecution was moribund; by 1940, interred, just sufficiently ahead of its old master to cede him his rightful place of chief mourner.

At long last Padre Pro's México was done with dictators, done with army rule, done with persecution. It had shaken itself awake, out of the horrendous nightmare, to take its place in the community of forward-looking nations. And it arose with the added blessings of a strong religious revival of its ancient Faith and—its own modern-day martyr to intercede for Heaven's favors upon it.

The tomb of Miguel Agustín Pro which, from the great day of his burial, constituted an unofficial national shrine, was never neglected, never alone. Always the focus of a public conscience and courage reborn, it stands, the symbol of their new liberty, before the eyes and hearts of "the thirty million."

[9] At only fifty-eight (1935).

XXIV

QUARTER-CENTURY MILESTONE

THE preliminary *escritos* (to prove that there is nothing against faith and morals to impede the introduction of the cause of the beatification and canonization of Miguel Agustín Pro Juárez) were approved by the Sacred Congregation of Rites on June 1, 1947. Those establishing the non-existence of a premature public cult were issued July 21, 1951. The way was now open for the presentation of the petition for the introduction of the Process of Fame of Martyrdom. This petition was approved by the Congregation, December 18, 1951, followed by the ratification of His Holiness Pius XII on January 11, 1952.

The introduction of the Process of Fame of Martyrdom (proof that the Servant of God has enjoyed a popular, spontaneous, continually-increasing fame as a martyr regionally or in the world, born of the facts and quite outside of any artificial provocation) is not, in itself, the official verification of martyrdom. This must await subjection of the evidence to a crucial examination to establish the fact that this fame is founded upon incontrovertible reason. The Holy See does not, however, approve the introduction of this Process without moral certainty that it will prosper.

With this "moral certainty" the Mexican nation, anticipating in joyous reverence the Vatican's definitive decree on the martyrdom of Padre Pro, launched the great jubilee of November 23, 1952, to commemorate the twenty-fifth anniversary of his death.

The newspapers of that day carried the account: "In the chapel of the Templo de la Sagrada Familia more than six hundred persons of our best society assembled for the solemn Mass celebrated by the Reverend Luis Cabrera, S.J., to commemorate the quarter-century anniversary of Padre Pro's sacrifice. . . .

"At the Chapel of the Inmaculada Concepción a fervent sermon was delivered during the solemn Mass by a classmate of Padre Pro, the Reverend Rafael Ramírez, S.J., who most effectively evoked anecdotes and considerations of Padre Pro's student days; and expounded upon the high qualities always evidenced in his work. . . .

"From a very early hour the public was streaming to Padre Pro's new memorial monument [at Dolores] to make the virtuous priest its reverent spiritual and floral offerings; and later these were joined by the large groups which had already been in attendance at the functions held at the Inmaculada.

"An interminable human river in five streams flowed through the entrance [of the cemetery] three abreast in each queue. But the love, the devotion, and the tranquillity of these devout souls maintained total order and repose throughout the immense defile. . . .

"The call to the final Mass in the cemetery chapel came at noon; and this was celebrated before an enormous concourse embracing the most diverse social classes, all inspired by a single concern—to render fervent homage to Padre Miguel Pro Juárez on the twenty-fifth anniversary of his tragic death. At this Mass (as at the preceding ones) there were present: the Reverend Father Provincial Roberto Guerra, S.J.; the vice-postulator and active organizer of these acts, Reverend Rafael Martínez del Campo, S.J.; and Reverend Marcel Izaguirre, S.J. The voices of these [dignitaries] mingled with those of the Señorita Pro, sister of the martyred, and the enormous company which filled the chapel. . . ." (*Novedades*, November 24, 1952.)

Besides the commemorative Masses and the impressive dedication of Father Miguel's new memorial monument there was one other resounding popular demonstration of love and gratitude tendered to him on this red-letter day in Mexican history. This took place in a busy downtown thoroughfare before the National Lottery Building which now rises upon the site of the old *Inspección.* Here on the exact spot where, murmuring, *"Viva Cristo Rey,"* he had joyfully died for them, his countrymen assembled to install the plaque which reads:

> "On the facing sidewalk in a line
> perpendicular to the end of the stairs,
> died
> R. P. MIGUEL AGUSTÍN PRO, S.J.
> shot the 23 of November of 1927
> R. I. P."

His heroic sacrifice and prayers for his people had not been in vain.

"Amen, amen, I say unto you, if you ask the Father anything in my name, He will give it to you."

BIBLIOGRAPHY

Acta de Inspección de la Policía. México, D. F. (November 19–20, 1927). Photostat reproduction published by *Novedades,* México, D. F.; November 12–December 11, 1952.

Araujo, Armando. *Últimas Noticias.* México, D. F., August 13, 1942.

Beals, Carleton. *Porfirio Díaz.* Philadelphia, Pa.: J. B. Lippincott Company, 1932.

Chapela, Gonzalo. *El P. Pro Inocente Mártir.* México, D. F.: *a.b.c.,* August 9, 1952.

Cuevas, Mariano, S.J. *Historia de la Iglesia en México.* 5 vols. Tlalpam, D. F., México: Patricio Sanz, 1921.

Dragón, Antonio, S.J. *Vida Íntima del Padre Pro.* México, D. F.: Buena Prensa, 1952. (Second edition.)

Excelsior. México, D. F.: November 14–25, 1927.

García Gutiérrez, Jesús. *Acción Anticatólica en Méjico.* México, D. F., 1939.

Junco, Alfonso. *Un Siglo de Méjico.* México, D. F.: Ediciones Botas, 1934.

Kelley, Francis C. *Blood Drenched Altars.* Milwaukee, Wisconsin: Bruce, 1935.

——— ———. *The Mexican Question.* New York, N. Y.: Paulist Press, 1926.

Magner, James A. *Men of Mexico.* Milwaukee, Wisconsin: Bruce, 1943.

Méndez Medina, Alfredo, S.J. *El P. Pro Mártir de Cristo Rey.* México,

D. F.: Report to Society of Jesus, December 5, 1927. Published by *Lectura,* December 1, 1952.

Portas, Bernardo, S.J. *Vida del P. Miguel Agustín Pro.* México, D. F.: Buena Prensa, 1944. (Second edition.)

Pulido, Adolfo, S.J. *Alborado de un Mártir.* México, D. F.: Buena Prensa, 1952. (Third edition.)

Simpson, Lesley Byrd. *Many Mexicos.* New York, N. Y.: G. P. Putnam's Sons, 1946.

Xavier, Adriano. *Entre Obreros.* México, D. F.: Buena Prensa, 1944. (Previous publications, Barcelona, Spain, 1934; Vallodolid, Spain, 1939.)